MORE WEALTH
from
Residential Property

by
Jan Somers

The laws relating to property investment are complex and constantly changing. Every effort has been made to ensure that this book is free from errors. No responsibility can be accepted by either the publisher, author or printer for any action taken by any persons or organisations, relating to material in this book. All persons should satisfy themselves independently as to the relevancy of the material to their own particular situation.

This book is copyright to J.B. Somers and is not to be lent, reproduced, resold, hired out, or in any way used apart from the strict usage permitted under the Copyright Act unless written permission has been obtained from Jan Somers.

Published by:

Somerset Financial Services Pty Ltd, PO Box 615, Cleveland Qld, 4163.

Ph: (07) 3286 4368   Email: sales@somersoft.com.au

Fax: (07) 3821 2005   Web: www.somersoft.com.au

First Released October, 2001

Printed in Melbourne by McPherson's Printing Group

Distributed by Herron Book Distributors

Copyright 2001, J.B. Somers of Somerset Financial Services Pty Ltd

A.B.N. 55 058 152 337

National Library of Australia

Cataloguing-in-Publication Data.

ISBN 0 9585672 5 5

About the Author

Today, Jan Somers is just your average millionaire housewife. Twenty years ago she was just your average high school mathematics teacher, who left the blackboard behind to raise a young family. With her teaching career on hold, she took advantage of her time at home to pursue other interests, namely property investment.

Jan's interest in property can be traced back to 1972, when she and her husband Ian bought their first house. Although they accumulated many investment properties over the following years, it was not something that they planned. In the early 80s, Jan was constrained somewhat by the needs of three very young children, but she used her time at home to read and to learn more about property. Introduced to a personal computer by Ian, a computer analyst, she relished the opportunity to analyse investment property in depth, playing with the figures to her heart's content.

At first she had trouble believing what the computer kept telling her, but no matter which way she looked at it, the answer always came out the same: *residential property, properly financed and kept long term, was a wonderful investment!* Jan now had an insight into why the family had been able to achieve so much through investment in property in the past 10 years, on just average wages, and for the most part, a single wage. As a result, Jan and Ian went on to buy many more investment properties and now have a multi-million dollar property portfolio.

Jan never did go back to teaching high school mathematics. In 1989, with Ian, she established Somerset Financial Services Pty Ltd and now enjoys sharing her knowledge with others through her lectures, books and computer software. Her first four books, *Manual for Residential Property Investors, Building Wealth through Investment Property, Building Wealth in Changing Times* and *Building Wealth Story by Story* were all runaway best sellers, with more than 400,000 copies being sold all up.

The Property Investment Analysis (PIA) computer programs developed by Ian have become industry standards and are now used by thousands of real estate groups, accountants, banks and investors throughout Australia and New Zealand.

Jan's new book, *More Wealth from Residential Property*, has been written in response to the countless requests for updates to her earlier books. However, while this book incorporates many of the changes in the property investment scene, her original simple recipe for success involving residential investment property remains unchanged and is shown to be just as effective in the new millennium as it was a decade ago.

Acknowledgement

I would like to thank my dear friend, partner and husband, Ian, for his continued support and enthusiasm. Thanks must also go to my wonderful children, Will, Tom and Bonnie, for enduring the countless hours while I was preoccupied with researching and writing this book. Thanks to Jenny Somers for bearing much of the work load during this time and to Robyn Heales, my editor, for turning my written thoughts into readable English.

CONTENTS

INTRODUCTION 9

PART I Deciding to Build

Chapter 1 About Wealth	15
Calculating your net worth	17
Calculating your nest egg	18
Towards more wealth	19
Chapter 2 Retirement Ready Reckoner	21
Spending time in retirement	22
Is $250,000 enough?	23
How much will you need?	24
How many properties is enough?	27
Chapter 3 The Risk of Doing Nothing	29
Age pension — right or privilege?	30
SGC — trick or treat?	33
What is the SGC?	33
What isn't it?	34
What can go wrong?	35

PART II Planning to Build

Chapter 4 Who Do You Ask For Advice?	39
The role of financial advisors	40
Who else will give you advice?	44
Chapter 5 The ABC of DIY Wealth Building	45
Attitude determines altitude	46
Blueprint your goals	47
Commitment to succeed	48
Debt allows leverage	49
Education versus school	51
Fear stifles wealth building	52

6   *More Wealth from Residential Property*

PART III Choosing the Bricks

Chapter 6 What Are the Options?	55
Pathways to wealth	56
Managed funds	57
Isn't superannuation the best?	58
Property trusts and syndicates	60
What about cash?	61
Chapter 7 Shares versus Property	63
Returns	64
Risk	66
Gearing ability	67
Tax effectiveness	68
Affordability	69
Liquidity	70
Control	71
Shares or property?	72
Chapter 8 Which Property Should You Choose?	73
Why not land?	74
'Vacant land' versus 'house and land'	74
Why not commercial property?	77
Which residential property?	79
Median-priced residential property	80
Choosing a suitable rental property	82
A typical rental property	85

PART IV Laying the Foundations

Chapter 9 Position, Position, Position	89
Position – which city?	90
Migration and immigration patterns	90
Returns from the capital cities	92
The growth/yield connection	93
Position – which suburb?	96
Other growth/yield factors	98
Position – which locality?	100
Chapter 10 Time — Not Timing	101
Property cycles	102
Property traders	105
Traders versus investors	106
Long term is the key	107

PART V Building the Framework

Chapter 11 Getting Started — Your Own Home   111
- Renting versus buying   112
- Saving the deposit   113
- Recognising reality   114
- Reducing your mortgage   115
- Improving your home   117
- Renting while investing   118
- Is one property enough?   120

Chapter 12 More Wealth from Residential Property   121
- Recipe for success   123
- Begin with your first home   124
- Buy an investment property   126
- Borrow the money   128
  - Security calculated using LVR   128
  - Serviceability calculated using DSR   129
  - Serviceability calculated using a budget   130
- Build a property portfolio   132
- Balance the debt on retirement   140

PART VI Financing the Project

Chapter 13 Sources of Finance   143

Chapter 14 How Much Money Can You Borrow?   147
- Status   148
- Security   149
  - Loan to Value Ratio (LVR)   150
- Serviceability   152
  - Debt Service Ratio (DSR)   153
  - Tips to help you qualify for a loan   156

Chapter 15 Which Loan Is Best?   157
- Loan types   158
- Loan terminology   162
- Loan arrangement   167

Chapter 16 The Costs of Borrowing   169
- How is the interest charged?   170
- What are the borrowing costs?   172

8 *More Wealth from Residential Property*

PART VII Taxing the Project

Chapter 17 Typical Tax Deductions	177
Capital costs	178
Revenue costs	179
Checklist of tax deductions	181
Chapter 18 Negative Gearing	193
Tax benefits	194
Negative gearing on low wages	196
Negative gearing; positive cash flow	197
Negative gearing and the GST	198
Varying your PAYG tax	200
Chapter 19 The Costs of Buying and Selling	201
Buying costs	202
Selling costs	203
Capital Gains Tax	204
Calculating the CGT	204
CGT – for better or for worse	207
Minimising the CGT	208

PART VIII Maintaining the Assets

Chapter 20 Financial Management	211
Chapter 21 Property Management	217
Chapter 22 Understanding the 'What Ifs'	221
What if the population declines?	222
What if there's too few tenants?	223
What if there's too many investors?	225
Some people never start	225
Some people never stay	227
What if negative gearing dies?	228
What if the inflation rate changes?	231
Links between inflation, growth and interest	232
Effect of inflation on returns	236
More what ifs ...	238
One more what if	240
Appendix A: Shares versus property	241
Appendix B: PIA Computer program	249
Appendix C: Internal Rate of Return (IRR)	256
Current publications available	254
Order form	256

INTRODUCTION

This book shows you how to build more wealth than you ever thought possible through long-term investment in residential property. In essence this is achieved by diverting some of your current income into assets that will provide an income in retirement. But don't be mislead. It is not a *get-rich-quick* scheme, nor are the principles new — but it is the surest path to personal wealth I know. Here is a recipe, in fact, for a personal superannuation scheme that offers far better returns and much greater flexibility than any institutional superannuation.

As the ensuing chapters will explain, residential property is a low risk investment that consistently produces high returns over the long term. Not only this, but there are no complicated and constantly changing rules governing how you can eventually get your money. There are no lump sum regulations, no reasonable benefits limits and no age barriers — none of the straightjackets associated with formal institutional superannuation.

This is my fifth book on the subject of property investment and, while much has happened since the first one was written a decade ago, little has changed: my views are the same today as they were yesterday, as they will be tomorrow. While the basic recipe is still the same, however, many of the figures used in the earlier books are now outdated following large rises in property values and significant falls in interest rates. This new book not only updates and consolidates much of the information from two of its predecessors, *Building Wealth through Investment Property* and *Building Wealth in Changing Times*, it contains much more material.

Something increasingly obvious is that people are wanting, but not getting, more information about investment in property. In search of help, many turn to a financial advisor, but are often confronted by a denigration of property and a sales pitch for managed funds. Why? Research by the Association of Independently Owned Financial Planners shows that:

Over 90% of the financial planning advice given to consumers is delivered by institutionally owned financial planning organisations.

Clearly, the majority of financial planners are not interested in assisting you to invest directly in property. They are really geared toward guiding you into indirect investments such as managed funds packaged by the large financial institutions who own and control their business. In my view, if you want to be a successful property investor, you should be seeking the advice of experienced, successful property investors. This book is the culmination of almost 30 years of research and experience in property investment, so you will be learning first hand how to build more wealth from residential property.

The philosophy

To build a property portfolio you need to formulate and stick with a consistent investment strategy. I didn't invent the formula outlined in this book. I don't have a franchise on it, and neither does anyone else. It is not new, but has been around for thousands of years. Yet many people do not embrace this strategy because they can not believe that something so simple can be so effective.

The formula is simply to buy income-producing residential property that is appropriately financed to achieve maximum tax benefits while you are working. As both cash flows and property values rise, you refinance so that your liabilities (your borrowings) increase with your assets, enabling you to build wealth by increasing your net worth. This will give you the opportunity to retire much earlier, and with more wealth, than you could otherwise. Then, if you wish, you can reduce your liabilities by selling a property or two.

Ultimately you will have a retirement package of residential investment properties that will continue to grow in value and produce a regular indexed income in the form of rent. In effect, you will be creating your very own pension and superannuation fund, but with returns that, in my family's experience and that of many others, will outperform all other investments over the long term.

This concept of 'buy and keep' is difficult for some people to accept because they believe the only way to make a profit is to buy and sell. But you don't have to sell to make a profit. By keeping the property you can borrow against the equity and invest in more property, putting your profit back to work.

Many property investors enter the market with a short-term view that is reinforced by some myopic media who report a myriad of short-lived crises to sell newspapers. Yet long-term investment in residential property is relatively unaffected by downturns in the economy, high interest rates, fuel crises, and high unemployment. This is demonstrated by the fact that in Australia for the past 100 years, the combined returns from capital growth and rental yields have averaged more than 15% per year compound. With gearing, in fact, those returns increase dramatically.

For short-term property traders, negotiating a bargain price, finding the best interest rate, and deciding when to buy and when to sell are extremely important. With long-term property investment, initial price, interest rates and timing are less significant because of the levelling effect of time. This means that the best time to invest in income-producing residential property is *today*. Time is always on your side.

Introduction 11

Summary

The ensuing chapters show you some of the basic steps involved in achieving total financial security through residential investment property.

PART I – Deciding to build takes you through the very first steps. It discusses the importance of deciding to start a wealth building program and helps you estimate how much you'll need in retirement.

- Chapter 1 discusses the concept of real wealth and helps you work out how wealthy, or poor, you are right now. It also gives you an inkling of how to go about building wealth in the future.

- Chapter 2 shows you how to estimate how much money or how many properties you'll need before you can be financially independent.

- Chapter 3 explains the dire consequences of deciding to do nothing and relying on government provisions to support you in retirement.

PART II – Planning to build looks at who will help you prepare a strategy for building wealth.

- Chapter 4 discusses the real role of financial advisors, who they are and what they do. You will discover that all is not what it seems.

- Chapter 5 examines the attitudes, information and skills you'll need to build wealth by the DIY approach, where *you* take responsibility for yourself.

PART III – Choosing the bricks lists the various options you have available to choose from as the basis for building wealth.

- Chapter 6 lays out the pathways to wealth and discusses managed investments, in particular institutional superannuation, and why it will never make you wealthy.

- Chapter 7 documents the history of capital growth and rental income from residential property over the past twenty years and compares the attributes of shares and property.

- Chapter 8 describes the rationale of why the average investor should choose residential property rather than commercial property or vacant land. It also describes the array of residential properties available and suggests some criteria for choosing a suitable one.

PART IV – Laying the foundations looks at location and timing in relation to investment property.

- Chapter 9 outlines criteria for choosing where to invest and makes some interesting comparisons between different cities and suburbs.

- Chapter 10 describes why time and not timing is one of the keys to successful property investment.

12   *More Wealth from Residential Property*

PART V – Building the framework outlines the steps involved in building a portfolio of properties beginning with your own home.

- Chapter 11 shows you how to get started by buying your first property. It is usually your own home but could even be an investment property.

- Chapter 12 *is the focal point of the book*. After learning about the basics of residential property, I believe that most people would like to discover the recipe for building wealth, before getting bogged down in tax and finance matters. This chapter describes how an average couple can easily build a million dollar property portfolio in 10 to 15 years.

PART VI – Financing the project looks at the financial aspects of borrowing and buying investment property.

- Chapter 13 examines the sources of finance with the aim of helping you make the best choice for your situation.

- Chapter 14 provides you with a simple formula to enable you to work out how much you can borrow.

- Chapter 15 helps you choose which loan is best and explores ways to make the most of your mortgages.

- Chapter 16 examines the fees associated with a loan and looks at how interest is charged and what borrowing costs to expect. It explains why interest rates are not the only criterion for selecting a particular loan.

PART VII – Taxing the project explains the tax implications of investing in property.

- Chapter 17 lists the tax deductions applicable to income-producing property to help you include everything to which you are entitled.

- Chapter 18 explains the principle of negative gearing and shows you how to get immediate tax benefits by having your PAYG instalments reduced. It also looks at how the new tax scales, brought in with the Goods and Services Tax, have affected investors in rental property.

- Chapter 19 details the costs of buying and selling property, and also explains how the Capital Gains Tax is now calculated.

PART VIII – Maintaining the assets shows you how to perpetuate your wealth by carefully managing your property and finances. It also answers many of the 'what ifs' that can intrude on your thoughts and cause you to stray from your wealth building plans.

- Chapter 20 shows you how to budget and manage your finances. Debt management plays an important role in wealth maintenance.

- Chapter 21 explains how to manage your property and the tenants.

- Chapter 22 answers the most commonly asked 'what ifs' concerning property investment.

Part I

Deciding to Build

1
About Wealth

Groucho Marx gave us an enlightened view of money when he said:

It frees you from doing the things you dislike. Since I dislike doing nearly everything, money is handy.

Being wealthy may not guarantee you happiness, but, as Groucho said, money comes in pretty handy at times. Most of us aspire to having that dream home or the holiday house by the beach; or to seeing the rest of the world while we still can; or being able to afford the best medical care if we need it; or to helping the kids financially should they need it; or giving to a local community group if we feel like it. I'm sure you'd have no trouble dreaming up ways of how you could spend your money if you were indeed wealthy.

But perhaps most importantly, wealth gives you the freedom to choose just *when* you retire: that is, to choose when to stop doing what you *have* to do and start doing what you really *want* to do. Wealth gives us *financial freedom* and it's my view that this is available to anyone who really wants it. This book sets out to show you a safe and easy way to build wealth and become financially independent. And the bonus is that it doesn't take rocket science to do it, just common sense.

You might ask, if it's so easy, why do so few of us achieve financial freedom? The answer is simple. The strategy I outline in these pages is a *get-rich-slow* recipe requiring 10 years or more. Our society, in contrast, prefers instant results. I want it now. I must have it right now. I can't possibly wait. We exhaust ourselves looking for quick and easy ways to riches, but spend little energy on learning the principles of building wealth. Consequently, the *get-rich-quick* schemes and gambling games designed to exploit our hunger for riches are overwhelmingly patronised. How many people do you know who have managed to achieve wealth in this way?

Perhaps patience is a lost virtue, but it's patience you need to build real wealth. How patient are you? Would you, back in your childhood, have passed the 'marshmallow' test? It goes like this.

16   *More Wealth from Residential Property*

Imagine you're a kid sitting at the kitchen table and your mother asks you to go on an errand. As a reward, you can have one marshmallow now before you go, or two if you can wait until you return. You just adore marshmallows, they're your favourites: the temptation is awful. So you sit there drooling, trying to make this very important decision. One now? Two later? Can I wait? What if I don't? Maybe Mum will come good with two later, anyway. What do you decide?

Would you like an adult version of the 'marshmallow' test? This time, then, imagine you're sitting at your own kitchen table reading a brochure advertising one of those super-duper stocktake sales to end all sales. Some of your favourite designer labels have been marked down, and buying new clothes makes you feel oh so good. You still have some money left from your last pay day. Will you spend it now on those bargains, or will you hold back and invest it for the future when you'll be able to buy anything you want, plus so much more? The temptation is awful. So you sit there pondering this important decision. Spend now? Save it for later? Can I wait? What if I don't? I can always start saving next week, or even next year. Maybe by the time I retire, the government will have increased the age pension, so I shouldn't need to worry about saving and investing right now. What's your choice?

Mostly, people who succeed financially are those who are able to delay gratification, and patiently follow the surer, slower paths to riches. As young children, they would probably have passed the 'marshmallow' test with flying colours and as adults, they'd be more likely to be savers than spenders. Would you have passed these tests of patience? More to the point, are you heading towards wealth or welfare?

We are talking reality here. The marshmallow test described above was first implemented by the renowned social psychologist Walter Mischel, who identified instant and delayed gratification in children as young as four. The implications of this telling test, reported by Daniel Goleman in his book *Emotional Intelligence*, were that it offered 'a quick reading of the trajectory a child will probably take through life'. Marshmallows and money obviously have a lot in common. Which description best fits your personality? Do you seek instant or delayed gratification?

The 'instant gratification' syndrome displayed by most of the children performing in Mischel's test corresponds to the 'live for today' outlook displayed by the majority of adults. But the good news is that it's never too late to learn the principles of building real wealth. How is real wealth measured, and what are these true and tried methods that lead to wealth, not welfare? If you'd like to know more about how average income earners can achieve financial independence, read on.

Chapter 1: About Wealth   17

Calculating your net worth

Imagine what would happen if you stopped work today and there were no government safety nets to help you out. For most people, their source of income would dry up — no job, no salary. For those few who run a business, it might be possible to maintain an income stream by allowing others to take over their work. For the very few who have learned how to invest, their income would be generated from their wealth. It depends on your ability to create a business or to build wealth by other means to provide an income stream from somewhere other than your own labour. This is why it is possible for a forklift driver to retire on a large income from owning rental properties, and why it is *not* possible for a highly skilled medical specialist with no net worth to retire. Doctors can not sell their skills as if they were a business.

Let's start you on your own path to more wealth by looking at how much you have right now. Add up the value of everything you own and subtract from it all that you owe — that's called your net worth. The table below may help you calculate this.

What's Your Net Worth?

Assets	Value	Liabilities	Value
Own home	_____	Home loan	_____
Investment properties	_____	Investment loans	_____
Shares	_____	Margin loans	_____
Other investments	_____	Other investment loans	_____
Superannuation	_____	Personal loans	_____
Cash	_____	Credit cards	_____
Car	_____	Car loans	_____
Boat	_____	Hire purchase	_____
Furniture	_____	Furniture loans	_____
Total assets	_____	**Total liabilities**	_____

Net worth = Total assets - Total liabilities

= $_____

The average net worth for couples under 35 years of age is $36,000. (NATSEM Report 11 Dec, 1999). Is that like yours? If your household income is also near the average of $67,000 a year (ABS Cat. 6523), a lot of money has slipped through your fingers — roughly a million dollars in 15 years! Where did it go, besides paying for taxes and food?

18   *More Wealth from Residential Property*

Calculating your nest egg

Being practical, we should really think of our wealth as a nest egg that can provide an income for us when we retire. How does a nest egg relate to net worth? You might be quite shocked to find that with net worth, what you see is not what you get. So if you thought the couple's average net worth of $36,000 didn't sound too bad, you might be about to change your mind.

Your net worth is not a true reflection of your nest egg at any time because it includes some assets that simply won't generate income for you when you retire. These assets include your home, furniture, boat, car and other possessions that do not produce income — not unless you want to sell up your home and furniture and live in a tent, then sell your car and ride a bike. So you must subtract the value of these personal assets from your net worth to find out how much wealth you have accumulated to generate an income for you when you retire.

$$\textbf{Nest egg now} \ = \ \textbf{Net worth now} \ - \ \textbf{(Home + car, etc.)}$$
$$= \ \$\underline{\hspace{3cm}}$$

This figure, which represents your nest egg right now, may be really sobering. I suspect that, like most couples, you've just discovered that your reasonable looking net worth makes a paltry nest egg. Once you take out the value of the family home and personal assets, the net value of the remaining assets is likely to be less than zero. As an example, suppose you are the average couple from NATSEM's study with $36,000 in net worth. If your home is worth about $180,000, the median value of a dwelling owned by a couple with children (ABS Cat. 4130), and you have around $50,000 worth of personal assets such as your car and furniture, your nest egg will be minus $194,000.

$$\textbf{Nest egg now} \ = \ \$36,000 \ - (\$180,000 \ + \ \$50,000)$$
$$= \ \$36,000 \ - \ \$230,000$$
$$= \ -\$194,000$$

Obviously, a very negative nest egg could never produce an income for you if you stopped work today. While most people acknowledge that their home forms the bulk of their net worth, they have trouble understanding that they can not count on it as part of their retirement nest egg. Don't despair. The purpose of this activity was not to discourage you, nor deflate your ego, nor to send you into a panic. It was mainly to give you a clear picture of your situation now so you can do something about increasing your net worth by generating more wealth in the future.

Chapter 1: About Wealth   19

Towards more wealth

You should realise now that most people need to build more wealth. But how? Have you ever wondered why the rich seem to get richer and the poor seem to get poorer? It's because the poor want instant gratification and spend money, usually borrowed, on things that make them feel wealthy today: cars and clothes, etc, that inevitably decrease in value. The rich delay gratification and invest money, again usually borrowed, into things that increase in value — such as property. But exactly how do you build wealth through property? What's the game plan? And when do you get to enjoy it all? First, let's review the figure on the next page to see what most people do with their finances, and then we'll look at what *you* can do.

Most young people are impatient and spend money as fast as they can, so that when they want to buy their first home, they only have a small deposit. They then have to borrow such a large amount that they struggle for years to repay it. What have they got to look forward to? On the plus side, despite a fast food diet, people now have longer life expectancies, and may well live another twenty five years or more after they retire. With no other savings, however, they may well be looking forward to spending this time on basic welfare.

You could be different. *You could look forward to an early retirement and total financial independence, and if you've already got some equity in your own home, you're on your way.* Using your own home as a base, you can borrow against the equity to buy an investment property, and then another one, and another... And so it goes on and on.

While you work, you continue to buy more and more rental properties until you decide that enough is enough, and you retire. If you need to, you could then sell a few properties to reduce your debt, and live off the rents from your remaining properties. In time you might sell another property or two to have an overseas trip, or buy a new car — the choice is yours.

Those of you who have scraped and saved all these years to make a dent in your first mortgage, you'll be thinking — why should I go back into debt? What you should know is that borrowing to buy the next property as an investment is so much easier. Why? Because the debt on a rental property is largely paid for by the tenant and the taxman and you are just left to pay the remainder. It can cost you less than $50 per week to get started! That's why borrowing to buy investment property is so much easier than borrowing to buy your own home where *you* pay the lot.

You will discover throughout this book just *why* residential property is the best vehicle for building more wealth and how it can be achieved on a very average income. Let's begin to find out.

20 *More Wealth from Residential Property*

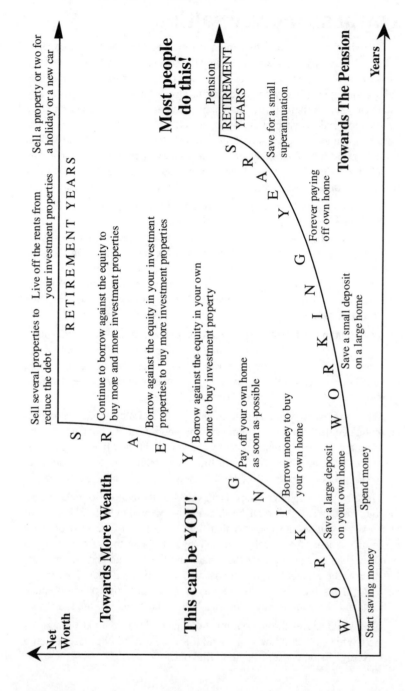

2
Retirement
Ready Reckoner

By now you've probably become aware that no matter which way you look at it, the nest egg you have won't be enough to retire on and the only way to financial independence in the future is to acquire more assets which generate income. But how much is enough? Have you ever sat down to really think about how much more you'll need to accumulate to enjoy a comfortable retirement?

How much you need depends on what you want from life. However, there's no reason to limit yourself, and, as you'll discover, most people need more than they really think. So how much is enough to allow you to enjoy a comfortable retirement for the whole time — not just the first two or three years? As one financial observer put it:

The only thing worse than dying is running out of money first.

I could add another line to this little gem. The only thing worse than running out of money first is the *worry* of running out of money first. According to Professors Sharpley and Yardley, writing in the *Journal of Applied Health Behaviour* (1999), concerns over finances rated the highest of all stressors for retirees on the Self-perceived Stress in Retirement Scale with, ironically, fear of death rating the lowest.

Retirement should be an exciting and enjoyable time — not just an enduring time between the end of work and the end of life. For most of today's retirees, though, the last years of their lives are definitely not the most exciting and enjoyable times that they could be. It is not a time of carefree living without financial constraints. It's a time when their income drops drastically below pre-retirement levels, but at a time when they are least able to cope with the change.

How do you know when you'll be able to retire with enough to last for the rest of your life? Or more importantly, with sufficient to generate enough income to allow you to live comfortably, in the way you desire, for that entire time? Is there some formula that will give you an idea?

Spending time in retirement

How times have changed. Figures from the ABS show that the amount of time now spent in retirement has dramatically increased, bringing with it a mixture of both good and bad news. This is shown graphically below.

The Pattern of Changing Times

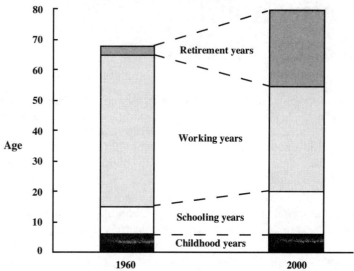

In the 1960s, the typical male left school at 15, worked with the same firm for the next 50 years, retired at age 65 and died aged 68. Retirement planning was unheard of — and really unnecessary — because governments could afford to pay the pension for three short years.

The story today, though, is different. Times have changed and the good news is that retirement now is not just a short-lived experience prior to death, but a major part of our lives. Today, the typical male remains in the education system until he is aged 20, works for several different firms for the next 35 years, retires at age 55 and spends an average of 25 years in retirement before he dies at almost 80 (Australian Life Tables 1995-97).

You should be excited about these figures. You'll now have even more time to do the things you really enjoy doing. There'll be time to take that overseas holiday, time to play golf or bowls all day long, and time to catch up with the hobbies you've been putting off all those years when you were still working. This really is great news! On the downside, although you'll enjoy the prospect of living a longer fuller life, financially, you'll need to be able to afford the extra years in retirement, and you'll have fewer working years to save for it.

Is $250,000 enough?

Does it really matter if your nest egg is small, or even negative, at the moment? Perhaps you think you'll be OK because you're expecting a quarter of a million dollars in super when you retire. It sounds like a lot. But do you know how long it would last an average couple who retired at 55? Most think they can live off the interest. But if they spent $50,000 each year, $250,000 would last less than six years, as you can see from the table below. It is probably stating the obvious, but sometimes we need to see this in print before things sink in. With an income of $17,237, assuming no tax (to be conservative), and living expenses of $50,000, there would be $217,237 left at the end of the first year. With income decreasing because of the now reduced capital, and living expenses increasing with inflation, it would take less than six years before the capital ran out.

How Long Will $250,000 Last?

Year	Start of Yr	Income	Expenses	End of Yr
1	$250,000	$17,237	$50,000	$217,237
2	$217,237	$14,979	$51,000	$181,216
3	$181,216	$12,495	$52,020	$141,691
4	$141,691	$9,770	$53,060	$98,401
5	$98,401	$6,785	$54,122	$51,064
6	$51,064	$3,521	$55,204	-$619

Assumptions: 7% gross return, 2% inflation, 0% tax, 1.5% management fees

However, *Australian Life Tables 1997–97* indicate that a male aged 61 is likely to live to 80, and a female to 83. If our couple still have 20 or so years to live *after* they've run out of money, what then? The age pension, if there is one? I'm sure you know many retired people who have returned to work, having badly underestimated their retirement needs. Suppose our couple decided to work until they were 60, when their super would be somewhat larger at $330,000. It too would be gone in just eight years, when they were still 68 years young, with the prospect of living a further 15 years. *Superfunds* (Jan, 2000) reported some sobering results from a survey conducted by the Association of Superannuation Funds of Australia (ASFA):

Financial advisors reported that clients frequently are surprised at how low the age pension is, often had poor funding for retirement, thought that $50,000 to $60,000 constituted substantial retirement savings, and greatly underestimated the cost of what they wanted to do in retirement.

So just how much is enough? Let's do some more sums.

24　*More Wealth from Residential Property*

How much will you need?

To estimate what you'll need in retirement, first work out how much you expect to spend each year, thinking in today's dollars. Then we'll use a formula to convert it to a lump sum. Have you picked an amount of around 75% of your present income? Then you're in good company. Most people who have attended my seminars over the past decade also want to retire on 75% of their pre-retirement gross income, a figure supported by a survey of financial planners and reported in *Superfunds* (Jan, 2000), the magazine of ASFA.

For the average couple earning $67,000 gross per year, 75% means about $50,000. Let's put this in perspective by looking at the incomes of our current retirees. As you can see from the table below, the majority of couples (62%) receive less than $20,000 per year — the median being just $18,500 per year — with most of them fully reliant on the age pension. Only 4.7% retire with the $50,000 they may have hoped for.

Annual Retirement Incomes for Couples

Amount ($)	%
less than 10,000	7.1%
10,000 - 20,000	54.9%
20,000 - 30,000	22.1%
30,000 - 50,000	11.2%
50,000 +	4.7%

Source: ABS Cat. 6523 (1999)

If you're having trouble guesstimating what you'll need, the following table may help you prepare a budget. It includes a budget for a pensioner couple on $17,000 per year, one for a couple on $40,000, the minimum needed to be comfortable, and one for a well-off couple on $50,000, all before tax. A rule of thumb to convert before-tax income to after-tax is to multiply by 0.8; and to convert after-tax income to before-tax, multiply by 1.25. So a before-tax income of $50,000 is $40,000 after-tax, and vice versa.

The difference between budgets is how much is allowed for the luxuries that make life just that bit more comfortable — a more modern car every so often, gifts for your friends and family, travel if you feel like it; or assisting your family while you can see them enjoy it. What have you decided? $40,000, $50,000 per year, or more? Write it down.

Desired income (before tax)= **$**_____ (per year)

Chapter 2: Retirement Ready Reckoner   25

Budgeting for a Couple in Retirement

Expenditure Essentials	Pension $/wk	Minimum $/wk	Well-off $/wk	You $/wk
Current housing costs	30	30	30	_____
Fuel and power	10	10	10	_____
Food and drinks	70	70	70	_____
Alcoholic beverages	10	10	10	_____
Tobacco	10	10	10	_____
Clothing and footwear	20	20	20	_____
Household furnishings	20	20	20	_____
Household maintenance	20	20	20	_____
Medical care	20	20	20	_____
Transport	40	40	40	_____
Entertainment	20	20	20	_____
Personal care	50	50	50	_____
Miscellaneous extras	7	7	7	_____
Luxuries				_____
Gifts		10	20	_____
Luxury food & drinks		10	20	_____
New clothes, shoes		10	20	_____
Personal beauty care		10	20	_____
Carpets, curtains, etc		10	20	_____
Extras for grandchildren		10	20	_____
Sporting, musical, etc		10	20	_____
Movies, plays, etc		20	30	_____
New furniture		20	30	_____
Family assistance		20	30	_____
Travel, holidays, etc		20	30	_____
Private hospital costs		20	30	_____
Dining out		60	80	_____
New car		58	73	_____
Total/wk (after tax)	327	615	770	_____
Total/yr (after tax)	$17,000	$32,000	$40,000	_____
Total/yr (before tax)	$17,000	$40,000	$50,000	_____

26　*More Wealth from Residential Property*

This income you have just decided you would like in retirement comes from the nest egg you've been saving during your working years. Let's now convert your income from the first step into a nest egg equivalent. We can use a simple formula to estimate the size of the nest egg you'll need to produce the retirement income you desire — in today's dollars.

$$\textbf{Nest egg} \quad = \quad \textbf{Desired income (before tax) x 20}$$
$$= \quad \underline{\$\qquad\qquad}$$

In other words, for an income of $50,000 per year, you'd need a nest egg of $1,000,000. What if you wanted $100,000 per year? Then you'd need $2,000,000, and so on. Is this much more than you ever imagined? Does it blow you away? You're probably saying to yourself: 'How on earth will I be able to get a million dollars before I retire? Win Lotto? The Casino? The TAB?'

We all know that the chance of winning a million dollars by gambling is zilch. And I should also be truthful and tell you that the average person can not possibly save this kind of money. How, then, can you do it?

You can easily and safely build one million dollars in net worth by borrowing to invest in residential property.

What is so magical about the number '20' used in estimating nest eggs from desired incomes? The answer is that the gross return on investments has two components, capital growth and income yield. If capital growth keeps pace with inflation, the before-tax yield is usually about 5% gross. Consequently, a nest egg of $1,000,000 would be expected to produce an initial yield of $50,000 (5% of $1,000,000), and the reverse calculation would be: $1,000,000 nest egg = $50,000 yield x 20. Do you see how a 5% yield is connected to the factor 20?

One further point on the use of the factor 20: this assumes that the capital base maintains its value throughout your retirement by keeping pace with inflation, and that it is not 'eaten into' to provide income. This means that your longer life expectancy is catered for and that you will also be able to pass your assets on to your dependents.

You could use a lower factor, of say 15, and aim for a smaller nest egg, if you were prepared to dip into the capital each time, but then you'd have nothing left when you die. Life companies are aware of life expectancy statistics and sell annuities and private pensions according to whether you are male or female, and how old you are at the date of sale. They are able to calculate how long it will be until you're expected to die, and pay you a pension according to this time, such that there will be exactly nothing left when you die. So use a factor of between 15 and 20 depending on whether or not you want to pass on any remaining assets to your children.

Chapter 2: Retirement Ready Reckoner 27

How many properties is enough?

Now that you know how to calculate the size of your retirement nest egg, let's continue our sums to see how many investment properties you'd need to own outright to produce the retirement income you want. To make the results easier to grasp, everything is in today's dollars. Ask yourself this question: 'If I retired today, what income would I like and how many properties will I need to give me this yield?' This provides a very good approximation of what you'll need in the future, regardless of inflation.

Suppose you'd like to retire with an after-tax income of $40,000 from your investment properties, which, as we've just seen, is $50,000 before tax. If the yield from your properties is 5% (net of expenses but not tax), you'd need to own outright about $1,000,000 worth of property in today's dollars, calculated by multiplying $50,000 by 20.

The next step is to work out the number of properties this represents. If you aimed for properties worth around $250,000 in today's dollars, you'd need four properties. The table below sets out this entire calculation.

Estimating the number of properties needed

Income desired (today's dollars, *after* tax)	=	$40,000
Income desired (today's dollars, *before* tax)	=	$40,000 x 1.25
	=	$50,000
Nest egg required (today's dollars)	=	$50,000 x 20
	=	$1,000,000
Value of 1 property (today's dollars)	=	$250,000
Number of properties needed	=	$\dfrac{\$1,000,000}{\$250,000}$
	=	4

You'll remember I said that you might need to sell some properties at the start of retirement to reduce the debt. It might, therefore, be necessary to accumulate six properties, so that after selling two, you eventually own four outright. The number you accumulate and sell is related to their values. If the properties you own are valued only at $100,000 each, you'd need to own ten outright with a total value of $1,000,000. If they were valued at $200,000 each, you'd need to own five, and so on.

28   *More Wealth from Residential Property*

In reality, your specific situation could be quite different. It could be that you want a higher income in retirement and are prepared to invest for a little longer; it could be that the properties are all of different values; it could be that the rental yield is much higher or lower than 5%; it could be that any number of things will differ and that you have any combination of these factors as well.

We, in fact, have a mixture of investment properties. Some are worth less than $100,000, some more than $500,000; some have 10% net yield, some just 3%. As you'll see consistently in this book, no particular combination is better. This is purely a guide to start you thinking about the value of your portfolio and the approximate number of rental properties you'll need to own outright in retirement. Filling in the table below should help you set a goal; then all you need to do is prepare a blueprint for how you are going to achieve it. If you have any doubts about starting today, you won't by the time you've read the next chapter.

Retirement Ready Reckoner

(All calculations are in today's dollars)

Spending money desired (*after* tax) = $_____

Gross income required (*before* tax) = $_____ x 1.25

= $_____

Nest egg required = Gross income x 20

= $_____

Value of 1 property = $_____

Number of properties needed = <u>Nest egg required</u>
Val of 1 property

= _____

3
The Risk of Doing Nothing

When talking about wealth and retirement, I often hear people say: 'I'm here for a good time, not a long time. Why not enjoy myself while I'm young and spend my money as soon as I get it. Besides, I pay taxes, so the government owes me a pension. And if there's not one, I'll still have all that super I'm being forced to pay into. She'll be right, mate.'

With life expectancies now beyond 80 and average retirement ages down to 58, the chances are that you'll be retired for a long, long time. This is good or not, depending on what planning you have done. When longer life expectancies and earlier retirement ages are coupled with lower fertility rates and fewer working taxpayers, our ageing population creates huge pressures on economies — on governments.

The World Bank, in its publication *Averting the Old Age Crisis*, has recognised this enormous problem emerging in developed countries and has described what it calls the 'three pillar' approach to providing funding for people in retirement. In Australia, those pillars are:

Public: Governments fund age pensions from general revenue.

Compulsory: Individuals compulsorily contribute to a government legislated scheme called the Superannuation Guarantee Charge (SGC) to fund their own pensions.

Voluntary: Individuals voluntarily invest for their own retirement.

In this chapter we'll look at the first two pillars, the age pension and SGC, to establish whether they could provide you with anything resembling a comfortable retirement. We investigate what could happen, for better or for worse, to the government-funded age pension, as a result of our ageing population. Is the pension a right or a privilege? Then we'll analyse the SGC in depth to determine its real benefits. Are you being tricked into forgoing future wage rises in the expectation that the SGC will treat you to a wealthy retirement? Then it will be up to you to decide if 'she'll be right', or if you really need to do something yourself.

More Wealth from Residential Property

Age pension — right or privilege?

Part of the problem societies have in funding age pensions is a belief that it is a due right. Today's pensioners are not entirely to blame for this myth, as for the past fifty years all Australian governments have actively promoted the idea that they will look after older people in their retirement.

At one stage, following World War 2, a special levy called the Social Services Contribution was introduced with the idea that it would be used specifically to fund age pensions in the future. But it only lasted for five years. Also, the age pension was originally available to *all* persons over age 65 — with no assets or income test. Only since 1983 has a means test existed. So today's retirees can be excused for believing that this pension is their right, not a privilege.

In contrast, today's young are growing up in an era when governments are admitting that they can no longer afford to fund age pensions and that in future, these will be reserved for the disadvantaged as a privilege, not a right. Let's look at some factors connected to age that have 'crept up' on our governments, so you'll appreciate why things can only get worse.

Ageing population

The projected greying of the population is perhaps the greatest single factor creating a crisis for welfare policies. An ageing population does not mean that we are just getting old, but that *more* of us are getting old. The prime cause is the baby boomer generation born in the years following World War 2. The table below gives a breakdown of the projected age structure of our population over the next 30 years.

The Ageing of Our Population

Years	2001	2031
	millions	millions
0 - 14	3.9 (20%)	4.3 (17%)
15 - 64	13.1 (67%)	15.9 (62%)
65 +	2.4 (13%)	5.4 (21%)
Total	19.4	25.6

Source: ABS Cat. 3222

By the year 2031 more than 5.4 million people, or about 21% of the population, will be aged over 65, compared to 13% in 2001, and 4% in 1921. At the same time the percentage of people of working age, from 15 to 64, will decline. This means that proportionately fewer workers will pay less in taxes to support more retirees on a pension.

Chapter 3: The Risk of Doing Nothing 31

Increased life expectancies

Healthier life styles and better medical technology have greatly extended the life expectancy of Australians, which, in turn, has increased the time of possible reliance on a pension. Forty years ago, males were expected to live to age 68. In contrast, today's males are expected to live to almost 80, and soon it could well be over 90. These are exciting statistics — or they should be. However for governments trying to balance national budgets, it foreshadows economic disaster; and individuals trying to balance household budgets may be landed in a financial nightmare.

Earlier retirement age

Another factor has been the trend towards earlier retirement. In 1960, the average retirement age for males was 63. Today it is 58. This in itself does not cause an immediate demand for age pensions. But double dipping (see below) means that people tend to spend their lump sum payouts from superannuation early, thereby qualifying for the age pension much sooner. Already there are indications of attempts to reverse this trend by forcing up the age at which women can receive the age pension from 60 to 65, and likewise by increasing from 55 to 60 the age at which superannuation can be claimed. Even newly elected politicians, who previously would have had access to their super at any age when they retired from parliament, now have to wait until they turn 55.

Aged health costs

Government spending on each person aged over 65 is 3.7 times higher than those aged under 15, mainly due to health factors (EPAC: *Economic and Social Consequences of Australia's Ageing Population*). With our population ageing, these costs will be even higher in future, particularly as a result of the increasing numbers of people over 75. In a recent analysis, the Australian Institute of Health and Welfare found that for those aged over 75, about half of health expenditure was outlaid on the 13% who died within two years. As one observer put it, we are now facing agonising ethical questions of whether we wish to add 'years to life' or 'life to years'.

Double dipping

Many people who retire with superannuation spend their lump sum payout immediately in order to access and maximise the age pension. This practice is called 'double dipping' — first you dip into your lump sum, then when it runs out, you dip into the pension. Current government policy does not require retirees to invest their superannuation lump sum into income-producing investments, nor to spread their consumption over a number of years. A research paper by the Reserve Bank and reported in *The Australian* (25 July, 2000) suggests that because the SGC benefits are so low, 'the incentive to engage in double dipping is most severe'.

32   *More Wealth from Residential Property*

Governments have several choices for balancing future budgets. As I see it, here are a few.

Option 1. Reduce or eliminate age pensions

One of the simplest options would be to drastically reduce or eliminate age pensions while still maintaining essential services such as education and defence. This would probably create an outcry from future retirees who have so far failed to act to provide for themselves. Nevertheless, it has already happened in Germany, Italy and the Greece, three countries with an even faster rate of population ageing than Australia (ABS Cat. 3102).

Option 2. Eliminate essential services

Pensions could be maintained but to the detriment of other services. This would benefit pensioners, but at what cost to the community? Would the country be worth living in?

Option 3. Borrow more money

Of course, the government could always borrow its way out of trouble. Governments are notorious for operating at a loss and have not hesitated in the past to borrow their shortfalls. Over the past 20 years, the public debt has grown from $9 billion to almost $200 billion, with interest currently tipping $14 billion. How much more can be borrowed before the interest bill completely overwhelms the budget? And then what?

Option 4. Increase the taxes of future workers

Perhaps the most contentious decision would be to increase the taxes of the workers of the future — your grandchildren. If you, along with others, decide to rely on your country for a pension, you had better be kind to your grandchildren: they could be paying dearly for it.

Option 5. Increase the tax base

Rather than increase the tax rates, it is possible to broaden the tax base. We have already seen the introduction of a Goods and Services Tax (GST). This was the first step by any Australian government to set in place a mechanism for easily increasing taxes across the board in the future.

Option 6. Increase the number of workers

Another method of increasing the tax base is the controversial one of bringing in young immigrants as productive workers. This tactic has been adopted in Germany where 30% of the population is classified as 'foreign'.

Option 7. Introduce a special levy

In the 1940s the government introduced a special pension levy, but it was soon absorbed into general revenue. Again, in the 1990s, a special levy called the Superannuation Guarantee Charge (SGC) was introduced. But what exactly does it guarantee? Let's see.

Chapter 3: The Risk of Doing Nothing 33

SGC — trick or treat?

Remember the slogan on television back in the early 90s promoting the government's Superannuation Guarantee Charge (SGC) scheme? The tune was catchy. The message was clear. It went something like this:

Super? What's Super?

Super's here for everybody right across the nation.

The 3% you're getting now provides a good foundation.

Any more than that and you'll have cause for celebration.

To plan for your retirement think of superannuation.

Now I must preface this section by pointing out that I applaud the initiative of forcing all Australians to take much more responsibility for their retirement. The intentions of the scheme are noble. However, I seriously question several elements.

First, because of the way in which the SGC has been promoted, there is a real danger that people will become complacent about their retirement needs, believing that the SGC will provide a pot of gold at the end of the rainbow. And secondly, there is a serious risk that the end benefits will be 'lost'. To fully understand why the SGC is no cause for celebration, we must look more closely at all its implications. What exactly is it, or isn't it? And more importantly, what will it do for *you*? Is it a trick or a treat? Are you being tricked into forgoing wage rises in the expectation that the SGC will treat you to a wealthy retirement?

What is the SGC?

With savings in Australia at crisis point, compulsory superannuation was seen as a mechanism for forcing Australians to save for their own retirement. Subsequent legislation made superannuation compulsory for the majority of employees from 1 July, 1992. The level of payment was to be phased in over 10 years, beginning with an employer contribution of 3% of salary, rising to 9% by 2002.

These contributions are invested on behalf of the employees, who can access the accrued benefits when they retire. An employer who provides less than the minimum superannuation support is liable for a charge to be levied by the Australian Taxation Office (ATO). The formal term for this is the Superannuation Guarantee Charge.

Here, then, we have a scheme with the potential to lower inflation, boost industry, lower unemployment, and provide Australians with a wealthy retirement. Sounds good, doesn't it? It seemed like a win-win situation all round. It not only kept the unions and workers happy, but also our policy makers. So what's the catch?

34   *More Wealth from Residential Property*

What isn't it?

Let's be clear: the SGC is not a road to wealth. It was never intended to provide an income high enough to give anyone a luxurious retirement. It *was* intended to make average and below average income earners, who had no intention of planning their own retirement, help pay for their own pension. Even the Reserve Bank has recognised that the SGC 'may not deliver enough money to cover most people's retirement' (25 July, 2000).

Suppose we take an average family where the husband and wife are both aged 31. Let's assume their joint income is $67,000 per year, with the husband earning $47,000, the average male adult wage, and the wife earning $20,000 part-time, half the average female adult wage (ABS Cat. 6302). The table below shows the amount they would accumulate for a particular time period, if they had started 10 years ago, at the time of introduction of the SGC, when their joint income was $44,000.

Estimated SGC Benefits for an Average Family

Period	Amount
10yrs	$20,645
20yrs	$79,945
30yrs	$156,201
40yrs	$250,851

Assumptions: SGC phased in as scheduled; 15% contributions tax; 4% return above inflation (ASIC guidelines); 10% tax on earnings (assuming imputation credits); 1.5% wages growth above inflation; 1.25% admin. charges; 2% inflation; no tax on lump sum.

After 40 years, with around $250,000 in super, this couple would *not* be wealthy — the income generated would be so low that according to the Reserve Bank, they would still qualify for a part-pension. Remember too, the baby boomer generation is already 45 years old, and with fewer than 20 years left until retirement, their SGC benefits would be even less.

Furthermore, not only could our average scenario be worse for many older people, it could be worse for young ones. It would be nice to believe that this world is perfect and that the benefits from the SGC — as modest as they are — will at least be there to be collected in retirement. As Dr Norman Zadeh said on the SBS program *The Cutting Edge*:

The problem with [superannuation] funds is that they are basically a gigantic IOU. You don't have the money now; they're supposed to pay you the money later; and between now and the time that you actually get your money, a lot of bad things could happen.

Chapter 3: The Risk of Doing Nothing 35

What can go wrong?

What are the 'bad things' that can happen to a superannuation fund?

Fund guarantee?

Although the name Superannuation Guarantee Charge implies that a guarantee is involved, the guarantee refers to the contributions you pay *in*, not the benefits you get *out*. With almost $600 billion now invested in superannuation, Senator John Watson, from the Superannuation Committee, commented on the SBS program *Not So Super* (26 April, 2001):

With so much under investment at the present time, there's always a tendency for those of evil intent to defraud the system. Now, as that pot of gold rises, and it's going to rise very significantly in the next 10, 20 years, there will be entrepreneurs out there, as we called them in the late 1980s corporate cowboys, who will want to get in there and rort the system.

Already several superannuation funds have collapsed in controversial circumstances (see page 59), despite the presence of two government watchdogs — ASIC (Australian Securities and Investments Commission) and APRA (Australian Prudential Regulatory Authority). And in Great Britain, front-page headlines in the *Daily Mail* (15 Aug, 2001) read: 'How safe are big company pensions?' after surveys revealed huge cash shortfalls.

Privately operated — government owned?

Although the SGC is a government scheme, the funds are managed privately by complying companies, so are ostensibly free from political interference. However, the temptation for governments to put their sticky fingers into the pie is a real possibility. This was recognised very early on when Hugh Morgan, managing director of Western Mining Corp Holdings Ltd, was quoted in *The Courier Mail* (2 Nov, 1993) as saying:

The big problem with superannuation is that because of the advantageous tax regime, governments fall into the habit of believing that those funds belong to them.

Management fees?

Fees charged by managers can destroy potential gains. On the SBS program *The Cutting Edge*, Peter Costello, the shadow Finance Minister at the time, stated that the SGC is 'where you will never see a return because you will have your funds eaten up by administrative costs'.

Unrealistic time frame?

The most generous calculations for the SGC are based on continuous employment for 40 years. With governments trying to keep people in the education system longer to ease unemployment, and people pushing to retire earlier, working for 40 years may be a time frame from a bygone era.

36 *More Wealth from Residential Property*

Change in government policy?

A shift in government policy could see the implementation of a totally different scheme. A change to a Labor Government could see a complete overhaul of the SGC as it stands, with the Australian Council of Trade Unions (ACTU) pushing to increase the level to 15%. While this may be a step in the right direction, it may breed even further complacency, as it has been recognised that the level needs to be closer to 40% to be effective.

Lump sum benefits?

Although the SGC benefits can currently be taken as a lump sum, there are noisy undertones that could lead to the abolition of lump sums in favour of indexed annuities; ie as pension payments. The present government has already indicated a desire to encourage retirees to take their benefits as an income stream in the form of a pension, rather than as a lump sum.

Boosting the economy?

One of the arguments put forward for the instigation of the SGC was that the monies invested would provide industry with much needed capital and boost the economy. This, in theory, would reduce our foreign debt by lowering our dependence on foreign investment. And yet, as Dr Clarke, Senior Lecturer in Economic History at the University of NSW points out:

If you don't get good rates of return from investing the funds at home, they have to go offshore.

If the superannuation funds continually exercise their right to invest 20% of their funds offshore (as is now allowed), how effectively would this stimulate industry at home?

Preservation age?

The age of preservation of superannuation benefits is currently being raised from 55 to 60, and there is no guarantee that this won't be altered as life expectancies rise. Already, the government has legislated to phase in the receipt of the age pension for women from 60 to 65. What next?

Amalgamation?

A rather frightening prospect is that any Australian government at any stage could abolish the SGC altogether, and redirect future payments away from the control of the superannuation companies into their own coffers. Governments have a history of amalgamating special contribution taxes into general taxes. The precedent was set in 1950 when the government of the day absorbed the Social Services Contribution into personal taxation. Who is to say it won't happen again?

Obviously, as Dr Norman Zadeh said of pension funds in general:

... a lot of bad things could happen.

Part II

Planning to Build

4
Who Do You Ask for Advice?

'After reading all your books, my wife and I thought seriously about getting into investment properties as a means of building wealth for our retirement. But we wanted to do it the right way, so we decided to talk to a financial advisor who we thought could arrange it all correctly for us. We looked up "financial planning" in the Yellow Pages and finally chose a reputable company that advertised its services as "Investment Structuring, Wealth Creation and Negative Gearing" among a host of other things that seemed to be relevant to property.

'The signs were there that they could help, so we made an appointment. But after two hours of "advice", we left completely bewildered, seriously doubting we had made the right choice to invest in property and believing that we were incapable of making any investment decisions for ourselves.

'In the beginning, it was fine, as the advisor seemed to ask all the right questions about our finances and aims, and he established that we could easily afford to borrow to invest. But after discussing with him our strong preference to invest in residential property, and explaining that we were seeking his assistance to do this, we were warned that it was the worst possible investment strategy. We'd be far better off, he advised us, to invest in a managed fund, and of course he had many that we could choose from.'

Does this story sound familiar? I couldn't count the people who have phoned or written, or told me after my seminars, of similar encounters with financial advisors. The tragedy is that many people who experience this scenario then begin to doubt their own confidence, question the facts in my books, and become disillusioned about investing at all.

The problem is not with the content of my books, nor with investment in property. It is that most people do not understand the true role of the financial services industry. So it's time to explain just who they are, what they do and where else you can go for advice about investment in property.

The role of financial advisors

The terms financial advisor, financial planner and investment advisor may conjure up images of professional people who provide *independent* financial advice to clients on *all* investment strategies and *all* investment types, whether indirect investments such as managed funds, or direct investments, such as cash, shares and property.

And yet, according to Sections 77 and 92 of the Corporations Law (*scaleplus.law.gov.au*) and Policy Statement 116 from the Australian Securities and Investments Commission (ASIC) (*www.asic.gov.au*), the terminology used by the financial advisory industry has quite specific meanings — none of which even vaguely suggest that financial advisors, by whatever name, provide general financial advice on every area of investment. Let me clarify some of these definitions for you.

Investment products means securities.

Securities means debentures, stocks or bonds issued or proposed to be issued by a government; or shares in, or debentures of, a body; or interests in a managed investment scheme (eg unit trusts, bonds and superannuation products); or units of such shares; or an option contract. (But according to ASIC, *not* property. Whilst property is often referred to as being a security for a loan, it is *not* classified as a security by the Corporations Law.)

Advice means personal securities recommendations or general securities advice.

Advisor means a natural person who provides advice relating to securities and includes a licensee and a representative of a licensee.

Investment advisory services means advice on securities, whether provided with another service or on its own. It is used interchangeably with the terms advisory services and securities advice.

Licensee means a holder of a dealer's or an investment advisor's licence.

You don't need to understand all these terms, and I'm sorry to bore you with such detail, but you need to see the real picture. In plain English, the fact is that almost all financial planners, investment advisors, financial advisors, etc, are simply licensed to sell managed funds, shares, trusts and superannuation, and provide financial advice limited to these securities. Property is definitely *not* one of them. On the other hand, licensed real estate agents, with no pretentious claims to calling themselves financial planners, are licensed to sell property and provide financial advice restricted to property (pers. com. Daryl Smeaton, President REIA). Most of the problems relating to the role of financial advisors arise, therefore, because of the public's misperception of their name, and what they do.

Chapter 4: Who Do You Ask for Advice? 41

I think it's pretty understandable that people have the wrong idea about what financial advisors and planners do, as for many years even I, in my naivety, thought that financial advisors and planners provided all round, big picture financial advice. After all, most goods and services are supposed to be labelled well enough so that you know what to expect before you buy. In other words — what you see is what you should get. For example, if you go to a bakery, you won't expect to be sold meat. But you'll expect to see an array of breads, cakes and other associated goods. If you go to the Toyota dealer, you won't expect to be sold a new Ford Falcon, but you'll expect to see all the latest in Toyota cars.

It was a complete revelation when I realised some years ago now, that the majority of financial advisors do not give that large scale, independent advice on *all* types of investments, but instead deal only in securities, which does *not* include property.

Even the Institute of Chartered Accountants (ICA) and the Australian Society of Certified Practising Accountants (ASCPA) have recognised the flagrant misuse of the term 'financial planner'. An article by Simon Hoyle in the *Australian Financial Revue* (23 Nov, 1995) states:

The provision of financial planning advice in Australia had been hijacked by a group of people with dubious qualifications, the accounting profession's peak representative bodies said yesterday.

The article defines investment advice as focusing on selling investment products as defined by ASIC, and it includes this comment made by Robert Brown, a spokesman for the ICA and ASCPA:

One of the problems is that the term 'financial planning' is not defined anywhere, and the term has been hijacked. The financial planning industry has used that term whereas in my view most of them are doing investment advice, not financial planning.

Yes, indeed! There is no question that the terms 'financial advisor' and 'financial planner', or whatever else, have been seized by an industry that purports to provide big picture financial advice when in fact the majority simply sell investment products such as managed funds. Why and how has this arisen?

Part of the reason is that most financial advisors are not trained in the area of property investment. The Diploma of Financial Planning (DFP) tertiary level course provided by the Financial Planning Association (FPA) for advisors wishing to attain the highest level, titled Certified Financial Planner, does not include the study of investment in property. According to the FPA's website (*www.fpa.asn.au*), the curriculum includes securities and futures markets (ie shares), superannuation and managed investments, as well as life and general insurance. But *not* property.

42   More Wealth from Residential Property

Also, financial planners and investment advisors, or whoever, are not at all remunerated for recommending investment in property unless they are licensed real estate agents — which of course most of them are not; or if they are independent financial advisors and charge a fee for service — which again does not usually apply, and is not likely to happen. Michael Rice confirmed this in the Nov, 2000 issue of *Asset* when he explained:

Despite frequent predictions in recent years that investment advisors would shift towards fee for service or fixed dollar retainers, almost all practitioners still receive commission from financial institutions as their prime means of payment. With the riches available for the major dealer groups, it is hard to see a shift in industry practice in the foreseeable future.

A rich gold mine, indeed — and already being mined! Writing in *The Sunday Mail* (6 May, 2001), Gerard McManus advised:

Australia's banks and foreign-owned institutions have quietly swallowed as much as 90% of the country's leading independent financial advisory firms over the past few years.

In which case, if you invest through a financial advisor, there's a good chance that your life savings could fall into the hands of a multinational company whose headquarters are overseas. If you go to a financial advisor knowing all this, that's OK. However, if you were under the misconception like I was, that financial/investment advisors or whoever, are independent gurus of advice in *all* areas, at least I have put you in the picture; so now you can make up your own mind whether that's what you want or not.

Rather than trying to correct the perceived image of who they are and what they do, many of the financial advisory profession have taken to deriding investment in property as a viable strategy. Once, I believed that all I had to do to correct the constant barrage of criticism from the industry was to educate them in the wonderful benefits of investing in residential property. They were not interested in learning, but were still prepared to make irrational statements. One major financial planning group during 1996 was promoting seminars with captions on brochures such as:

Why residential property could be the worst investment in the 90s!

Five years later, they were producing newsletters with the headlines:

Housing goes off the boil ... experts are warning that the housing bubble is about to burst.

Pray tell, what happened in the meantime? How many people would have been discouraged or disillusioned and so missed out on the residential property upturn during this time? Those investors who stood by their own judgement and invested in residential property instead of listening to those advisors who decried property are probably thousands of dollars better off.

Chapter 4: Who Do You Ask for Advice? 43

Obviously, finding an independent financial advisor who gives strategic advice on property is going to be a challenge. What criteria should you use? ASIC defines an independent advisor as one who:

- avoids commissions, trailing commissions, soft dollar arrangements and other benefits from product providers which may tend to create bias;
- operates free from any direct or indirect restrictions relating to the securities recommended; and
- operates without conflict of interest created by ownership links to product providers.

However, according to the National Information Centre on Retirement Investments (NICRI) which is a free, government sponsored service aimed at improving the quality of information provided to people investing for retirement, getting independent financial advice is difficult. They advise:

The vast majority of organisations and people providing investment or financial advice at present do not meet the above criteria to promote or advertise their services as 'independent'. Investors should be aware of this and take into consideration in their decision-making the fact that the advice provided may be biased in some way.

Choice magazine, in its review of the financial advisory industry in 1998, also discovered that independent strategic advice is hard to come by:

If you're in the wealth accumulation stage in your life — still working, saving for retirement, with dependents — you are more likely to need strategic advice. The difficulty is that many planners don't provide strategic advice on a simple fee-paying basis because they don't consider it cost-effective to do so.

In other words, as already pointed out, most advisors make more money from selling commission-based products. NICRI suggests:

To minimise the possibility of advice being biased, investors may want to make it clear to the advisor at the outset that they will not be buying any investment products from or placing any investments through him or her. This will separate the financial planning process from the sales and marketing of the products.

By now it should be fairly clear to you that if you want to find out more about investing in property, it is highly unlikely you'll receive help from the financial advisory industry unless you can find an advisor who is truly independent. Yet as Rob Sitch of *The Dish* and *The Castle* fame wrote in *Business Review Weekly* (23 Nov, 1998) in response to that often heard comment, 'I suggest you seek independent financial advice':

That sounds good, but then you need independent advice on who is independent.

44 *More Wealth from Residential Property*

Who else will give you advice?

If you can't get independent advice on *all* areas of investment from a financial advisor or financial planner, who else can you turn to? Your accountant? Maybe, maybe not! The financial advisory industry has become so lucrative that many accountants are now expanding their traditional role of dealing with tax related issues to include financial planning. So after rebuking the industry for hijacking the name 'financial planner', it seems that accountants have now taken the view that if you can't beat 'em, join 'em. Daryl Corpe, chair of the financial planning committee within the Australian Institute of Chartered Accountants, argues in *Asset* (Nov, 2000):

The financial planning industry is driven by commissions at the moment and accountants just have to accept that, and accept that they have to provide financial-planning services or find it very difficult to survive.

That proposal is hard to swallow, considering that accountants have been inundated with compliance work since the introduction of the GST. Accountants are in a unique position to understand their clients' financial situations, so it's a worry that they have succumbed to financial expediency.

If most financial advisors and accountants can't advise you on property, who can? You could talk to those who will benefit most from your plan to borrow and buy property: the financiers and real estate agents. Or, you could simply talk to other property investors, often with mutual benefits.

Financiers are in the business of lending or 'selling' money. They not only profit from the upfront fees and ongoing charges but also from the margin between the borrowed and deposited interest rate. So they are keen to provide as much information as they can.

Then of course there are real estate agents. Yes, they do get paid a commission and yes, they are biased towards property. At least what you see is what you get, and there is little misleading about what they do. In recent years, with property investors becoming very frustrated at the lack of information available, many agents have become quite knowledgeable about the physical attributes and financial aspects of investment property.

Perhaps the most useful and unbiased information comes from other property investors. There's no need to join an association, for you'll often meet them at work or while playing sport. Alternatively, we host a very popular forum on our website (*www.somersoft.com.au*) where you can freely interact with other property investors and share their experiences.

No matter how much you learn from others, I believe that *you* are the best person to help yourself! Self education is the key and this book is designed to inform you about investment in property. First you need to learn the basic 'Do-It-Yourself' principles of building wealth.

5
The ABC of DIY Wealth Building

If wealth can provide all the wonderful things you desire, you might well ask: Why is it that only 5% of the population ever become wealthy, while the remaining 95% are content to dream? Patience is the real key and lack of it is why most people fail. The truth is that most people desire and strive for wealth. However, rather than taking the time and making the effort to learn the principles of wealth building, most opt for the quick and easy way and gamble on schemes that purport to bring quick riches.

In a recent survey Thomas J. Stanley, author of the best-seller *The Millionaire Next Do*or, found that poor people played the lottery almost three times more often than wealthy people. He noted that wealthy people held the common belief 'that it was better to burn a few dollars with a match each week than to lay money down for the lotto!'.

It is indeed true that even if you strike it lucky against all odds and win your millions, the chances are that you will not stay wealthy. I'm sure you've seen the headlines in the newspapers such as 'Lotto pair on the dole', 'Battlers blow a fortune' and 'Pools winners now broke', telling the woeful stories of people who have won or inherited a fortune, then lost it. Why? Because the same principles apply to preserving wealth as building it, and unless you know those principles, you will never stay wealthy.

Wealthy people are not gamblers, but simply ordinary people who understand the wealth building principles necessary to succeed. Once you know these principles, you too will be able to make confident investment decisions for yourself, without having to pay other people to do it for you.

Let's look at the facts and philosophies underlying these principles. I call them the ABC of DIY wealth building. We begin by discussing why having the right 'Attitude', preparing a 'Blueprint' and staying 'Committed' are so important. We analyse two different kinds of 'Debt' then compare 'Education' with schooling. Finally, we investigate why 'Fear' can stifle any well laid wealth building plan.

46   *More Wealth from Residential Property*

Attitude determines altitude

Being positive, and having the right attitude, is probably one of the most difficult of the principles of building wealth, but it plays a huge part in determining how high you will travel up the ladder of success. William James, the famous psychologist, put it this way:

The greatest discovery of my generation is that a person can alter his life by altering his attitude of mind.

Today, economists are realising that people's attitudes have a powerful influence on a country's economy. Some larger Australian institutions have even been introducing a 'confidence indicator'. If confidence is such an important economic factor at the national level, think what it could do for you on a personal level. It doesn't matter how well you understand the principles of success, you will never become wealthy unless you possess that bit of something extra — confidence. The formula below represents my measure of the state of the economy — the economy of the country, and yours personally.

$$E = MC^2$$

where	E	=	Economy
	M	=	Money
and	C	=	Confidence

How you think and feel can influence your confidence to such an extent that it affects what you do. It's a case of wrong attitude, no confidence, no action, no wealth. Positive thinking can enhance all aspects of our daily lives, including the way we think about wealth and success. Thinking positively means overcoming all obstacles that get, or rather *appear* to get in our way. In his wonderful book *Think and Grow Rich*, Napoleon Hill describes some of these obstacles. Here are just a few of the countless 'alibis for failure' that he lists:

If I had a good education; If I could get a job; If I had good health; If I did not fear what 'they' would say; If I could save some money; If I only had time; If I could just get a break; If my family were not so extravagant.

The list is endless and you will recognise how easy it is to find an excuse, or 'alibi', for doing nothing today, or deferring it until tomorrow. To become wealthy you must learn to see the positive attributes of a seemingly bad or hopeless situation. Don't allow negative thoughts to undermine all your well-intentioned plans. If you listen to negative people around you, you'll become one of them — one of the 95% of the population who fail to achieve the wealth they're capable of.

Blueprint your goals

Have you made out a will? Most people take the trouble to put pen to paper and set down exactly how they are going to distribute their assets when they die. Very few bother to set down their financial goals. We take more time to plan what we're going to do with our money when we're dead than while we're alive. It pays to *plan* if you really want to be financially free. The mind is a powerful force and visualisation can help turn goals into a reality. Most people live up to their expectations: so if you expect nothing, you'll more than likely get nothing.

A social worker in the United States once asked a young man standing in a dole queue what it was he expected to do with his life. He said that his father had been on the dole for his whole life, his grandfather had been on the dole for a lifetime, so more than likely he too would spend the rest of his life on the dole. It's sad to think that negative expectations are often fulfilled, simply because they're expected.

Last year, my husband and I both turned 50. To mark this momentous occasion we decided to go in the Sydney marathon being held as a trial run over the course planned for the Sydney 2000 Olympics later in the year. Being reasonably fit to begin with, we decided that a time of less than four hours was achievable, providing we followed a training blueprint and stuck to it. The plan was that for each major training session we did on a Sunday, we would increase our run by 2 kilometres until we got within reach of the marathon distance of 42 kilometres.

Three months and 1,000 kilometres of road later, we flew to Sydney to compete. The course was much more difficult than we had expected, with long hard hills over the latter part towards Homebush. What kept us going was knowing that our blueprint for running the race was sound and that our goal was achievable, if we kept to it. We both finished in less than four hours, though I had a more difficult time sticking to the plan, managing to finish with only 49 seconds to spare.

Achieving your desired level of wealth is a bit like running a personal best, or a PB, as they say, in a race. You may not win the race, but by running your very best, you will achieve just as much satisfaction as the winner. Investing is the same. You don't have to be the richest person in the land. You may be happy to become financially independent without becoming a millionaire. But at least set a goal, no matter what it is, then set about planning how and when you'll achieve it. You might start with a plan as simple as paying off your credit cards, then reducing your home loan, before laying out a blueprint to buy investment properties every other year, until you retire at 55, or even 40. The sky's the limit, only when you plan it that way.

48   *More Wealth from Residential Property*

Commitment to succeed

Once you've set yourself a blueprint for building wealth you need to stay committed to that goal and make it work. It has been said that people generally fall into three categories: those who make things happen, those who watch things happen and those who wonder what happened. Being committed and taking responsibility means that you, and you alone, have to make it happen. Don't simply *decide* to do it — *do* it.

Many years ago my eldest son, who was nine at the time, came up to me while I was cooking dinner and posed this question. 'If there are three frogs on a lily pad, and two decide to jump, how many are left?' Thinking deeply, I replied, 'One'. 'Wrong,' he said gleefully. 'Three — they only *decided* to jump — they haven't jumped yet.'

Don't be like a frog on a lily pad. Once you decide to do something about increasing your wealth, you have to take the next step and go for it. Staying committed means you can't let obstacles get in your way. As my mother often said, 'Where there's a will, there's a way'. On the counter of my local bank there is a plaque inscribed with a quotation from Vincent T. Lombardi, who coached the Green Bay Packers football team to five World Championships. It reads:

The difference between a successful person and others is not a lack of strength, nor a lack of knowledge, but rather a lack of will.

I often wonder how many people standing in the queue at the bank take any notice of this little gem. Setting goals and deciding to do something is a great start, but you then need the willpower and commitment to follow it through. When things go wrong, as they often will, we tend to blame everyone else but ourselves. Shifting the blame for our woes may appease our conscience, but it rarely solves our problems. It's the government's fault that I'm unemployed or it's the children's fault that I'm overweight and it's society's fault that I committed a crime. There are many people who not only blame others for their problems, but expect others to solve their problems for them. They want someone else to make their decisions for them, to help them lose weight, or to support them in old age. After abusing our bodies for 40 years with fatty foods, alcohol, and cigarettes, we expect doctors to find a miracle cure for our ills.

So too with our finances. We prefer to leave our financial well-being to Lady Luck, and if that doesn't work, we leave the responsibility to the government. For most people, their only commitment is to live for today, often borrowing to buy consumer goods to help make today even better. In the next section, we see how a commitment to debt of the wrong kind will eventually lead to financial ruin.

Debt allows leverage

Many people wrongly believe that good and bad debt are synonymous with small and large debt. For example, they think that it's OK to borrow $16,000 for a new car, but not to borrow $160,000 for an investment property. In fact, a small debt for consumable items can destroy wealth. A large debt on appreciating assets can build wealth.

Let's imagine two people who each can spare $2,700 a year. Bill Poor can't wait to get behind the wheel of a new $16,000 car that will cost him $2,700 a year over 10 years. Richie Cash decides that with his $2,700 a year, he can buy a rental property for $160,000. Why should a property worth ten times that of a car cost the same amount each year? Let's see.

Bill Poor gets a great deal from his local bank and borrows the entire $16,000, with a personal loan at 11.5%. In the first year, his repayment of $2,700 consists of roughly $1,793 in interest and $907 towards the principal, but over 10 years, he will clear the loan and own the car outright.

Richie Cash borrows $166,000 ($160,000 property price and $6,000 purchasing and borrowing costs) at 8.5% on interest-only. (See page 194 for more details.) His interest bill is $14,110 a year, but with no principal payments, after 10 years he still owes $166,000. However, in the first year, with $10,400 in rent and a tax refund of $3,626, Richie pays only $2,684 of his total expenses of $16,710 ($14,110 interest plus $2,600 in property expenses). The table below shows what happens over 10 years.

The Way to Wealth — Car or Property?

Car ($)				Property ($)		
Value	**Debt**	**Equity**	**Yr**	**Value**	**Debt**	**Equity**
16,000	16,000	0	**0**	160,000	166,000	-6,000
14,240	15,093	-853	**1**	167,200	166,000	1,200
12,674	14,076	-1,402	**2**	174,724	166,000	8,724
11,280	12,936	-1,656	**3**	182,587	166,000	16,587
10,039	11,658	-1,619	**4**	190,803	166,000	24,803
8,934	10,225	-1,291	**5**	199,389	166,000	33,389
7,952	8,618	-666	**6**	208,362	166,000	42,362
7,077	6,817	260	**7**	217,738	166,000	51,738
6,299	4,797	1,502	**8**	227,536	166,000	61,536
5,606	2,532	3,074	**9**	237,775	166,000	71,775
4,989	0	**$4,989**	**10**	248,475	166,000	**$82,475**

Assumptions: Car depreciates at 11%; property value increases at 4.5%

50   More Wealth from Residential Property

After 10 years, Bill would have paid a total of $27,000 (10 years at $2,700) for a car, which at 11% depreciation per year, is worth just $4,989. If he had sold the car at any time up to the seventh year, he would have been going backwards. For most of the time he owed more than the car was worth. However, Richie would have paid only $21,579 over the 10 years for a property now worth $248,475 (at a conservative capital growth of 4.5% per year). He still owes the original $166,000, but this gives him an equity of $82,475!! And by this stage, the rent would be almost equal to the interest payments!!

Let's go one step further. After 10 years, poor old Bill is left with a worthless car. To buy another new one he would need to borrow $20,000, because by then, that's what a new car would cost with inflation. On the other hand, cashed up Richie, if he wants to, can sell his property and then pay cash for a brand new car. He'd also have more than enough to buy one for his wife and one for his son and to go on a holiday too!

Which Path Would YOU Choose?

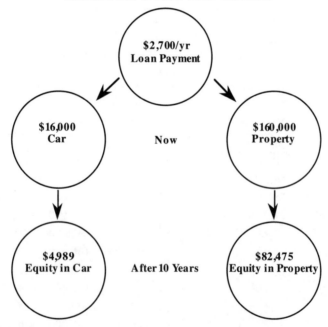

When you next think that big debt is bad debt, think of the following conversation between two young boys.

1st boy: We are so poor that my Dad owes the bank $2,000.

2nd boy: We are so rich that my Dad owes the bank $2,000,000.

Education versus school

Knowledge takes the worry out of investing. It gives you confidence and arms you with sufficient information to sensibly evaluate each step in your wealth building plan. I've learned over time, sometimes the hard way, that knowledge maximises gains and minimises risks. Ultimately, you must become your own expert. To do that, you need knowledge and you will only acquire it if you have a real desire to learn.

When I was teaching, it was more than evident that students needed a reason to learn and study. Classes progressed with the usual amount of disruption and disinterest, until that magic word 'exam' was mentioned. The transformation was nothing short of miraculous. Students suddenly discovered an overwhelming desire to learn because they had found a very good reason. Perhaps if the word 'pension' was linked to 'poverty' more often, people might become more aware of their need to learn more about investing.

What's your own attitude to learning? How many books have you bought in the last year to help you make decisions? Who have you talked to about your financial ideas and goals? Have you actively sought any information, or are you going to sit and wait for it to come to you?

The subject of 'how to build wealth' is generally not taught in schools. Indeed, most people do not become financially literate until they are adults, sometimes older adults at that. This is a sad reflection on our education system. I for one did not become aware of the difference between saving your own money and investing with other people's money, or OPM, until my thirties, even though I'd completed a university degree 10 years earlier.

As a teacher, it worried me to see that courses in finance were just not available to most students. Topics such as Financial Maths were directed mostly at non-achievers and even then, the emphasis was more on how to budget and save money, rather than how to invest and make money. The more academic students often completed a high school education knowing little about interest rates and even less about assets and liabilities. How can we expect them to manage their finances? Presently, the education system teaches the skills needed to earn money, but ignores the skills involved in managing and investing the money you get.

If this emphasis were better balanced, we might not need to spend so much money on saving people from their self-inflicted financial crises. However, even without the help of our education system, and no matter how old you are, you can still educate yourself in the principles of how to become wealthy. As Henry Haskins put it:

The man who is too old to learn was probably always too old to learn.

52 *More Wealth from Residential Property*

Fear stifles wealth building

Perhaps one of the most common reasons why people never start to invest, even though they *want* to, and *do* realise that they need to, is fear. They are afraid of going it alone when everyone else around them is living for today; they have a profound fear of failure so it's easier to do nothing; and they suffer an attack of the nerves at the thought of borrowing a large amount of money. Franklin D. Roosevelt, in his inaugural speech in Washington, summed it up:

First of all, let me assert my belief that the only thing we have to fear is fear itself — nameless, unreasoning, unjustified terror which paralyses needed efforts to convert retreat into advance.

Fear! It stops us dead in our tracks. It prevents action when we know we should act. Yet most of our fears are completely unfounded. They are based on illogical perceptions of what 'might' happen. Most people have a dreadful fear of sharks. They are afraid to go out in the water further than anyone else, nervous about dangling their toes over the side of a boat, and suffer a panic attack if they fall off a boogie board in deep water.

These same people willingly get into a car and drive it around town, or up the coast for a holiday, or a thousand kilometres for a wedding, without any fear of a car accident whatsoever. Their fear of sharks and lack of fear of a car accident are out of whack with reality. According to the Australian Bureau of Statistics, on average, only *one* death per year has been caused by shark attack in Australia over the last two hundred years, while over *one thousand* people are killed on our roads in car accidents *every* year. What should we be more fearful of — sharks or cars?

Most people are fearful of starting an investment plan, in the same way as they fear sharks. Perhaps if I remind you of some statistics I've already quoted, it might help you put this in perspective. The median income of couples aged over 65 is just $18,500 per year, with the majority dependent on an age pension. Keep in mind, too, that with an ageing population, the age pension right now could be as good as it gets, so it could be much less when it's time for you to retire. Only 4.7% of couples retire on $50,000 per year, the income that most had hoped for in their retirement.

If you are afraid of plunging into an investment strategy, you need to keep in mind the alternative of being reliant on a pension that may or may not exist in the future. In the next part of this book you will learn enough about investing in residential property to overcome your fears so that you can be confident and comfortable about starting an investment program. We'll start by looking at, and comparing, the various investment options to give you enough information to get you off and running.

Part III

Choosing the Bricks

6
What Are the Options?

Many years ago, when my three children were pre-schoolers, I remember giving them each a dollar for doing a few small jobs and they asked to go to the local school shop to buy some lollies. So off we went in the old station wagon.

Never had they been in a position before to make their own decisions on such important matters. They stood staring at the huge array of bottled lollies, trying to pick the best ones. They walked up and down looking first at one bottle, then another, often selecting one then deciding not, sometimes asking the patient shopkeeper which ones the older school kids liked best. After twenty minutes, with not a lolly chosen, I gave them an ultimatum — decide in the next five minutes or we'll leave with nothing. With only a minute left, they each hurriedly picked their lollies, but then complained all the way home that there were some they didn't like.

Once people realise they must invest for their future, they are faced with a bewildering array of options and, quite often, like my kids in the lolly shop, they can't make up their minds what to do. It is understandable that people become confused, sometimes making hurried decisions they later regret, often doing nothing because it's all too hard. So I want to make the investment decision easy for you by narrowing down the choices.

If you look carefully at *all* possible investment options, you find that they boil down to just three choices — cash, shares or property. They may be disguised as something completely different, such as a managed fund or a superannuation scheme, but they all ultimately entail cash, shares or property. As well as making a choice, you must also decide if you want to DIY (Do-It-Yourself) or PSE (Pay-Someone-Else) to do it all for you.

This chapter will guide you through the maze of pathways that lead to cash, shares or property when you Pay-Someone-Else to do it all for you. These include managed funds, of which superannuation, property trusts, syndicates and even cash investments, require a special mention. In the succeeding chapter we will then compare the Do-It-Yourself investments of shares and property.

Pathways to wealth

This diagram shows you the maze of pathways that ultimately lead to cash, shares or property.

Which Way to an Early, Wealthy Retirement?

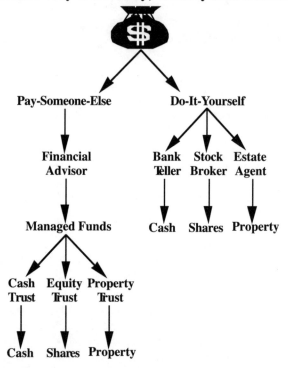

When you set out on the route, your very first decision is whether to Pay-Someone-Else or Do-It-Yourself. We discussed the role of financial advisors in Chapter 4, and noted that they primarily sell managed funds. So it's important for you to understand that if you *do* decide to see one, you will already have unwittingly allowed someone else the potential to take control of your finances. You may have gone to them intending to get help to Do-It-Yourself, but as I have already pointed out, most financial advisors are *not* in the business of providing strategic advice on which you can then act. By following the DIY path, you are assured of taking control of your financial destiny with far more rewards. The choice is yours.

> *Two roads diverged in a wood, and I —*
> *I took the one less travelled by*
> *And that has made all the difference.*
>
> Robert Frost

Managed funds

Not long ago, in a book on investment, I saw a chapter headed 'Money for a Rainy Day — Superannuation, Rollovers, Annuities'. I think this sums up what these funds will do for you. Although managed investments may not be the greatest wealth generators, for many people these funds will provide their *only* form of income when they retire.

Managed investments are exactly what they say they are — managed. Someone else takes all the effort out of investing for you — *and* all the cream. Most people who choose this option do so because they believe they lack the time, knowledge or skills to become a DIY investor. Many also think they lack the funds necessary for direct investment, believing they couldn't possibly afford to buy a property with a $160,000 price tag.

On the contrary. Direct investment in residential property does not require special expertise (most people have a basic knowledge of residential property), does not dominate all of your time (do-it-yourself does not mean do-it-*all*-yourself), and doesn't cost an arm and a leg (it may cost less than $60 per week to buy a $160,000 rental property).

How do the returns from managed funds compare to DIY investments? Let's look at this logically. Fund managers invest your money into cash, shares, or property, usually via trusts. So your money ends up where you could have invested it anyway, but with returns significantly reduced by the middlemen between you and your money. According to *Asset* (Nov, 2000), upfront fees are from 1% to 4% of the sum invested, while ongoing fees or trailing commissions range between 0.25% and 1% per year. Then there are administration charges plus the costs associated with churning, the process of unnecessarily moving funds, ostensibly to a better investment, when more often than not it is an exercise in boosting commissions.

Perhaps you're thinking that fund managers are more capable of making good investment decisions than you. Let me remind you, then, of how many of them were caught in the stock market crash of 87, the collapse of the commercial property market not long after, and the failure of many dot com companies just recently. Yes, there are some good fund managers in the market place, but choosing the astute ones can be a daunting task and defeats the very purpose of why people invest indirectly; that is, to be free of such decisions.

At the very least, choosing managed investments is better than doing nothing. But farming out your profits to all and sundry along the route may not allow you to achieve your goal of retiring early or wealthy. What about superannuation? Where does it fit into the scheme of things? Isn't it a special option? Let's see how good it is.

58   *More Wealth from Residential Property*

Isn't superannuation the best?

Superannuation is simply a managed fund with a notoriety for rather questionable tax concessions. Any good returns are, in fact, swallowed by taxes and fees. Taxpayers Australia, in *DIY Superannuation* (June, 2000), listed seven taxing points within the superannuation process and classed the scheme as a 'Super Tax Rip-off'. They went on to say:

So much for the fairy story kept alive by politicians that superannuation savings are concessionally taxed! The government's greedy revenue grab is destroying the benefits of superannuation.

It sounds good when you hear that superannuation is only taxed at a concessionary 15%, but this is just the start. This 15% tax on income is combined with 15% tax on your contributions, plus 15% surcharge for high income earners, plus 15% exit tax on the lump sum, which rises to 47% if this amount exceeds the Reasonable Benefits Limit (RBL). Then there's 10% Capital Gains Tax (CGT) and 10% Goods and Services Tax (GST) levied at other points.

After taxes have skimmed the cream from superannuation, management fees milk what's left. Unlike property, where management fees are paid only on the rental income, super fund fees are paid on the whole asset. A 2% annual super fund fee might sound far less than the 7.5% management fee charged for rental properties. However, 2% of $160,000, or $3,200, is much more than 7.5% of $10,400, or $780, the property management fee you'd pay on a $160,000 investment property renting for $10,400 per year.

However, the main reason why superannuation can never be as good as investing directly in property is its lack of gearing ability. Consider a person who wants to invest $2,700 per year from a $47,000 annual salary. If it's invested in a super fund, this $2,700 is all that is growing in value. However, if it costs $2,700 to invest in a $160,000 investment property, then $160,000 in assets is growing in value. If both the super fund and property increase at 4.5% per year, it's easy to see that 4.5% of $2,700, or $122 from super, is a lot less than 4.5% of $160,000, or $7,200 from property. Why the difference? Leverage is the key. You can't borrow to invest in normal superannuation, but you can borrow to invest in property. This debt, or leverage, can multiply your returns and accelerate your wealth building much faster than any superannuation fund.

Most of us believe that despite the possibility of poor returns from superannuation, at least there will be a small nest egg awaiting us when we retire — which will be better than having done nothing. However, there is a real possibility that as well as receiving no return *on* your money you could well get no return *of* your money.

Chapter 6: What Are the Options? 59

Many superannuation funds are not guaranteed and this is highlighted by the number of them that have collapsed. The most recent were CNAL (Commercial Nominees Australia Ltd) and EPAS (Employees Productivity Award Super) in 2001. In both these cases, not even the two government regulatory bodies set up to oversee the superannuation industry — ASIC and APRA — could save them. According to the SBS television program *Insight,* screened on 26 April, 2001:

Thousands of Australians, many of them close to retirement, have lost most or all of their savings, because of the failings of two separate trusts. This, despite regulation by two government authorities whose duty it is to oversee the management of superannuation funds.

In recent times, Great Britain has witnessed the collapse of many of its pension funds, the equivalent of Australia's superannuation. Headlines in the *Daily Mail* (13 Dec, 2000) screamed 'Organised Theft' following the implosion of Britain's oldest mutual insurance group Equitable Life, while *The Sunday Times* (10 Dec, 2000) described it as 'A disaster for investors'. In scenes reminiscent of Australia, the UK government watchdog, the Financial Services Authority (FSA), allegedly 'stood in the shadows'.

This collapse followed hot on yet another pension scandal to rock Great Britain, in which millions of people lost billions of dollars through the improper selling of pension plans. This saga is still being sorted out by the UK government, in what has been called the 'scandal of the century'.

Another drawback with superannuation is that you can not touch your funds until you turn 55. Superannuation is not a redeemable asset and you can only access it early in cases of severe hardship; so money can not be withdrawn simply to pay for your daughter's wedding. However, property can be sold at any time; and if you've set up a credit line to enable immediate withdrawal of funds, you may not even need to sell.

I'm often asked if I have superannuation, and when I explain that my super fund is mostly my properties, they don't understand. Some people have firmly entrenched ideas that superannuation must be obtained through an institution such as a life insurance company, or a bank. But ponder for a moment. What do you expect from your super? You want it to give you long-term security and income on your retirement. Don't you? Doesn't investment in rental property accomplish all of this and more? Doesn't investment property give you long-term security and income for your retirement in the form of rent? And don't you contribute to it year after year by paying the shortfall between your rent and interest? So you see, it's really the same as superannuation — yet a far more powerful and more flexible form. It just takes some rearrangement of our thoughts, and a little lateral vision, to think of it that way.

Property trusts and syndicates

Since this book is about investment property, it seems appropriate to look at two special types of managed funds that involve property. These are property trusts and syndicates.

When you buy units in a property trust, you become a beneficiary of a trust which directly owns property. In most cases, property trusts buy large commercial properties such as suburban retail shopping centres or Central Business District (CBD) office blocks, as they often have pooled funds worth hundreds of millions of dollars. Property trusts may be listed, meaning their units can be traded on the stock exchange at the listed price, which is subject to market fluctuations. If they are unlisted, they are often controlled by a fund manager and can be bought and sold directly at the nominated valuation price, so long as there are no time limits on tenure which might restrict their sale for a set period. While some property trusts have done well, it is extremely difficult to separate the wheat from the chaff and determine which ones are solid.

I might add that we have invested a small amount of 'play money' into a listed property trust, albeit through our company's superannuation fund. While this fund is very small compared to our large property portfolio, our company can contribute a little bit to property each year in a tax effective way. The only asset of this trust just happens to be one of my favourite shopping centres, so my husband believed that if I was going to continue to spend extravagantly at this centre, this trust was likely to do well. From my point of view, it seemed a good way of feeling better about spending so much, knowing that some of it would be returned as a dividend.

In a property syndicate, you become a registered part-owner of a specific building. Usually, property syndicates consist of a small consortium of investors (about 20) with a selected fund manager and a property manager. Each syndicate is established to purchase a specific property, and because of the minimum of overheads and middlemen, these syndicates can be quite profitable, particularly since they can be geared to a high level. You can only retrieve your money when the syndicate is terminated and the building is sold, although some syndicates do make provision for on-selling shares at the discretion of the manager.

Property trusts and syndicates have limited use as a compromise for those people who are interested in property investment, yet don't want to commit themselves to outright ownership. While some have been highly successful, many have not. The downside is that as well as incurring management fees, they are often associated with the higher risks inherent with commercial properties such as volatile property values and higher vacancy rates.

What about cash?

Cash, in a sense, is just another managed fund. It's certainly a different concept to consider cash in this light, but think about it for just a while. The banks are really borrowing the money you have deposited, to invest on your behalf, and as they see fit. They pay you interest for the privilege then lend the capital to others at a higher rate. You have no control over where the money goes, so in effect, it's a managed fund.

More importantly, will the interest from cash investments make you wealthy? Do you know many people who have made enough this way for a comfortable retirement? A few? None? It's likely that you do know someone with cash in the bank who *thinks* they have enough to retire on, but in fact have been getting poorer each year. Most people feel secure with cash in the bank. But they don't see that the twin ravages of inflation and taxation make it unprofitable.

People relying on interest from invested cash are in a no-win situation, no matter what the interest rate. If rates are high, cash investors receive an apparently good income from the interest. Taxation takes away up to half the income and then, because high rates are usually coupled with high inflation, the buying power of both the income and the base capital is continuously eroded, generating fewer and fewer 'real' dollars. In recent times, with low rates, cash investors have been complaining about the pittance they've been receiving in interest. The only positive thing with low interest rates is that the tax liability is less and the capital devalues more slowly.

Let's take a look at the track record of cash over the past five decades. The chart on the following page tracks the inflation rate based on the CPI (Consumer Price Index; ABS), the interest rates based on two year fixed term deposit rates (Reserve Bank) and the real return, taking into account inflation at the time and a 40% tax rate. (This tax rate is conservative in view of the fact that in the 1950s and 60s, top marginal rates were 60+%.)

The dark line on the graph shows the *real* return after allowing for tax and inflation. For the most part, the real after-tax, after-inflation returns were negative, reaching a trough of minus 25% in the early 50s and again at minus 12% in the mid 70s. In only a few years was this real return positive, and even then, at most 4%.

Cash investments are clearly not your pathway to wealth and will never allow you to retire early and wealthy. Ironically, investing in cash, which is really saving money, not investing, allows someone else to borrow and invest in more profitable areas so they can retire earlier and wealthier than you.

After-Tax, After-Inflation Returns from Cash

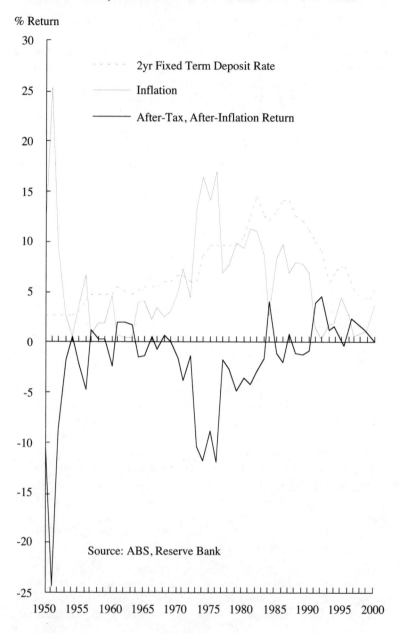

Source: ABS, Reserve Bank

7
Shares versus Property

You could be forgiven for thinking that, as this book is about property, a comparison of shares and property might not be as balanced as it should be. Let me assure you that this is not the case. In fact, I want to acknowledge upfront that it *is* possible to make a fortune by investing in shares. For example, had you invested $1,000 in Westfield shares in 1960 they'd be worth $109 million today and you probably wouldn't be reading this book. On the other hand, if you'd bought a small flat on the outskirts of Sydney, it would probably be worth only $100,000 today, a pretty good result, but not quite a fortune. Yet, as a result of the study presented in this chapter, I am more convinced than ever before that residential property is the key to building wealth for the average investor.

Everyone likes to back a financial winner like Westfield, but as you probably already know, few, if any, of our 19 million Australians have achieved such results or ever will. There are no flashing neon signs that signal future share market winners — so you either need the foresight of a Nostradamus, a reliable source of inside information, or a big helping hand from Lady Luck. For instance, in 1960, had you invested in a company such as Centralian Minerals, your shares would now be worthless: the company liquidated in 1962. Is there any residential property in Sydney that is worthless now?

The age-old debate between shares and property is often sensationalised in the media, but rarely are the articles in depth, and they are invariably one sided. One day you read that property is better than shares, only to read the next day in the very same paper that shares are better than property — and it all sounds so very convincing! Which propaganda do you believe? The problem with many of these articles is that they seem to carefully choose the variables (either growth or yield or both) and the time frame (usually a short term of less than 10 years) that suits the answer they are looking for.

In this chapter, I have tried to provide a comprehensive and objective comparison of the two investment vehicles using all of the criteria that are important to investors and to draw from the experiences of the past twenty years (1980 to 2000). Obviously, such an analysis must consider the

64   *More Wealth from Residential Property*

gross returns and the associated risk, but there are many other criteria that investors consider when making decisions. For example, the level of risk will determine how much lenders will allow you to borrow, which in turn will influence how much the returns can be magnified through gearing. The tax effectiveness will be very important to many investors, as will the affordability and liquidity. Last, but by no means least, I compare the level of personal control that each asset class offers, an issue that has become of critical importance to many investors in recent times.

Thus, the aim of this chapter is not so much to show you whether property or shares is the better investment, but rather to help you understand which of the two best suits your particular needs and aspirations.

Returns

One of the reasons why many people become confused with the various arguments put forward by proponents of shares or property is that 'returns' can be measured in different ways. Let me explain the terminology. Gross returns represent the capital growth and yield from the asset. Net returns allow for the costs of getting those gross returns. However, the most comprehensive measure of return is the Internal Rate of Return, or IRR, but it is rarely used. It takes into account *all* relevant factors, including loans, tax and the investor's income; and if inflation is considered, it can also be expressed as a 'real' return. The IRR used here and throughout this book has been calculated using the Property Investment Analysis (PIA) software and is described in detail in Appendix C on page 251.

To make it easy for you to understand what all this means to you, the investor, I have gone one step further. I will simulate an investment in *either* shares *or* property over the past 20 years and compare the wealth accumulated in each case. To do this, we must make some assumptions.

Let's slip back to 1980 when a fictitious couple, whom we'll call Tom and Jenny, had just paid off their home worth $40,000, the average of median-priced property in all capital cities at the time. Tom earned the average male wage of $13,500 and Jenny worked part-time earning $6,500, giving them a total annual income of $20,000. In both wealth building scenarios, Tom and Jenny start by using their home as security to borrow and buy the assets, and with equity and cash flows increasing each year in line with the relevant inflationary statistics, they borrow to buy more.

A study of this magnitude clearly requires more than just a cursory analysis. So rather than bog you down in facts and figures, I'll first review the results for those readers who simply want the gist of the comparison, then do a more detailed analysis in Appendix A on page 241 for those who would like to validate the results for themselves.

Chapter 7: Shares versus Property 65

Gross returns

For shares, the annual gross return between 1980 and 2000, based on the All Ordinaries Accumulation Index (Source: ASX) was **13.2%**. Based on the Residential Investment Property Index (Source: REIA) for the six major capital cities over the same period, for property it was **15.6%**.

Net returns

Maintaining a portfolio of either shares or property costs money. For shares, there are transaction costs associated with mimicking the All Ords Index, as it does not consistently represent the same companies. In 1980, 265 companies were in the All Ords Index, but by the year 2000, only 109 remained. To achieve *exactly* the same returns as the Index, it would be necessary to buy and sell shares. According to Professor Terry Walter from the Faculty of Economics at the University of Sydney, such transactions cost between 2% and 3%, *excluding* Capital Gains Tax (CGT). Here, the selling costs *including* CGT were conservatively estimated at 1.7%, giving a net return of **11.5%** for shares. (Note: A further 1.3% was allowed for purchase costs.) In calculating the Residential Investment Property Index, Professor Graeme Newell from the University of Western Sydney allowed 20% of the rent for expenses, leaving a net return for property of **14.0%**.

Wealth returns

In 1980, Tom and Jenny started their wealth building plan with nothing but the ability to borrow against their own home. As you will see next, residential property is a lower risk than shares so lenders prefer to use it as security for a loan. For Tom and Jenny, this meant that property could be geared with Loan to Value Ratios (LVRs) of up to 80%, while shares could only be geared to 50%. Keeping below these LVRs for each asset, and within the limits of loan serviceability as measured by Debt Service Ratios (DSRs), they were able to continually borrow and buy more assets. (LVRs and DSRs are defined on page 165.) After 20 years, Tom and Jenny accumulated **$1,060,637** from shares, but with better net returns and higher gearing they amassed **$1,894,195** from residential property.

Internal rate of return (IRR)

The internal rate of return, explained in depth in Appendix C on page 251, takes into account *all* factors such as capital growth, yields, expenses, interest, tax benefits, gearing levels and wealth returns. Using the PIA software to calculate the IRR on the entire portfolio, for shares it was found to be **11.9%** compared to **17.2%** for residential property.

Clearly, for an average couple like Tom and Jenny, investment in residential property can provide greater returns and more wealth, as you might like to now confirm for yourself by reading Appendix A. But what about the other attributes of shares and property. Let's move on.

66 *More Wealth from Residential Property*

Risk

If you don't take some risk with your money, however slight, you'll run the risk of having to live on the bread line later in life. We can not eliminate risk altogether, but we can try to choose an investment that is powerful enough to build wealth, yet secure enough to let us sleep.

Investing in shares is risky. According to the ASX report *Delisted Companies,* 7,661 companies have registered since 1929. Of these, 4,402 have been delisted for legitimate reasons such as takeovers, mergers and name changes, but a worrying 1,896 have been removed for reasons such as 'failure to pay listing fees' or 'no official reason given'. This leaves only 1,363 companies today. Risk can be reduced by manipulating your portfolio to mimic the All Ords Index, but this might incur significant costs, as we have already noted. Even if you achieve this, however, the All Ords Index still reflects a very volatile market compared to residential property. For example, it took nine years for the Index to recover from the 1987 crash from an all time high of 2239 to just 1227.

If you borrow money to invest in shares, you run the risk of a margin call, usually requiring you to sell shares in a down market to reduce the LVR to a limit acceptable to the lender. Between 1980 and 2000 the All Ords Index experienced negative quarterly growth 31 times. While you may not have needed to sell shares on each occasion, you'd have certainly been sitting on the edge of your seat waiting for the phone to ring.

How do we measure risk? Residex measured it by the deviation above and below the average return, and by the probability of a return being less than inflation (*Housing Investments Why? A Complete Comparison with Other Asset Sectors*). They found that standard deviation for shares was 22.4% compared to 6.8% for property, while the probability of returns being less than inflation was 34.1% for shares, but only 14.5% for property.

Comparing the Risk of Shares and Property

Risk	Shares	Property
Standard deviation	22.4%	6.8%*
Probability of returns less than inflation	34.1%	14.5%*
Number of returns less than -1%	24	3

* Source: Residex (1999)

Perhaps one of the simplest measures of risk is to compare the number of negative quarterly returns for shares and property. During the 20 years from 1980 to 2000, quarterly returns from shares have been significantly negative (less than -1%) on 24 of the 80 possible occasions, whilst those from property have been negative only 3 times out of 80.

Chapter 7: Shares versus Property   67

Gearing ability

Why is the high risk factor for shares so important even when you intend to be a long-term investor in shares? *The simple answer is gearing!* You can gear or borrow against residential property to a much higher level because of the lower risk, ensuring you of a huge leverage advantage that ultimately increases your returns and your wealth.

Lending institutions prefer to use property as security for their loans, because they see the volatility of the share market as meaning a high risk. Residential property can be geared with a Loan to Value Ratio (LVR) of up to 95% for owner occupiers and 80% for property investors, or higher with mortgage insurance. It is possible to borrow to buy shares; however the level of safe gearing is much lower, with lending institutions preferring to keep the LVR down to 50%. Ironically, the very first question often asked by a lending institution of someone wanting to borrow to buy shares is, 'Do you have a property, preferably residential, to use as a security for the loan?'

You can borrow to buy shares in many ways. You could use a Margin Loan, where only the value of the shares is used as security, or you could borrow against the value your family home by itself, or in combination with shares. However, all of these methods are risky. Deutsche Equity Lending points out:

The higher the level of gearing, the more likely it is that a margin call will be made at some time during the life of the portfolio. Using a conservative gearing ratio of 50% to 60% will reduce the chance of having to sell into a falling market to meet margin calls.

To expand on margin calls, this is when the value of the asset you've geared falls, increasing the LVR above the limit acceptable to the lending institution, and you get called on to offer more security to lower the LVR. While you can sell a few shares to cover a margin call, you wouldn't want to be caught trying to sell a piece of the family home if you had geared it so highly to buy shares that there was no equity left. On the other hand, margin calls on residential property are unheard of, primarily because the median price of residential property rarely falls more than a few per cent in any quarter.

How does gearing affect your wealth building capacity? Higher gearing increases the returns and this allows you to accumulate wealth much more quickly. How quickly? At what rate? And how much? For our couple Tom and Jenny, in the 20 years between 1980 and 2000, they would have been able to build twice the amount of wealth through residential property than by shares.

68   *More Wealth from Residential Property*

Tax effectiveness

Shares and property both have unique tax advantages. To encourage share investments in Australian companies, a scheme called 'dividend imputation' was implemented by the government in 1987. The scheme gives a tax credit to the shareholder for tax already paid by the company, thereby averting double taxation. In the Tom and Jenny scenario, this had the effect of increasing the dividend yield by 40% for most of the shares for two-thirds of the time.

Property also has special tax advantages through depreciation provisions in the tax laws which allow the building and the fixtures and fittings to be 'written off' over a period of time. These non-cash items, so called because they are a tax deduction without necessarily incurring a cash outlay, are discussed in detail later in Chapter 17. During Tom and Jenny's 20 year investment period, they contributed significantly to the tax effectiveness.

Further tax benefits are possible through negative gearing into either shares or property. However, as we have just seen, because of its greater stability, residential property can be geared much higher and more safely than shares, resulting in greater tax benefits. Higher gearing means higher interest payments, which creates a larger shortfall between the rent and expenses. This loss can then be offset against other income, lowering the tax payable, resulting in a tax refund.

A study by the Economic Planning Advisory Council (EPAC) in 1993 found that 'geared property investment is highly tax favoured', with an effective tax rate much lower than interest bearing deposits, owner occupied housing, unincorporated enterprises and publicly listed companies. With the government's GST induced tax reforms of 1 July, 2000 now firmly entrenched, though, many have suggested that the lower marginal tax rates may cause negatively geared property to lose favour with investors.

This could well be the case. Investors have a habit of jumping ship if they perceive it to be sinking. I say 'perceive', because in most cases, people who jump ship do not stop to think about why they are jumping. If they did, they would realise that although the tax effectiveness may be less, everything is relative and all other tax-advantaged investments will also be affected. If residential property was more tax effective than all other investments before, there is no reason to suspect that this will be any different in the future.

Chapter 18 deals with negative gearing in much greater detail. At this point it's important to understand how these tax benefits would have made investment in residential property very affordable for Tom and Jenny. Let's look at that now.

Chapter 7: Shares versus Property 69

Affordability

It is thought that shares are a much more affordable investment because they can be bought in small lots compared to the cost of a rental property. While there is no question that investment in shares is within the reach of most people, I want to show you why investment in residential property is also easily affordable.

For Tom and Jenny, $40,000 was a lot of money back in 1980. How then, you might ask, could they possibly have afforded $120,000 to buy three rental properties in the first year and then embark on a 20 year wealth building program involving millions of dollars? Let's start by breaking down the price of $40,000 into smaller chunks. By borrowing $41,600 for the property plus the purchase and borrowing costs, their outlays were only $4,784 in the first year, consisting of the interest of $4,160 (at 10%) plus the property expenses of $624. This made it much more affordable, but more was to come. The tenant contributed $3,030 in rent and, as a result of negative gearing, the taxman refunded $917.

All things considered, the $40,000 rental property really only cost them $837 per year or $16 per week — not much more than the cost of a carton of beer at the time. In terms of the annual cost of the property of $4,784, the graph below shows who paid what, with the tenant contributing the most at 63.3% ($3,030), the taxman refunding 19.2% ($917), leaving Tom and Jenny to pay just 17.5% ($837).

The Real Cost of a Rental Property

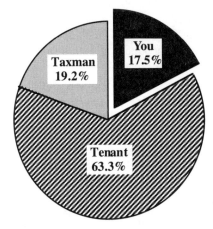

Can you see now why investing in residential property is so affordable for the average person? In Chapter 12 (page 194) we'll do this exercise again with the new tax scales and a $160,000 property with similar results.

70 *More Wealth from Residential Property*

Liquidity

In discussions comparing shares and property, people often suggest that shares are highly liquid and therefore provide greater flexibility, whereas property not only takes a great deal of time to liquidate, but it involves selling all or nothing. But this proposal is only perpetuated by those who don't know how to extract cash from a property without selling.

First, let's look at shares. True, shares are extremely liquid, and it's this liquidity and spontaneity that adds to the excitement of playing the sharemarket. Ironically, though, this easy liquidity contributes profoundly to the sharemarket's volatility. A person can respond to good or bad news by buying or selling shares instantaneously — but so can everyone else, creating an immediate supply and demand crisis.

It's the thrilling prospect of picking an instant winner that attracts the white collar punter to the sharemarket. How very appropriate to see an advertisement for the TAB in the midst of the sharemarket columns of a national newspaper. It read:

EASY MONEY
QUICK RESULT
GREAT FUN

It seems that the TAB and sharemarket attract a similar type of person. Unfortunately, because of the highly volatile nature of the sharemarket, exactly *when* you liquidate shares can be critical. You can sell when you want, but with no guarantee that you'll get your initial capital back, even if you wait many years before selling.

Property is perceived as illiquid, a distinct disadvantage in the eyes of many investors. You can't sell off the back bedroom in a hurry if you need some cash quickly, the argument goes. This perceived illiquidity is one of the very reasons why property is so much more stable than shares. Usually, when property investors need money they put their property on the market and then wait several months to finalise the sale and 'see' the money. This time-lag insulates property from the 'buy and sell' mentality that drives the sharemarket to all-time highs and lows.

I said that property is 'perceived' as illiquid because most investors think that a sale is the only way to extract cash from an investment. But one of the greatest attributes of property is its borrowing potential. If you need money in a hurry to visit Grandma in England, you can easily borrow it through a credit line set up with your property as a security. This not only eliminates the need to sell at short notice, it may eliminate the need to sell at all. It is advisable to set up a credit line well before you need the money, as banks have a habit of lending you lots of money when you don't need it, and nothing when you do.

Chapter 7: Shares versus Property   71

Control

Last but not least, any investment that you will be dependent on for your long-term financial security must offer complete personal control. For your own peace of mind, you should have control over every aspect of your assets. You can decide just what the investment will be in the first place and how it fits into your wealth building plan. This does not mean that you have to do everything yourself. What it does mean is that you have the capacity to delegate to others those aspects of your investment which you either have no desire to be part of, or no time to complete.

While shares offer greater control than a managed fund, unfortunately, you are at the whim and mercy of the directors of the company. And although there are shareholders meetings, voting is usually in proportion to the number of shares you hold. Small investors have very little say in the destiny of a company and control usually lies with larger institutions. *The Weekend Australian* (9–10 March, 1996) reported that:

The takeover rules say next to nothing about how the interests of small shareholders are to be looked after during a takeover battle.

Yet even being a large shareholder does not guarantee complete control. Take the case of the recent collapse of One.Tel where two of the directors who represented the largest shareholders apparently knew little about the true financial situation of the company.

The Australian Financial Review (16 Nov, 2000) bemoaned how little control investors really have over the salaries of Chief Executive Officers (CEOs). It seems as though the CEOs want more money when their company does well as a reflection of good results and they also want more money when their company does badly as a reflection of the amount of time and energy needed to lift performances! Ultimately, average investors have little control over the companies in which they own shares.

In contrast, direct investment in property gives you complete control over all aspects of your investment. If you choose to, you can even add value to your investment by doing something as simple as mowing the lawn. It is impossible to add value to shares. More importantly, you can decide if you want a property manager or not, and choose who you like. Don't think for one moment that using a property manager is relinquishing control of your assets, for they do not control the financial aspects of your property, just the tenant.

When you buy residential property, the ultimate control of your wealth building plan lies with you. You can choose your extent of involvement and do as much or as little as you like.

72　*More Wealth from Residential Property*

Shares or property?

We have seen in the preceding pages, both shares and property offer returns that far exceed those from superannuation or savings accounts. We also observed that it was possible for average income earners like Tom and Jenny to accumulate around twice as much wealth from residential property compared to shares over a 20 year period. Why was this so when the net returns from property (14.0%) were only marginally more than those from shares (11.5%)? The main reason was that lenders recognise residential property as a low risk compared to shares, enabling property to be highly geared (80% compared to 50%), magnifying the returns even more — in our example, 11.9% for property and 17.2% for shares.

We have also seen that higher levels of gearing create more tax benefits for residential property compared to shares — or for that matter, any other investment. This makes property investment very affordable. Considering liquidity, we saw this to be one of the greatest strengths of shares, but also one of its greatest weaknesses. Yet we saw that if the finances were correctly structured, residential property could be just as liquid — without the need to sell. Lastly, we saw that investment in property offers total personal control, something that is largely non-existent with shares.

If residential property is such a wonderful investment, why then, do less than 7% of Australians opt for it, while more than 50% invest in shares? A single answer is not obvious but a few comments might help. Firstly, our comparison has not shown that shares are a bad investment, just not as good as property. Secondly, about 10% of people own shares indirectly through superannuation or other managed funds. There must be other reasons why so many people are attracted to shares. The most obvious is that while investing in property can be downright boring, playing the share market can be exciting — nowadays, you can log on to the internet and, with a few clicks of a mouse, find out how much you've made, or lost. You can even buy and sell a few shares while you are there. What's even more appealing is that, like a ticket in Lotto, you have a small chance of making a fortune with the next Westfield. How exciting is that? Why wouldn't the average Australian punter be attracted to the share market?

Investment in median-priced residential property for the long term may not be exciting, but it is relatively safe and rewarding, as we have seen. You don't have to rely on a crystal ball, nor count on Lady Luck, and you don't need inside information for it to work for you. Most of us know something about property. Add a dash of common sense to what you already know, talk to other property investors and learn enough about financing, and you will have the surest and safest path to financial security. Just don't expect to get there overnight with the click of a mouse.

8
Which Property Should You Choose?

The term property and words associated with it spark much confusion. So before you jump to conclusions, you need to know precisely what type of property is being referred to when you read newspaper headlines such as:

Property prices slump 40%

Couple lose all in property deal

Vacancy rates at all time high

Quite often you don't find out the type of property concerned until the third or fourth paragraph, if you read that far, and by this stage you've probably become perturbed about *any* property being a good investment. In fact, those headlines were referring to an industrial property close to the CBD of Melbourne in 1994 when Victoria was in recession; a 500 hectare farm more than 300 kilometres north-west of Sydney after a flood in 2000; and a hotel in Cairns during the midst of the airline pilots' strike in 1989.

It is a bit like saying that fat is bad for you. Are all fats bad for you? Or are some fats worse than others? For sure if we categorise fat into saturated, unsaturated, monosaturated or polyunsaturated, we are in a far better position to decide how bad it may be.

Property is much the same. Do all types make good investments? Or are some types better than others? Property is an all encompassing word that takes in land (including vacant building lots and rural land), commercial property (including industrial, retail and office) and residential property; and even then, there are numerous categories, with some, such as serviced apartments, bordering on commercial. So we must know which type of property we are talking about before we can make any judgement.

In a nutshell, I believe that median-priced residential property is the best vehicle for building wealth for the average investor. Let's take a look at why neither land nor commercial property is appropriate, then examine in more detail why residential property is better for the average investor.

74   *More Wealth from Residential Property*

Why not land?

Throughout the centuries, the thought of buying cheap land and making big money from it has caught the imagination of land speculators often masquerading as property investors. Typically, they speculate that land values will increase astronomically in the short term as a result of frenzied buying and selling, or over a long time from rezoning and development. Fortunes have indeed been made this way, but the high returns possible generally reflect the huge risks involved, so speculating and investing need to be clearly distinguished.

A classic tale of short-term speculation in Melbourne during the 1880s is recounted in Michael Cannon's historical study, *The Land Boomers*:

Business boomed. Banking boomed. Money poured in from overseas. The frenzy grew and fed upon itself. Thousands of acres of suburban land were subdivided and resold many times, each time at a higher price.

The bubble burst eventually when 'there was no greater fool left to pay the higher price'. Two pioneers of the time, C.H. James and M. Davis, became instant millionaires through land speculation, but according to Cannon, were worth nothing following the crash.

Buying vacant land with a view to development down the track can also be fraught with danger. I have known many people who have bought land with a view to developing it, then found they couldn't afford the million or so dollars needed to fulfil its real potential. Instead of reaping the rewards themselves, people can find they must on-sell to a professional developer, thereby passing on the big profits to someone else. To top it off, if treated as a trader, they may have to pay tax on the proceeds at their marginal tax rate, without the Capital Gains Tax concessions available to an investor. Speculating on land is *not* investing in property. It is gambling that a market will rise enough to enable buying and selling with large margins. In the long term, ironically, land by itself has the greatest potential for the highest capital growth of all types of property. Let's explore this issue.

'Vacant land' versus 'house and land'

Figures from BIS Shrapnel's *Residential Property Prospects* (1990) show that in Melbourne between 1960 and 1989, median-priced residential property, meaning 'house and land', averaged 10.4% annual growth, while 'vacant land' averaged 15.1%, almost 5% higher! It was similar in Sydney over the same time frame: house and land prices grew 10.6% annually while land by itself experienced 12.4% annual growth. Inflation averaged 6.9% per year during this period, implying that while residential property grew at around 3.5% above the rate of inflation, the capital growth of vacant land was much higher, between 5.5% and 8% above inflation.

Chapter 8: Which Property Should You Choose? 75

Why is there a difference between the growth rates of 'house and land' and 'vacant land'? The costs of building materials, land development and other inputs into housing continually rise at the roughly same rate as inflation. (Source: ABS Cats 6401 and 6408). This affects property values which, in theory, should then grow at the *same* pace as inflation. But do they? BIS Shrapnel has observed:

In a growing market, long term property values rise above inflation, with marked cycles around this growth trend. In Australia, the growth trend in most markets is around 2% to 3% per annum [above inflation].

Another factor affecting *just* the land must be responsible for this growth above inflation. That factor is simply supply and demand. Will Rogers once said:

They're not making any more land.

How very true. It's so easy, in our technological world, to manufacture more goods such as cars and computers. But no matter how clever we are, we can not make more land. Scarcity of desirable land is the key force driving growth, and through supply and demand, land with good attributes will increase in value faster than land that is less popular or more plentiful.

One interesting point is worth mentioning here. Over the long term, a building usually depreciates to such an extent that the value of the entire 'house and land' will eventually equal the 'land only' value. From then on, the value of the house and land grows at the same rate as the land only. So, when analysing the returns from median-priced residential property using capital growth, it's not necessary to account for any improvements to the building, a factor that some believe needs considering.

If capital growth of land is higher than property with a building on it, why is vacant land not a good investment? It comes back to measuring the IRR on an investment, taking everything into account. Unless land is generating revenue, your investment dollar is not working hard enough. The reason for this is two-fold. First, there is no rent. Then, without income, there are no tax deductions for expenses such as interest. So unless you can generate revenue by grazing or the like, vacant land is not as good as a house and land for investment, and will have lower returns, all factors considered. We'll make a comparison now so you can see why.

Suppose an average couple, Bill and Mary, are contemplating buying a house and land package for $160,000. The building, fixtures and fixtures are worth $95,000; the land is valued at $65,000. The table on the next page compares a house and land package with the land only. The average capital growth in each case is assumed to be 4.5%. As you can see, in the last column, growth of 20% would be needed for the land to achieve the same rate of return as property over five years.

76 *More Wealth from Residential Property*

Comparison of Returns from Property and Land

	Property (house&land)	Vacant land (no building)	Vacant land (no building)
Value	$160,000	$65,000	$65,000
Loan	$166,000	$67,000	$67,000
Capital growth	**4.5%**	**4.5%**	**20.0%**
Inflation	2.0%	2.0%	2.0%
Growth above inflation	2.5%	2.5%	18.0%
Interest payments	$14,110	$5,695	$5,695
Rent	$10,400	0	0
Tax credits	$3,626	0	0
Expenses	$2,600	$1,300	$1,300
Bill and Mary's cost	$2,684	$6,995	$6,995
Value after 5 years	$199,389	$81,002	$161,741
Equity after 5 years	$33,389	$14,002	$94,741
Rate of return (IRR)	**41%**	**-29%**	**41%**

If Bill and Mary borrow $166,000 (including purchase and borrowing costs of $6,000) to buy the house and land package at 8.5%, their annual interest would be $14,110. With rent of $10,400, expenses of $2,600, and a tax refund of $3,626, their contribution to the total cost in the first year would be $2,684. (See page 194) If capital growth was 4.5%, the annual compound rate of return, or IRR, would be 41% over five years.

If they borrowed $67,000 (including costs of $2,000) at 8.5% to buy *just the land*, their annual outgoings would be $6,995, including interest of $5,695 and expenses of $1,300, as they still pay rates, and mowing, etc. But these costs are *not* offset by a tenant or taxman. With growth of 4.5%, the annual return (IRR) would be -29% (yes minus 29%). Think about it.

Their holding costs for the five years would be $35,240 (about $7,000 per year), but with growth at 4.5%, the capital gain would be just $14,002! They are losing money real fast! The next question is: what growth is necessary to achieve the same rate of return as the house and land of 41%? You would need to achieve astronomical capital growth of 20% each year for five years, a return which may be possible, but unlikely.

Over the years, some large corporations have made a lot of money by spending millions on large rural acreages, and holding on for many decades in the hope that future rezonings will add value and produce large capital growth. However, most people do not have the time nor the money to invest this way, and that is why vacant land may not be the best option for building wealth for the average investor.

Chapter 8: Which Property Should You Choose? 77

Why not commercial property?

Allow me to make a statement about commercial property before I go into the reasons why it may not be as suitable as residential property for building wealth. It *is* possible to make money by investing in commercial property. Some of the benefits include the large capital gains that can be made in a short space of time, the high yields that may far exceed those of residential property, and the lower expenses because the tenant pays for most of the ongoing costs. Overall, commercial property has the *potential* to be a very sound investment.

This said, there are greater *risks* associated with commercial property as it is closely tied to the corporate and business sector and consequently can be almost as volatile as the share market with many ups and downs. Town centres can move from strip shops to suburban malls. Councils can zone and rezone commercial areas as needs change. Businesses can move from outlying areas and become more centralised — for example the banks, who have been closing down branches. For the average investor, these situations can create huge risks beyond an individual's control. Such risks are often reflected in volatile capital growth, low rental yields and high vacancies, which we'll look at in more detail.

Commercial property does not have long term *steady* growth and many commercial properties in the past have suffered substantial falls in value. Some, in fact, sold for less than half their valued price at the peak of the markets in 1989, a situation that median-priced residential property has never encountered. The fact that financial institutions mostly lend to a maximum of 70% of the value of commercial property further testifies to its volatility. While the potential is there to make large capital gains, there is also the risk of making large capital losses. And since commercial property usually comes in very expensive chunks, these losses are more likely to be serious.

Moreover, although the yields from commercial property can be much higher than residential property, the vacancy factor can also be quite high, with capital cities experiencing vacancy rates of between 15% and 40% in recessionary times. In places like Sydney and Melbourne, one in three office blocks was vacant in 1992. Rates this high negate the potentially high rental yields, and introduce a large element of risk which I believe to be unacceptable and unnecessary to the average investor.

Yes, high yields of up to 20% are possible from commercial property, with the tenants paying many of the outgoings such as rates, insurance and maintenance. But *potentially* high yields are of no use if the premises are vacant for long periods.

78 More Wealth from Residential Property

Contributing to the higher vacancy problem is the changing usage of commercial property, particularly offices and retail shops, brought about by the communications revolution. Technological advances have already, and will continue to transform the way in which both the business world and ordinary citizens go about their daily affairs.

Offices in the Central Business District (CBD) have borne the brunt of this revolution with the advent of the personal computer being one of the main catalysts for the change. Not only have personal computers reduced the need for office workers, lessened the requirement for office space and eliminated the necessity for offices to be centrally located, but they have enabled many people to work from home. I believe that this trend will continue at an incredible rate, weakening the demand for commercial office space. *The Courier Mail* on 18 April, 2001, highlighted the growing number of home offices:

More than two million Australians currently work away from an office, representing more than a quarter of the entire workforce. With the arrival of the internet and other electronic add-ons, for these people, working for themselves full-time from home is already a reality.

With the rise and rise of the internet, Australians now have unlimited opportunities to not only work from home, but also to shop from home. According to the ABS in its *Communications and Information Technology* report in May, 2000:

About one-third (33%) of households (2.3 million) had internet access, a 53% increase over May, 1999.

The report continued that almost 50% of Australian households were expected to be connected by May, 2001. With almost 802,000 Australian adults already using the internet to purchase goods or services for their own private use in the 12 months to May, 2000, the overall implications for commercial property are mind boggling. Retail shops, as we know them today, may change significantly in the not-too-distant future. But on a much brighter note, instead of looking at all the negatives, perhaps the astute investor may see this as a great opportunity to utilise commercial property in a completely different way from the standard thinking.

Obviously, as a result of technological advances, commercial property is experiencing changing times. People can indeed successfully invest in commercial property, but the average investor can not be expected to have the experience necessary to identify the changing needs of commercial markets and cater accordingly. However, if you're in business and you own your own premises, you are, in effect, your own tenant, so the risks will be under your control.

Chapter 8: Which Property Should You Choose? 79

Which residential property?

Vacant land may be as solid as a rock with good capital growth, but as we have just seen, it does not provide income and without income, there are no tax advantages, making the land less affordable with lower returns. Commercial property, while potentially having high returns, can be very volatile and requires not only a substantial outlay of capital, but a great deal of skill. For the average investor, count *me* in that category, neither of these types of property is suitable as a building block for accumulating more wealth. I believe that residential property is best because it has *all* the attributes of a great investment, and doesn't require specialist skills.

Residential property has g*ood returns* coupled with *low risk*, allowing it to be safely and *highly geared*, providing even better returns. It is *tax effective* and *easily affordable* for the average investor. It also is *highly liquid* so you can easily redeem your money and it offers total *personal control*.

You have already seen in the previous chapter that residential property has *all* these attributes. But exactly which residential property fits the bill as they come in all shapes and sizes and at varied prices? I suppose you're now thinking that you need to be an expert in picking the right property. Absolutely not! If you were investing in shares, you'd need to be skilled (or lucky) in picking the right company, because most people have a lot of trouble deciphering company prospectuses and annual reports and don't have an intuitive feel for shares.

Choosing a residential property for investment is easy. Everyone has a good feel for the kind of property they would like to rent, as most people have rented a place at some stage of their lives. So in terms of the above criteria, I'm sure you'd intuitively know that a waterside mansion may not be affordable either for you to buy, or your tenant to rent; while at the other extreme, you would recognise that it may be difficult to find tenants for a fibro shack under a railway bridge, no matter how low the rent.

But with or without your intuition I can make it easy for you. Imagine a scale of one to ten where a fibro shack under a railway bridge is a '1' and a waterside mansion is a '10'. I believe that it is best to aim for residential property in the 3 to 5 category, as these properties would more than likely have *all* the attributes of a good investment.

While this simple scale might provide a good rule of thumb, there will be those who want to know a little more detail. *Reasonably priced* and *reasonably suitable* is a good description of this category of residential investment property, and in the next few pages I will elaborate on both of these features.

Median-priced residential property

A more concrete way to think about 'reasonably priced' property is to think 'median-priced'. This term is a little confusing to many people, but most of the published statistics relate to it, so I'll define it for you first. 'Median-price' has a specific statistical meaning and for property, it is:

The price at which half the properties sell for more and half sell for less.

According to the Real Estate Institute of Australia (REIA), median prices are 'not affected by unusually high or low values' and are therefore the best ones to use in any statistical analysis.

To help us better understand how 'median price' is calculated, let's look at a specific example in an imaginary place called Middletown. The graph below was produced using the values of all residential properties sold in the past year. A total of 980 properties were sold with prices ranging from a low of $50,000 to a high of $500,000. The individual sale prices of these properties, together with the number of sales at each price, are graphed below. In this particular case, the median-price is $180,000; ie the price at which half the properties (490) sold for more and half (490) sold for less.

Defining Median-Priced Residential Property

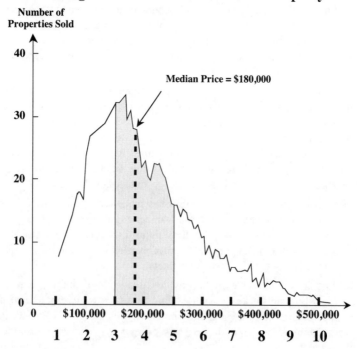

Chapter 8: Which Property Should You Choose? 81

Notice that if, instead of dollars, we apply our scale of 1 to 10 to this graph along the bottom line, median-priced property falls within the range of 3 to 5. So you shouldn't think of a property in terms of its exact price, but where it fits on the scale of 1 to 10.

I'm often asked the question: 'I want to invest $200,000 in property. Should I buy one at $200,000, two at $100,000, or four at $50,000 each?' My answer is always the same: 'It really depends on the median price of property in the area. If you are buying in a very small country town, a $200,000 property might get you a riverside mansion, probably rated at a number 9, or a 10, on the scale. But if you bought on the North Shore of Sydney, your $200,000 might get you a hovel, rated down at 1 or 2. And neither property would fall in the category of 3 to 5. So in a country town you might buy four properties at $50,000 each, whilst on the North Shore, you might need to spend much more than $200,000 to buy just one.'

Why is median-priced residential property the best suited for investment? As already pointed out, properties at either end of the scale are not suitable for investment. Properties scaled at number 10, such as a penthouse, are expensive for the investor to buy, with high loan payments, and expensive for a tenant to rent, so a lower rent is usually offered, giving a lower than average rental yield. Properties in this category may also be difficult to sell, should the need arise, as no one else can afford them; consequently they are more likely to be volatile in price. In terms of a good investment, they are likely to have poor returns and can not be geared as highly because of the volatility.

Properties scaled at number 1, such as our fibro shack under a railway bridge, while being cheap to buy, are usually difficult to rent at any price. Would you like to rent one there? They are also difficult to sell, should it be needed, for exactly the same reason — no one else wants to live there. So in terms of a good investment, they also have poor returns.

Properties scaled at between 3 and 5 fit the bill perfectly. As you can see in the graph by the number of properties bought and sold in this particular category, they are highly desirable properties that suit the average person as either a first home or an investment property. So they are easier to buy and sell if people need to. Also, with regard to rent, the yield is better than that at the top or bottom end of the scale as these properties appeal to, and can be afforded by, a larger number of tenants.

So in terms of a good investment, they have good returns and can be very highly geared because they are the least volatile of any category of residential property. But this is not to say that you shouldn't buy a rental property worth $1,000,000 in an upmarket area, or one worth $20,000 in the slums — *if* the figures stack up.

82 *More Wealth from Residential Property*

Choosing a suitable rental property

An investment property must be suitable for both you, the investor, and your tenant. There's no point in buying an old Queenslander if you shudder at the thought of maintenance costs, or a one-bedroomed flat in an area where prospective tenants consist of Mum, Dad, two kids and a dog.

When it comes to choosing an investment property, no two people are exactly alike, and what's perfect for you may not be so for someone else. Obviously, the more you are involved, the greater the financial return, but it isn't necessary to squeeze out every last dollar to achieve great returns. Learn to recognise your own level of involvement and delegate accordingly. You can paint, collect the rent, build the carport and fix the taps, or simply sit back and appoint a property manager who will organise these things to be done for you. Below are some of the questions you need to ask yourself to help you understand your own profile as an investor.

Do you want to be involved with people in a committee?
(Units and townhouses usually operate under a body corporate.)

Do you like the possibility of redevelopment in the future?
(Old houses on larger blocks might provide this opportunity.)

How often do you want to be concerned with painting?
(Timber properties need to be painted every few years.)

Do you enjoy organising tradesmen?
(Older properties require more repairs than newer ones.)

Do you like one-bedroomed units?
(You could buy near a University and rent to students.)

Do you like the idea of investing in a large house with a family room?
(Have a look in an area the locals call 'nappy valley'.)

Do you want to holiday in your investment property?
(A holiday unit may provide a good investment and a good holiday.)

Do you eventually want to live in your investment property?
(Perhaps a more upmarket property might be one to aim for.)

Do you like adding value to a property?
(Properties advertised as needing a little TLC might suit.)

Do you prefer units to houses?
(Consider buying in an area with young professional couples.)

No type of investment property is substantially better than another. The returns depend on a combination of growth and yield — and personal circumstances. With this question resolved, the next aspect to consider is the physical attributes of a property.

Chapter 8: Which Property Should You Choose?   83

Once you've learned to recognise the kind of property that suits, there are many physical attributes to consider. Some of them are described in the list below. Not all of the more desirable ones will be found in the same property and sometimes it might be a case of trading off better attributes for price. For example, properties on a busy main road may not be ideal, but a big reduction in price may still make it a viable investment. Heading the important attributes are:

Construction style

The style of the property (ie flats, units, townhouses or single houses) largely determines the type of tenant you are seeking. For example, an expensive upmarket townhouse may suit a professional couple with lavish tastes, and a suburban low-set brick house is good for families.

Construction material

Whether the exterior is constructed of brick, weatherboard, chamferboard or fibro, etc, you must consider both the maintenance and the price. For example, a weatherboard house bought for $95,000 may prove to be just as good an investment as a $110,000 low-set brick, since the lower cost will offset higher maintenance.

Condition

The condition of the building must be linked to the price and to your desire to be involved with repairs. If you are a handyman, you might get a great deal of enjoyment by doing the maintenance yourself. If not, a newer property requiring much less maintenance may be preferable.

Age

The age of the building can affect maintenance, but it should be just one of many considerations. The tax implications relating to the capital allowance and depreciation claims for newer properties must be considered in conjunction with the potential for higher growth with older properties.

Land size

Land size will depend on your choice of unit, flat or house as well as location. We have already discussed the importance of land content in the growth/yield equation and this must be weighed up against the overall price, maintenance, rents and tax benefits.

Land features

Look for easy-to-maintain yards, because most tenants dislike spending their leisure hours maintaining your gardens. Corner sites might provide better access to multi-tenanted dwellings, but our experience with normal suburban corner blocks has shown them to be noisier and a lot more effort to maintain because of the additional footpaths.

More Wealth from Residential Property

Building size

The size of the building must be considered with tenants, price and location in mind. Inner city properties vary from small bedsits to studio apartments to units, all usually with little land content in relation to the building. While in the suburbs, three-bedroom (or more) houses with larger land content (for kids and dogs) tend to dominate.

Car accommodation

It may suffice to have off-street parking with inner city properties, but it is usually better for suburban properties to have a garage or at least a covered carport. Quite often, tenants are in the process of building their own home, and a lockable garage is a desirable attribute as a storage area.

Fencing

Fencing is a distinct advantage in suburbia but again, it depends on your tenant market. It makes your property appeal to a wider selection of tenants who may have children or pets to consider.

Building aspect

The aspect of a building does not necessarily affect property valuations, but it is important to have a property that is comfortable for your tenants. In hot climates, tenants dislike hot houses, so lounge, kitchen, and dining room arrangements should be away from the afternoon sun. The tenancy will be prolonged if the tenants are comfortable.

Internal fittings

There is no need to have lavish fittings, but it doesn't cost much to make a place attractive with curtains and carpets. Kitchen cupboards and built-in wardrobes are standard in new buildings, but for older ones without built-ins, it is inexpensive to supply one or two wardrobes.

Furniture

I prefer unfurnished investment properties because tenants tend to treat your building with the same respect as their own furniture. Good tenants should have accumulated some assets in the way of furniture, and those without any at all would make you wonder why. Also, if tenants have their own furniture, they tend to move less often because of the effort and expense. Holiday units are an exception and are usually let furnished.

Zoning

Different councils have different zoning regulations that could limit or enhance your options later, but don't speculate on possible rezonings. Too many investors buy houses with a 'higher use' zoning (suitable for units or commerce, etc), but rarely do they achieve better returns and usually the property is on-sold 'as is'.

Chapter 8: Which Property Should You Choose? 85

A typical rental property

Despite the fact that we would all like a recipe for the perfect rental property — there is *no* such property. Like the perfect child, the perfect property does not exist. Too many investors buy with their heart rather than a calculator. Property investment and building wealth are all about dollars and cents, not colours of curtains. If you have assessed the property as an excellent investment, except for the purple curtains and the vicious dog next door, go with the figures. If you are buying property for the long term, most of these things won't be around after a few years.

The guidelines you have read in this chapter should give you an idea of what to look for but there are many properties that ultimately serve the same wealth building purpose. The following is an excerpt taken from *Building Wealth Story by Story* that briefly describes some of our own experiences in choosing property:

While recognising that commercial property worked well for others we stuck with residential because, with less risk and requiring less homework, it suited our passive style. Also, we were not prepared to boldly alter a recipe that had worked so well for us. But within the realms of residential property we did vary the recipe, as this list of features illustrates.

The properties include some as old as sixty years, some brand new, with some of those bought off the plan; some are timber, some fibro, some stucco and many are brick; some have a tiled roof, some corrugated fibro, some tin; some are free standing houses, some are townhouses and some are units; some are on individual titles, some are on strata titles and some are on group titles; most have three bedrooms, some have one and one has seven; most are unfurnished permanent rentals, some are fully furnished holiday rentals; some have a perfect north-east aspect, most don't; some are within one kilometre of where we live, others are hundreds of kilometres away; some are close to a central business district, some are out in suburbia; most are on land zoned Residential A, a few on land zoned Residential B; on a scale of one to ten in terms of price and style, most are around the three to five category, some are nudging eight and just a couple are at level two.

Nowadays, we tend to stretch the parameters a little and have been prepared to include more expensive properties at the more volatile end of the holiday market. But the mainstay of our portfolio has always been the median-priced properties that make up the bulk of our collection. Adding value with extensive renovations or rezonings is not our cup of tea but we have been involved in many small DIY exercises that mostly resulted in a learning experience rather than a cost saving, value adding exercise.

86 *More Wealth from Residential Property*

To be more specific, below is a description of two of our properties to give you an indication of the variation that still works.

House A

Currently valued at around $200,000, this low-set weatherboard house on timber stumps is an older style worker's cottage that's now 70 years old. It's on 1,000 square metres of very desirable land in a quiet street near the seaside. A double carport was added soon after purchase. The kitchen is older style with removable cupboards. None of the three bedrooms had built-ins, so four free-standing wardrobes were added. The bathroom is small and in the same condition as when the house was first built. Rent is $150 per week and long term I expect that the property will continue to have capital growth greater than the norm, primarily because of the larger land content and good position. However, this anticipated higher capital growth will most likely be offset by higher maintenance and lower yields. The house has already had expensive termite treatment costing around $2,000, but I consider this to be quite insignificant in view of its great capital growth already, and its potential in the future.

Unit B

This suburban brick unit in a quiet street is currently valued at around $120,000. The building is worth about two thirds that of the property. It is modern, being only three years old, but small — a very basic 10 square unit with a small single carport. The two bedrooms both have built-in wardrobes. Rent is now $170 per week and I anticipate average capital growth but good yields, as the property will need minimal maintenance.

Which type is better? *Both!* The difference between the two properties lies in the fact that Unit B provides more net income with average capital growth, while the older House A provides less net income in return for potentially greater capital gains. In the long term, both will have produced pretty much the same overall rates of return, exceeding 20% per year, depending on financing.

To be perfectly candid, I doubt if any property we own stands head and shoulders above the rest. What has worked best for us is simply time. We were prepared to sit back and wait, and we did very little apart from keeping up the maintenance and organising the finance. Value adding has not been our style, but obviously it works very well for many people. Trading has not been our style either, but again, many successful long-term property investors trade profitably along the way.

The message is that the basic recipe for building wealth can be varied to suit. Providing you finish up with a bunch of properties that allows you to retire on the rent, it doesn't really matter how you get there. There is no right or wrong property; there are only different ones.

Part IV

Laying the Foundations

9
Position, Position, Position

'I'm just about to buy an investment property. Where's the best place for capital growth?'

This would be *the* most common question I am asked about choosing where to buy investment property. And when I answer with a 'Yes, that's an easy one', their ears prick up and eyes light up in anticipation, but they are often deflated by my answer:

'A good place for growth would be the Sydney Botanical Gardens! It's a large waterfront block with unrestricted water views, not to mention the spectacle of the Harbour Bridge and Opera House. It's close to shops, transport, with plenty of job opportunities nearby and it's also a highly desirable place as I'm sure there would be millions of people wanting to live there. So it has all the criteria for potentially high capital growth. But of course, the reality is that neither you nor I could afford to buy even a small piece of it. What you really want to know is where's the best place for a great return on your investment!'

Many property investors believe that capital growth is the only factor to consider in deciding where to invest. They constantly search newspapers for clues as to which city or suburb is about to boom, hoping they can jump on the band wagon early. This preoccupation with capital growth leads to another line of questioning, of which this line is typical:

'I've owned this rental property for almost 20 years now and its value has barely kept pace with inflation. Do you think I should sell up and buy in an area with better capital growth?'

'What's it worth and how much does it rent for?' I ask.

'It's probably worth around $60,000 and it rents for $150 a week,' was the reply. A quick calculation tells me the yield is 13%, so I reply with:

'With such a good yield, it seems to me that you already have a great investment, why would you need capital growth as well?'

In this chapter we examine the unique relationship between capital growth and rental yield with some fascinating results that may challenge your preconceived ideas on what makes the best investment.

90   *More Wealth from Residential Property*

Position – which city?

If you're investing in property for the long term, you will obviously want to buy in an area where there will still be a demand to either rent or buy your property in 20 years time. Where should you buy? In Australia, for better or for worse, people are moving away from the rural countryside and into more urban areas (towns of more than 2,500 people) as shown in the table below. In 1851, more than half (60%) of Australia's population lived in rural areas, but over the past one hundred and fifty years this has decreased to just 13%. One of the key factors precipitating this trend has been the mechanisation of farming, with the consequent reduction in the need for farm labourers.

Urbanisation of the Population

	1851	1891	1921	2001
Urban	40%	50%	62%	87%
Rural	60%	50%	38%	13%

Source: ABS

If people are moving to urban areas, exactly where in Australia are they going? Furthermore, where do overseas immigrants go when they arrive here?

Migration and immigration patterns

People move interstate for all sorts of reasons, such as better climate, better employment prospects, or better facilities. Queensland, with its catchy slogan 'Beautiful one day, perfect the next', has attracted many 'southerners'. With their own warmer climates, Western Australia and the Northern Territory have also attracted many interstate migrants. The result is that these particular states are often singled out as better places to invest. However, as I'll show you, looking at the figures for interstate migration alone does not give a true picture of population trends in Australia.

While there is a net movement of people within Australia from the southern states of Victoria and New South Wales to the warmer states such as Queensland, those two southern states have been prime destinations for overseas immigrants. Let's look at the figures so that you'll understand why it is misleading to look at *only* the internal migratory patterns. I have chosen to look at just these three states because they are representative of why you must look at the whole picture — not because I have forgotten about the others. The table on the opposite page portrays the figures for the numbers of people who have moved either into or out of Victoria, New South Wales and Queensland over the past five years between 1995 and 2000.

Chapter 9: Position, Position, Position 91

Interstate Migration and Overseas Immigration
NSW, Vic, and Qld (1995 – 2000)

	Vic	NSW	Qld
Net interstate migration	-6,300	-70,600	107,000
Net overseas immigration	111,500	198,400	65,000
Net intake	105,200	127,800	172,000

As you can see, Queensland has been a target for 'southerners', with a net interstate migration of 107,000 people over the past five years. Most overseas immigrants, however, prefer to move to New South Wales and Victoria to be close to their already-settled family and friends. As a result, more than 300,000 people have immigrated to these two states in the same five year period. Yes, Queensland's net intake from interstate and overseas is higher than other states, but changes to these patterns could easily upset this balance in the future. Even as I write, Victoria is reversing the trend with a positive net intake of people from interstate in the past two years.

If you are looking at population growth as a criterion for choosing the best place for investment, then, you must look at the whole picture, not just interstate movements. The map below shows the circuitous route of people moving into Australia through the southern states, hence to the north and west.

Pattern of Interstate and Overseas Movements

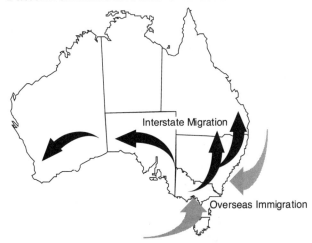

It's impossible to select one state or one city over another based solely on movements of people. Perhaps if we looked at the past returns from residential property in each city we might see a different picture.

92   *More Wealth from Residential Property*

Returns from the capital cities

And the winner is — no, not Syd-a-ney! In fact, the city with the highest capital growth between 1980 and 2000 was Melbourne (9.2%), followed by Brisbane (8.3%) and then Sydney (7.8%). Had the time frame been from a year or two earlier, Sydney would most likely have been the winner as it was approaching the end of a growth cycle in 1980 while Melbourne and Brisbane were just beginning. At the other end of the scale was Hobart, with capital growth of just 5.8%, barely managing to exceed inflation (5%) over the 20 year period.

But capital growth alone does not determine the best investment return. The reality is that if you'd invested in median-priced residential property in any Australian capital city or large regional town during the past 20 years, your average annual gross returns (capital growth plus rental yield) would most likely have been around 15%. The figures for the capital cities were surprisingly similar, ranging between 15 and 17%, as shown in the table below. I am not sure where the magic figure of 15% comes from, but it is interesting to note that Residex found the annual gross returns for Sydney for the past 100 years to also be around 15% (*Past Returns from the Sydney Housing Market*).

Gross Returns from the Capital Cities

	Syd	Mel	Bri	Ade	Per	Can	6-City	Hob
Cap growth	7.8	9.2	8.3	6.7	7.0	7.5	7.8%	5.8
Gross yield	7.6	7.9	7.4	8.5	8.0	7.7	7.8%	10.0
Gross return	15.4	17.1	15.7	15.2	15.0	15.2	15.6%	15.8

Hobart has long been maligned as a poor investment area compared to cities like Sydney and Melbourne, based solely on its relatively lower capital growth. However, while it might have the lowest growth, Hobart has the highest rental yield (10.0%) compared to the other six cities which average 7.8%. Also, while Adelaide has the second lowest growth rate of 6.7%, it has the second highest yield of 8.5%. On looking closer, the cities with the highest capital growth, namely Melbourne, Sydney and Brisbane, have some of the lowest yields. These figures suggest that there is some sort of an inverse relationship between growth and yield.

Further evidence of this growth/yield inverse relationship can be found by comparing capital cities with country towns, or inner city with outer suburbia. But the question is not so much as what the exact relationship might be, but which makes the better investment — properties like those in the larger capital cities, with higher growth and lower rental yields, or like those in places such as Hobart and Adelaide, with lower growth and higher rental yields? Let's look into this very interesting phenomenon further in a revealing study of the growth/yield connection.

Chapter 9: Position, Position, Position 93

The growth/yield connection

We would all like to buy investment properties that have both great capital growth and high rental yields. However, while this combination is possible, it is not the norm. Let's think about why this is so.

Consider an investment property valued at $100,000 which rents for $10,000 a year, giving a gross yield of 10%. Suppose capital growth for the year is 50%, increasing the value to $150,000. The property market is driven by both investors and owner occupiers clamouring and competing for desirable properties, whereas the rental market is driven by tenants with a limited capacity to pay and a limited time frame in which to choose. So it would be highly unlikely for rents to simultaneously jump by 50%. Rent of $10,000 on a $150,000 property would then reduce the yield to 6.6%. While this is an extreme example it serves to show how rents, yields and capital growth are inextricably linked.

If a place like Hobart produces gross returns similar to the other capital cities, even though capital growth has been low, which combination of growth and yield is better for wealth building? Could high growth and low yield be better than low growth and high yield?

In the previous chapter we saw how Tom and Jenny could accumulate a million dollars worth of property over a 20 year period, using growth rates, yields and interest rates which were the averages for the six capital cities, *excluding* Hobart. An interesting question now is, would they have been able to accumulate the same amount of wealth using the parameters unique to a city like Hobart, or for that matter, any city or town where the capital growth barely exceeds inflation, yet yields are high. The table on the next page lists the variables used in a computer analysis of property with either a high growth/low yield or low growth/high yield combination.

The bottom line is that Tom and Jenny would have been able to amass almost the same amount, with no significant difference between $1,892,435 with Hobart type parameters, or $1,894,195 using the major capital city averages. Just as importantly, the rate of return, or IRR, on the entire property portfolio for each scenario was the same at 17.2%.

Please note that it was not the object of this exercise to convince you to rush off to buy properties in high yielding towns. It was simply to point out that a relationship exists between growth, rents and yields, and to explain why growth should not be used as the sole indicator of a good investment. You will, no doubt, encounter a whole range of growth/yield combinations for residential property, and the gross returns will probably not be exactly 15%. However, it's most important for you to judge each situation on its merits so that you can decide whether or not it suits your wealth building strategy. The discussion following the table might help.

Comparison of
Low Growth/High Yield to High Growth/Low Yield

	High yield	High growth
Gross return (20yr av)	15.8%	15.6%
Capital growth (20yr av)	5.8%	7.8%
Gross yield (20yr av)	10.0%	7.8%
Expenses	30%	20%
Net yield (after expenses)	7.0%	6.2%
Net return (20yr av)	12.8%	14.0%
Initial 1st wage (1980 male av)	$13,500	$13,500
Initial 2nd wage (1/2 1980 female av)	$6,500	$6,500
Wages increase (20yr av)	6.5%	6.5%
Marginal tax rate	30%	30%
Initial living expenses (30% of income)	$6,000	$6,000
Inflation rate (20yr av)	5.0%	5.0%
Margin of growth above inflation	0.8%	2.8%
Initial value home (cap city av in 1980)	$40,000	$40,000
Initial purchase (based on safe LVR)	$120,000	$120,000
Initial LVR	78%	78%
Average LVR over 20 years	72.8%	52.6%
Vacancy rates (20yr av)	5.0%	2.9%
Purchase costs	3.0%	3.0%
Borrowing costs	1.5%	1.0%
Interest rates (20yr av)	10%	10%
Depreciation on fixtures	20%	20%
Depreciation on building (for 3/4 time)	2.5%	2.5%
Return (IRR) (20yr av on portfolio)	17.2%	17.2%
Number of properties accumulated	37	17
Investment wealth after 20yrs	$4,570,620	$3,054,107
Investment loans after 20yrs	$2,678,185	$1,159,912
Net investment wealth after 20yrs	**$1,892,435**	**$1,894,195**

Sources: REIA, BIS Shrapnel, Reserve Bank, ABS

Notes: The relevant statistical information on property values, wages, rents, expenses, interest rates, growth rates, rental yields, vacancy rates, depreciation, inflation, etc, has been entered into the PIA software to calculate the rates of return (IRR) and the wealth generated over the 20 year period.

Chapter 9: Position, Position, Position   95

Most of the variables such as property values and interest rates remain the same in each case. But there were also some important changes. The growth/yield combinations reflected the Hobart averages of 5.8% and 10% respectively, and the major cities' average of 7.8% for growth and 7.8% for yield. A few other subtle differences need explaining.

Expenses

Not always, but sometimes, higher yielding properties incur higher expenses. One of the reasons for attaining high yields is that it may be the kind of area that many people are attracted to, but in which they don't want to buy their own home as they consider it a transient measure. This may result in either a higher tenant turnover with more letting fees, or greater wear and tear with higher maintenance costs. Also with higher yields, it is possible to buy a greater number of properties, incurring extra accounting fees. Consequently, expenses were set at 30% for high yielding properties.

Vacancy rate

High yielding properties being prone to a high turnover of tenants, there is more likely to be time between tenancies. In Hobart in the past 16 years for which there is data, the vacancy rate averaged 4.5%, while the national capital city average was just 2.9%. To be conservative, a vacancy rate of 5.0% was used for properties with low growth/high yield.

Borrowing costs

Properties with a higher capital growth may have a greater amount of equity in them at any point, so the LVR is usually not the limiting factor in borrowing money. More often than not, people with these kinds of properties are limited in their borrowing capacity by their Debt Service Ratio, or their ability to service the loan. However, with high yielding properties, the DSR is usually no problem because of the higher rental income. The limiting factor is often the LVR, since it may be higher, sometimes incurring mortgage insurance. Hence the borrowing costs for the high yielding properties have been set at 1.5% instead of 1%.

Number of properties

With high yielding properties it might be possible to borrow to buy more often because of the higher DSR. So by the end of the 20 years it may have been possible to have accumulated 37 high yielding properties instead of 17 higher growth properties. While the value and debt of the portfolio will be much higher, the investment equity is almost the same.

• • •

If you've read this section hoping to find out exactly where to buy, I'm sorry to disappoint you. Our experience has been that most cities and towns are different, not better! Perhaps the suburbs differ? Let's see.

96   *More Wealth from Residential Property*

Position – which suburb?

When you've chosen a particular city or town, the next step is to decide where to buy within the city. Should it be in the inner city close to the CBD, or in the outer suburbs close to the fringe?

Many years ago, I had a sociable debate with a friend who insisted that his portfolio of inner city properties would be worth much more than our suburban ones in ten years time. And he quoted some long-term capital growth figures for both areas to support his argument.

'See,' he said, 'capital growth is higher closer to the city, so I'll be wealthier than you in the future!'

In a wide-ranging study of Melbourne housing between 1967 and 1992, Dr Ian Hopkins of the Australian Property Information Centre also found that capital growth was significantly higher in suburbs closest to the CBD, and tailed off towards outer suburbia (pers. com. 2001). Does this support my friend's argument? Or is it another case of a growth/yield connection? More to the point, does this have an effect on our wealth building capacity? My answer to my learned friend should shed some light on this.

'Yes, I agree that capital growth can be higher towards the city centre, and you're right – all the statistics verify that to be the case. However, our net worth will be just as much as yours in 10 years, as the higher rental yield in the outer suburbs will allow us to borrow to buy a lot more properties more often. The end result will be the same and we'll have just as much net worth, give or take.'

Some ten years later, we were both right. Yes, each of his properties was now worth much more than any of ours, based on their individual values. And yes, over the same time, we had been able to accumulate more properties with lower growth and higher yield. With many more properties working for us, our net worth accelerated just as fast as if we had bought fewer higher growth/lower yielding ones. The important point here is that the situations are just different – not better – and today, we own a mixture of properties with all kinds of growth/yield combinations.

So this growth/yield connection is very relevant even at the suburban level of property selection. The diagram on the opposite page should help you visualise how the relationship works, with property very close to the CBD typically experiencing high growth and low yield, while growth is lower and yields higher out towards the suburban fringe. Given that BIS Shrapnel found that capital growth averages 2% to 3% above inflation for capital cities, you would expect that very close to the CBD, growth would be much higher than this, while further out in the country it's more likely that growth would barely keep pace with inflation.

Growth and Yield with Distance from CBD

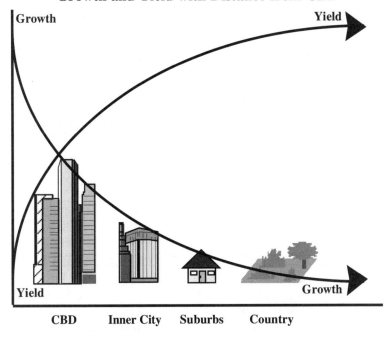

While this graphically illustrates the connection between growth and yield, it needs to be acknowledged that it is a very simplistic overview. In reality, there is not an exact balance between growth and yield, and there will be many other factors that interplay creating all kinds of growth/yield combinations. Sometimes the growth/yield factors in various areas will be out of kilter with other areas, as capital growth tends to start in a particular spot before spreading outwards. We should think of growth areas as like the radiating ripples created by throwing a stone into a mill pond. And if several stones are thrown in different places, you'll have many centres of wave action spreading and interacting with adjacent ones.

Likewise with property. Even within capital cities, there will be other epicentres of growth which spread and interact, and sometimes join. Take Brisbane, for example, which is the centre of a large population. Thirty years ago, when we bought our very first property in Kippa Ring on the northern outskirts of the city, our street was really verging on country. Now, with the spread of Brisbane, this suburb has become the hub of a mini growth area with main roads, shops, schools and other infrastructure contributing to much higher capital growth than previously. At the same time, mind you, with higher growth the yield has fallen.

98 *More Wealth from Residential Property*

Other growth/yield factors

As well as the capital city/regional town and inner city/outer suburban correlation between growth and yield, there are many other factors in the growth/yield equation that are just as influential. The list below is not intended to portray one combination as being better than the other. It should, however, give you a better understanding of the phenomenon.

Growth/Yield Connections

High Growth/Low Yield	Low Growth/High Yield
Major city	Country town
Inner city	Outer suburbs
Large land content	Small land content
Houses	Townhouses
High density zoning	Low density zoning
Older properties	Newer properties
Expensive properties above an '8'	Cheaper properties below a '2'
Unique position (views/water front)	Common position (no views/dry lot)

Properties with a higher proportion of land content, such as those with a small house on a large block, tend to have high growth and low yield. This analogy might also apply to older properties where the value of the building is low compared to the cost of the property. Expensive properties in a category above 8 on our housing scale usually have higher growth and lower yield, while the reverse is true for cheaper ones.

Properties with smaller land content, such as town houses and studio apartments, tend to have high yield and low growth as do newer properties and those with a low density zoning. Yet another factor is the uniqueness of a property which endows a much higher value to the land due to its position, position, position — as is so often cited as the main reason for buying property. While properties with superb views or water frontage may have potentially higher capital growth, this is not the whole answer to the question of whether or not it is a good investment.

Then, of course, there is a whole array of properties in between with a combination of average growth and average yield. Such a property might be a townhouse near the inner city or an older property in the suburbs. But if you can find a property with both great capital growth and high rental yield that is sustainable, then go for it!

An interesting aside is that this growth/yield phenomenon is unique to residential investment property and does not apply to commercial property. On the contrary, commercial properties are valued on the basis of their yields as the commercial property market and prospective business tenants are generally driven by similar market forces.

Chapter 9: Position, Position, Position   99

While various combinations of growth and yield tend to produce similar results, there are some instances when an individual may be better off choosing an investment that favours one combination over another. In such cases, it may be worthwhile investing in a particular style of property or even a different area, to maximise the benefits.

Under what circumstances should someone go further afield to look for properties that provide a different combination of growth and yield to the one they might experience in their own area? The following list should be used only as a guide and is certainly not to be seen as a reason for selling up and buying elsewhere.

- High growth/low yield may suit higher income earners as there's likely to be more tax benefits if the rent is much lower than the interest.
- Low growth/high yield may suit lower income earners, as the extra rent may allow them to buy into more properties more quickly.
- You may finish up with a combination of growth/yield mixes, having bought them at different stages of your earning capacity.
- Different cities may be at different stages of the property cycle, which might allow you to buy sooner than you could at home.
- Buying properties in different states may minimise land tax, as each state levies taxes on property owned in them.
- Buying properties in different areas may have tax advantages stemming from travel.
- A couple with very different incomes might buy properties in different names to take advantage of different growth/yield combinations.
- People just starting out might prefer higher yielding properties, as it enables them to kick-start the process.
- People close to retirement might prefer higher yielding properties as a source of future income.

This exercise is really to emphasise that overall returns are much more important than either growth or yield alone. So the growth experienced in capital cities of 2% to 3% above inflation can not be directly compared to lower growth in other areas throughout Australia unless yield is taken into account. When growth *and* yield are considered, it can be shown that it is possible to accumulate the same wealth and achieve the same rate of return, or thereabouts, regardless of whether the properties have high growth/low yield, or low growth/high yield.

As living proof, we have accumulated properties with both kinds of combinations of growth and yield. We have no preference for one over the other, as you will have already seen on page 86 where I describe two of our own properties — one with high growth potential but low yield and the other with low growth potential, but high yield.

100　*More Wealth from Residential Property*

Position – which locality?

Beyond the city and suburb selection process, we are now down to the nitty-gritty of choosing the locality. With this decision, the needs of the tenant should be your guide in choosing the best position. I believe that the emphasis should be on 'handy', not 'prime', so it is not necessary for an investment property to be one street back from the shopping centre, providing it is handy to transport, schools, shops, parks and areas of employment. In general, tenants dislike properties that have the following detractions:

- on a busy road
- bus stop at front gate
- unsealed road in front
- next door to schools
- adjacent to industrial sheds
- across the road from a large sporting complex
- railway at back fence
- large shopping complex next door
- next door to public toilets
- overpowering unit complexes on both sides
- mobile phone towers next door
- no public transport within walking distance
- beneath a busy flight path

That being said, there might be circumstances where some of these unfavourable attributes should be overlooked. For example, in Brisbane, one of the most highly regarded suburbs lies beneath a busy flight path, and in another suburb, a dirt road separates prime real estate from the bay. And as a third example, we have friends who own a house with a towering unit complex next door, because they were able to buy it at substantially below the market value and could afford to accept a lower rent should the tenants see the units as annoying. In other words, sometimes — come to think of it, more often than not — the pros and cons have to be balanced.

People often believe that property should be selected on the basis of position, position, position, and for your own home where there is no yield to be taken into account, this might be true. But you can see now why this is a gross over-statement for investment properties, for while position is a consideration, it must be viewed in relation to other factors including capital growth and rental yield. It is the *overall* performance of property that is important, taking into account everything that affects the returns, not just position, position, position.

Now you know what to consider in deciding *where* to buy, so it is time to look at *when* is the best time to do it.

10
Time — Not Timing

During our thirty years of investing in property, we've been told many times that it was not the right time to buy. In the mid-seventies, with the OPEC oil crisis, we were asked: 'Why are you buying property in the outer suburbs? People won't want to rent way out there if they can't afford to buy petrol to get to the city for work.' In the early eighties there was a recession and we were told: 'Don't buy property now, the country is going down the gurgler and your tenants won't be able to afford to pay the rent.'

By the mid-eighties, with the abolition of tax benefits from negative gearing, we heard: 'Why bother to invest in property now when there's no tax refund?' In the early nineties, it had changed to: 'Now we've got low inflation, property investment is dead.' By the late nineties, it was: 'This Asian crisis will make property values plunge. Get out quick while you can.' At the turn of this century it became: 'The GST will put a damper on things. Don't buy property now.'

Following each crisis, after we emerged unscathed, still holding a large portfolio of properties, there have been those who have looked back on our achievements and commented: 'Gee you were lucky. You were just so lucky you bought all those properties when they were cheap!'

In fact, our properties weren't cheap at the time; we paid market price for them. And lucky? It takes a great deal of commitment, not luck, to stick to a plan and buy property when no one else is. In ten years time you too will look back and marvel at how cheap property is right now. We can all look back and pinpoint a particular time when property values were in the doldrums, and realise that it would have been a perfect time to buy. However, I don't own a crystal ball, and unless you do, the right time to buy property is right now, regardless of the economic clock. Building wealth is achieved through borrowing, buying and keeping residential property for the long term. It requires time — not timing.

In this section we will look at the time-related issues to understand why property cycles are driven by herd mentality, and why property traders, who rely on timing, are totally different from property investors.

102   *More Wealth from Residential Property*

Property cycles

Although capital growth for residential property in the major capital cities has averaged 7.8% per year for the past 20 years, it is not a constant growth rate each and every year. While property values do not experience the extreme ups and downs of the share market, there are times when they stagnate, and times when they surge, creating cycles. For very short-term property traders, the timing of these cycles is extremely important; but for long-term property investors, time smooths out these fluctuations. The diagram below shows the theoretical sequence of stages in an economic cycle. A boom is followed by a downturn that leads to a bust. This gives rise to an upturn before another boom, and so on.

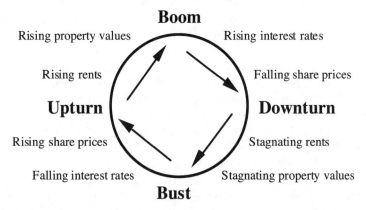

Let me describe how cycles affected the value of one of our properties in Brisbane. Over a 25 year period between 1976 and 2001, capital growth averaged 7.4% ($23,500 to $140,000). However, between 1983 and 1987, annual capital growth was only 2.4% ($50,000 to $55,000). Over the next five years, the annual growth averaged 14.2% ($55,000 to $107,000), and for the past nine years it has averaged only 3.0% ($107,000 to $140,000).

The cyclical nature of the property market is very much related to the herd mentality of human nature. Everyone builds when everyone else is building, buys when everyone else is buying, and sells when everyone else is selling. Now I'm not one for picking exactly the right time to invest in property, but there are a few months at the peak of any cycle when it may be best to steer clear because of the frenzied buying spree. One of the most interesting graphs I have put together is the one shown on the opposite page.

Chapter 10: Time — Not Timing   103

This graph is a combination of median-priced residential property in Sydney (although any city would show similar results), fixed interest rates, and the number of loans approved during the latter half of the 1980s and early 1990s.

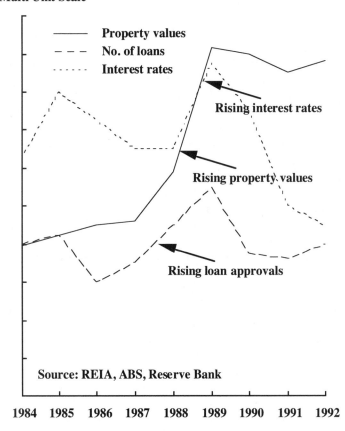

Source: REIA, ABS, Reserve Bank

This clearly shows that a lot of people got caught up in the buying frenzy of 1988/89 and borrowed to buy property in Sydney when values were going up faster than agents could put up signs, and interest rates had risen before contracts had even settled! This culminated in a downturn of the property market beginning in early 1989, with a fall in both interest rates and the number of loans approved. How does this happen? And why don't we have a level playing field with regard to property values?

104   *More Wealth from Residential Property*

In the mid 1980s, it was very difficult, if not impossible, to find rental accommodation in Sydney. This arose because of the abolition of some of the tax benefits from negative gearing and because developers had fled the scene during the preceding years of recession. This meant fewer property investors and fewer rental properties, and the demand for rental properties became enormous. With pressure mounting on the rental market, rents climbed through the roof, rising by an average of 44% ($160 to $230) in about 18 months.

Late in 1987, a rather unusual chain of events occurred. Reintroduction of the right to offset negative gearing losses against all other income, the share market crash, the lowering of interest rates, and rising rental yields together with the already pent-up demand for property, precipitated a huge onslaught of buyers into the property market. This was soon followed by substantial increases in property values as demand quickly outstripped the supply. The average prices of property in Sydney almost doubled in just two years, taking the median value from $92,100 in 1987 to $182,300 in 1989 (Source: REIA).

Out of the woodwork came all the property developers who had been 'mustering cattle out west'. They jumped on the band wagon, developing and building at a tremendous rate. New houses, unit developments and commercial buildings appeared almost overnight. What followed in 1991 was highly predictable. These developers, apparently oblivious to the laws of supply and demand, continued on their merry way. The resulting glut of properties, in particular units and townhouses, was as apparent to Mr Joe Average as it was to the astute property analyst.

There were now more than enough rental properties, and agents were having difficulty renting them, with rents falling back to a more normal $180 over the next two years. Meantime, developers were left holding the bag — or the properties. The stage was then set for a 'bust' with many developers forced to sell at bargain basement prices, before vacating the scene yet again. By 1996, with the inevitable return to prosperous times and a shortage of developments, tenants found it more difficult to find a property, rents rose sharply followed by a jump in prices as investors once again returned — and off we go again. The South American philosopher George Santayana said:

The only lesson history teaches man is that it keeps on repeating itself.

You'd think that human beings would be smart enough to learn from experience, but this appears not to be. Human nature drives us to do what everyone else is doing when everyone else is doing it. Those who want to achieve financial success must learn to fight against this basic instinct.

Property traders

Trading involves buying and selling property with the aim of making a profit, preferably in the shortest possible time. More recent terminology refers to this practice as flipping. But trading, or flipping, involves risk and requires specialised expertise: investing involves little risk and requires time. There are many books on property trading that describe how to negotiate a bargain, how to renovate, and how to pick the best time to buy and sell. This book is not one of them. Now I'm not saying that you can't make money by trading in property, but it's a specialist's occupation and requires expert skills in many different areas.

Some people expect to make money by trading in property just because they think they know everything about it. They live in a house or unit, walk on land and touch it every day and imagine that being familiar is synonymous with being an expert. Knowing a little bit about property does not automatically imply expertise in property trading. Most people are skilled in just one area and if you are, say, a teacher, mechanic, doctor or farm labourer, you can't expect to wave a magic wand and become a professional renovator or rezoning expert. Neither can you expect to be able to pick the best time to buy and sell property. I believe it's far better to use your skills in your normal job to generate the money to plough into long-term property investment. Traders include renovators, speculators and developers and it's important to distinguish between them and investors.

Renovators

Expert property renovators can buy a run-down property and transform it. They know all the tricks of the trade, and have the ability to improve property cosmetically with the least expense. Renovators often possess a trade such as carpentry or plumbing so that as well as minimising labour costs, they are more skilled in knowing what's possible and what's not.

Speculators

Professional property speculators may spend all day in their car with a mobile phone glued to their ear, just waiting to pounce on that bargain. They are well known to all the local real estate agents and have a finger on market conditions. Speculators live by their wits and should be clearly distinguished from long-term investors.

Developers

Developers are full-time traders who research demographics, market conditions and town planning, then add value accordingly before on-selling. For example, land developers buy large tracts of land, rezone and subdivide, add water, power, phone, road and sewage connections. Unit developers might rezone land to a higher density then build units.

106 More Wealth from Residential Property

Traders versus investors

There are factors that, although crucial to the success of any trading project, are almost unimportant to long-term property investors. Buying long term is a matter of borrowing and buying reasonably priced residential property at any reasonable time. Not so with trading. To be successful, traders must judge every detail with accuracy. Some of these details are:

Timing

Timing is critical to property traders and any little hiccup in the market can play havoc with a trader's profits. However, investing in property long term means that timing is of little consequence. Even though the property market may move in cycles, long-term investors don't need to be *when to* investors, as time irons out the humps and bumps. You should not be concerned with what the property will be worth by next year or the year after, but rather — what it will be worth when you retire?

Loans

Property loans for traders have to be flexible so that they can sell at short notice, and there is usually little chance of fixing the interest rate for a lengthy period. This leaves traders vulnerable to rises in interest rates, which can destroy a potentially good proposition. Long-term property investors can look for cheaper, but less flexible loans, where they can fix the interest rate and remain insulated from wild fluctuations.

Price

One of the real factors that traders need to consider at the outset is the price. Everyone loves a bargain and when you trade in property, the initial price can make or break a deal. However, when you buy long term, you only need to pay fair market value to achieve good returns.

Costs

As well as the renovation costs, which can escalate because people tend to over capitalise, there are also buying, selling and holding costs such as the interest on the money borrowed. Even if you buy with cash, there is an opportunity cost factor to consider. For long-term investors, all these costs would be insignificant compared to long-term gains.

Taxation

The tax implications for traders versus investors are totally different. Traders' profits are taxed at their top marginal tax rates, so taxes can wipe out any cream. Not only are long-term investors saving tax by borrowing money and using negative gearing to gain a tax refund, the Capital Gains Tax laws favour long-term investors by allowing a 50% discount on their gain before it is taxed.

Chapter 10: Time — Not Timing   107

Long term is the key

The key to building wealth through residential property is to borrow, buy and keep long term. How long is long? When AMP purchased $145 million worth of residential properties in Sydney in 1990, they planned to keep them for up to 21 years. If superannuation institutions see fit to keep property long term, so should you. In my view, property should be kept at least 10 years and if sold at all, it should be on retirement. In a 1997 survey, the ABS (Cat. 8711) found that almost 80% of people who were intending to buy investment property in the next two years were doing so with the aim of keeping it long term. This is seen in the table below showing the reasons people gave for investing in property.

Reasons for Buying Investment Property

Reasons intending to buy	% of Investors
Long-term investment	79.8%
Negative gearing	23.1%
Possible future home	12.8%
Capital gain	11.3%
Rental Income	9.6%
Other	9.7%

Source: ABS Cat. 8711
Note: The total is not 100% because of multiple answers.

Admirable intentions are quickly transformed, however, and in fact, very few people commit to the long term. In the same survey, the ABS (Cat. 8711) also found that in the previous five years, more than 30% of property investors had sold at least one residential investment property, while yet another 20% intended selling in the next two years. The reasons given for selling were:

Reasons for Selling Investment Property

Reasons intending to sell	% of Investors
Needed funds for family or business	20.4%
To invest in share market	0.8%
Inadequate return on investment	9.2%
To finance purchase elsewhere	30.5%
To realise the capital gain	6.9%
Couldn't afford to keep it	9.8%
Divorce/separation	4.1%
Other	18.3%

Source: ABS Cat. 8711

108 *More Wealth from Residential Property*

Many people (20.4%) needed money for those unforeseen events that may occur in business and family, although you can't cash in your normal superannuation just because your daughter's getting married. Some (9.2%) 'perceived' they were getting an inadequate return, but I would like the chance to prove to them otherwise. A large number (30.5%) were into the 'sell and buy again' mode, as they probably hadn't worked out the large changeover costs. Others (9.8%) thought they couldn't afford to keep the property, though I bet they hadn't looked at ways of reducing their cash flow commitment through interest-only loans and tax variations. Then there were those (6.9%) who just wanted to see how much they'd made, but a simple property valuation would have told them.

Investing in property for the long term can be dead boring. At first, it can be exciting finding the property, arranging the finance, doing some renovations and organising the tenants. Then there's nothing to do, which is when most people are vulnerable to 'Fidget Fever'. They renovate, add an extension and then sell when it's not necessary, just to see what it's worth. Of course you have to spend time looking after your portfolio of properties, but for the rest of the time, leave it be. It's far better to get on with your own career, the one you know best, and make extra money to pour back into your property investing. St Vincent de Paul epitomised it:

All comes at the proper time to him who knows how to wait.

Buying property to keep is a whole new way of thinking. Yet when people talk about superannuation they immediately think in phrases like retirement package, future security, income assurance, nest egg, and a time frame of 30 years or more. It's time to use these terms too, when talking about property because property can be the best form of 'superannuation', the best 'pension fund' and the best 'insurance fund' that you'll ever have.

Let me ask you — with 'normal' superannuation, do you ring up every few weeks to find out what it's worth? Do you change from one plan to another just for the sake of it? Do you fiddle with it night and day to see how to make it better? Do you plan to keep it for a short term, then cash it in? Of course not. So if property is to provide you with all you want from superannuation, it must be kept long term.

'If I buy property to keep long term, when do I get to see my money?' is the question people ask when they become aware of this buy and keep principle. I usually answer with another question: 'What do you want to see your money for?' Isn't the whole reason for investing to have future wealth and security? Then, when your property has grown in value, and the rent has outstripped your interest payments, you should be receiving a great income from your tenants. The only reason for selling is when you retire and you may want to balance the debt and reduce interest payments.

Part V

Building the Framework

11
Getting Started — Your Own Home

Most investment advisors agree on one point — your first investment should be your own home. Less than 70% of Australians currently own their home and despite well meaning governments providing tax advantages and monetary incentives for home ownership, this percentage is forecast to greatly decline. According to the Australian Housing and Urban Research Institute (AHURI), home ownership will fall sharply over the next few decades and by 2030 it is expected to be less than 60% nationally.

Although your own home is free of Capital Gains Tax, in borrowing to buy it, the drawback is that the interest is *not* tax deductible. And because there are mortgage repayments, living expenses *and* tax to be paid from your wages, there seems very little left. Nevertheless I believe that buying your own home is just as difficult today as it was yesterday, and will be tomorrow. In fact, in a previous book, *Building Wealth Story by Story*, I recount a letter to my old aunt written to her by a friend, bemoaning the fact that it is far easier for young couples to buy a home today than it was in her day in 1959. And she provided some very astute comparisons.

Once you have bought your first home, you should try to pay it off as quickly as possible. Then the increased equity can be used as a springboard to building more wealth, not as a stepping stone to spending more money. After the last round of property price rises, one of the local bank managers told me how they had written record 'home equity' loans. But those loans had been for boats and cars and other luxury items. The increase in home equity was mostly spent on wealth-destroying consumer goods, rather than wealth-creating assets.

This chapter examines many of the issues relating to home ownership and answers many questions such as: Is buying better than renting? How much deposit is enough? Is one property enough? How can you pay off your home loan quickly? The discussion and answers should help you get started on your road to wealth by getting you into your very first property.

112 *More Wealth from Residential Property*

Renting versus buying

While most financial advisors agree that owning your own home should be a top priority, there is a controversial school of thought that renting is better than buying. According to a report by the Australian Institute of Family Studies, 'many people would be better off investing their equity and renting'. While I agree that this is possible, particularly if you rent while buying an investment property, this kind of thinking fails on two points. First, it fails to acknowledge that home ownership benefits are not only measured economically but emotionally. And second, it presumes that the tenant-come-investor will be mentally disciplined enough to divert all loose change into other investments.

Owning your own home currently provides one of the few tax havens left untouched by the government, because it is not subject to the Capital Gains Tax (CGT). Badcock and Beer, authors of *Home Truths*, suggest that these 'tax advantages make it an excellent investment vehicle for most people — even better than superannuation'.

However, perhaps the best economic advantage lies in the psychology of taking on a home loan. For those who decide to rent rather than buy, with good intentions of investing their spare money, there is a high risk that their savings will be squandered long before they are invested. It only takes a moment of weakness to succumb to a new car, new clothes or a holiday, etc, and the savings are gone forever. In contrast, a home loan is not just a loan but a commitment to save, with equity being built up in a tax free asset. When people take on a loan they tend to pay the bank first, then spend what's left. Without a loan, it is human nature to spend first, then save what's left — which is usually nothing.

Greater than any economical advantages are the emotional benefits of home ownership. Badcock and Beer state that 'there are other intangibles and unpriced benefits' associated with buying and living in your own home. They talk about the satisfaction of putting down roots, the feeling of well being, forming bonds with neighbours, the freedom to keep pets, a sense of attachment, the memories, and the right to design and create your own living space. Perhaps most important is the security of tenure, providing the stability for raising a family. Few of these attributes are enjoyed by tenants. These views were confirmed in a report by Burgess and Skeltys, *The Findings of the Housing Locational Choice Survey,* where satisfaction amongst home owners was found to greatly exceed that of tenants.

Owning your home has always been the great Australian dream and is probably part of our primordial instincts to stake out our own territory. Any comparison with renting can not be based solely on economics.

Chapter 11: Getting Started — Your Own Home   113

Saving the deposit

It would take an eternity to save the full amount to buy your own home. Imagine a couple wishing to purchase their own home valued at $180,000. They have a joint income of $67,000. With tax of $13,865, rent of $10,400 and living expenses of $20,000, their maximum annual savings would be $22,735. Allowing for an increase in wages, rent and taxes, they would need 10 years to be able to save enough to buy their home. By then, it would cost $280,000 if capital growth was only 4.5%. The real danger over this 10 year period of intense saving, however, would not be that property values could rise much faster than the rate of saving. It would be the temptation to spend that readily available cash!

Forget about trying to save the lot: the best way of getting a foothold in the property market is to save a deposit and borrow the rest. Many lending institutions are willing to lend up to 95% of the value of an owner occupied home, requiring just a 5% deposit, and some schemes require no deposit at all. Saving this mere 5% to 10% of the value of a basic home should be an achievable goal for most young couples, especially if they start when they are young. I highly recommend that all young couples read *The Richest Man in Babylon* by George S. Clayson, hailed as one of the greatest works on the subject of wealth.

While only a small deposit is enough for buyers to get started, it may result in serious problems if the cost of the property is too high. Small deposits on cheaper properties are practical because the size of the loan is usually manageable. But small deposits on expensive homes require large loans. The resulting hefty mortgage payments can leave a young family vulnerable to rising interest rates, which often leads to economic woes.

Saving a deposit should be the first financial goal for everyone, even while you are still at school and even though buying nice cars and clothes and going to the movies seems so much more important. If you spend all your money when you are young, you suffer many times. First, because it takes longer to save a deposit; second, because ingrained spending habits are hard to break; and worse still, by the time you realise your mistakes the property costs more!

How can parents help their children raise a deposit for their first home? I believe the best way is by teaching them good saving patterns when they are young. I speak from experience in saying that this is not always easy. One innovative method of helping was suggested to me by a friend who is a bank manager. He had arranged a loan for a young man whose parents were willing to mortgage their home for him, so he could borrow the entire amount for his first home without the need for a deposit. While I don't suggest this to everyone, it's certainly food for thought.

114 *More Wealth from Residential Property*

Recognising reality

What kind of home would you like to live in? We all have our ideas about our dream house, with fantasies of owning a mansion on the harbour or a homestead on acreage. But very few of us ever have the opportunity to realise that dream first up. Nevertheless, it never ceases to amaze me that many young couples are prepared to mortgage themselves to the hilt to purchase their first property with all the mod-cons.

One of the reasons that young couples get into trouble with variable interest rates and large mortgage repayments is that for their first home, many will not settle for less than an upmarket house in a trendy suburb, complete with double lock-up garage and gourmet kitchen. One of the best ways to get into your first home is to buy an affordable property at the lower end of the market. The loan can then be kept to a minimum, which enables your equity in the property to build up much faster.

Our very first property, which we still own by the way, was purchased for $12,500 in 1972, our only aspirations being that one day we would own our own home. I was rather fortunate in that my husband Ian had been working for 12 months and had saved about $3,000, enough for a deposit; our parents helped out with the few hundred dollars needed for the stamp duty and other costs. This high-set chamferboard house near the mudflats in Kippa Ring, a suburb on the outskirts of Brisbane, was not handy to anything. No rail, no bus, no school, no entertainment and no shops except for a general store-come-post office. But it was all we could afford at the time.

It was just 7.4 squares with a combined kitchen-dining-lounge room, one small bathroom and three bedrooms. We later reclassified it as one bedroom and two studies when we found that we couldn't fit standard single beds into two of the so-called bedrooms. There was no carpet, no curtains and no concrete beneath the house, which flooded every time it rained. Our furniture was second-hand from St Vinnies and we borrowed my father's bait fridge. That's how we started almost 30 years ago.

We still own that house and it is now a first class rental property less than 500 metres from a huge shopping complex built some six years after we bought it, and less than 200 metres from a proposed railway station. It formed the basis of a large portfolio of investment properties, and I have no doubt that had we bought a big brick home in an upmarket area and furnished it with leather lounges and electrical appliances bought on credit, we would not be in the position that we are now in. So aim high, but take one step at a time. It won't take long until you can afford your dream home plus everything else you've ever wanted.

Reducing your mortgage

Once you have made your purchase you should aim to pay out the loan on the property as quickly as possible. Unfortunately, as I pointed out earlier, with no income from a tenant and no tax benefits, paying off the loan on your first home is the hardest of all.

Numerous mortgage products are available that purport to reduce your home loan in record time. First came fortnightly repayment options, then mortgage offset accounts, then credit lines (see page 160). Psychologically, it might help to have a gimmicky loan, but the only sure way to reduce your home loan quickly is to pay as much as you can, as often as you can.

Chapter 15 discusses credit lines in detail but they warrant a special mention here because, used in the right way, they can be a very effective tool in mortgage reduction. Converting your home loan to a credit line effectively creates a line of credit against the value of your own home to a predetermined Loan to Value Ratio (LVR) set by the bank. The idea is that you dump all your income into the credit line at the time you are paid, thus reducing the loan immediately. You then use your credit card to pay for all your expenses, paying no interest for 55 days in each period; and when this is due and payable, you withdraw funds from the credit line to pay out your credit card before any interest is due.

The theory is that money left in the credit line for up to 55 days before it is withdrawn will reduce the interest bill. While this makes a small difference of maybe a few hundred dollars per year, the real impact is made by simply cutting down on spending and redrawing less. This way, you can leave thousands of extra dollars in the account to reduce the mortgage.

Although these loans are fantastic tools for mortgage reduction, you need to make sure you don't pay a premium interest rate for the privilege. It may be better to take a low interest home loan with an offset account if the credit line interest rate is too high. Another danger with credit lines is that it's far too easy to redraw money to buy consumer goods; before you know it, your equity has been whittled away. If you do use a credit line, you need to be well disciplined to make it work.

Mortgage reduction ultimately builds equity — the difference between the property value and the loan. Exactly how much equity do you need before you can start borrowing against it to buy investment properties? There is no exact amount and it varies for each individual depending on income. We discuss this in Chapter 14: at this stage you only need to be aware that it is possible to start a wealth building plan while you still have a mortgage on your own home. With every possible effort, though, you should be striving to rid yourself of this non-tax deductible loan.

116   *More Wealth from Residential Property*

You can reduce your home loan in many ways and these tips should help you achieve first-home ownership faster.

- Make a commitment to put money into your mortgage *before* buying luxuries. In a few years you'll be able to buy all you ever wished for.

- Think carefully before buying a new car, and avoid getting a second one when it may not be necessary. Cars are one of the biggest guzzlers of money, and figures from automobile clubs (*The Sunday Mail* 6 Aug, 2000) suggest it costs almost $100 per week to run a small car. With interest rates at 8.5%, it's probably cheaper to pay $50,000 more for a property closer to work than to buy a second car. Alternatively, for much less than $100 you could take a taxi several times a week. Cars always seem to need something doing to them, usually when you have the least amount of spare money.

- Never buy consumer goods on credit. If you can't afford to pay cash, don't buy them. Reduce your use of credit cards. By all means have them, but restrict their use and pay them back completely before the interest-free period is up. Buying consumer goods on credit is one sure way to financial ruin and does nothing to reduce your mortgage.

- Restrict the money you spend on your children, or even defer having children until you have established your wealth foundations. Children seem to have only two words in their vocabulary, 'I want'. For many parents, this plea is difficult to ignore, particularly if you have had a deprived childhood yourself. You will be doing your children a big favour by showing them restraint and teaching them the real value of money. When children make demands, they usually need time spent with them, not money spent on them.

- Holidays needn't be extravagant and camping is a fraction of the cost of a high rise unit near the surf, but can be just as much fun. In the early years of our wealth building we travelled overseas several times on the cheap. On one of those occasions we cycled nearly 9,000 kilometres around Europe — during the wettest summer in 100 years!

- Mortgage-offset accounts are effective because they save you paying tax on the interest from your savings, while reducing the principal on your home loan. Rather than use these, I believe it is better to use a well managed credit line; or just put all your available cash into the loan, then reduce the payments when and if needed.

There are many techniques to help you pay off your mortgage quickly, but all require the right mental attitude. Try to get away from the instant gratification mentality and replace it with an understanding of the great benefits that will follow if you take care, think ahead, have restraint, and delay. Your reward will be having what you wanted, and much more.

Chapter 11: Getting Started — Your Own Home   117

Improving your home

As well as reducing your mortgage, you can build equity by improving the family home. This can be done by adding value, or moving upmarket.

Adding value

If you buy a finished house that looks great right from the start, the value is already built in to the price with little room for improvements. The best way to add value is to buy a run-down place and improve it by renovating the building or landscaping the grounds. This can be done in your own time with your own money and even by your own labour.

However, be careful not to over-capitalise. There is no sense in paying $40,000 for a new kitchen if the property is worth only $100,000 to start with. One further point needs mentioning. Renovating definitely does not suit everyone — myself included. If you are prepared to cook in a kitchen juggling pots and pans between ladders and trestles or sleep in a bedroom with paint fumes and plaster dust, then go right ahead — it's a great way to build equity. But keep in mind that value can also be added by cosmetic changes, which is far less messy and sometimes a lot more cost effective.

Moving upmarket

With renovating your home, there is only a certain amount of value you can add before you over-capitalise. The next step then should be to borrow to buy investment properties. However, there are those who like to 'ride the escalator' by moving upmarket. This is achieved by selling the home you have just improved then buying into a better property, again with potential to add value. By doing this several times you could finish up with a large mansion. The advantage of this approach is that you get to enjoy a better home each time in a capital gains tax free environment, as present laws exempt the principal place of residence.

The only time you should contemplate selling is when it will help you to build equity. Many books tell you how to buy, how to renovate and how to present your property when you sell. Suffice to say that it is just one method of building equity and that it will only suit some people.

Although adding value or upgrading are good for building equity, I don't believe they are best for building wealth. If you are working and paying tax, this method does not provide personal tax relief and furthermore, your improvements are paid for from your after-tax dollars. I believe it is far better to build wealth by remaining in a comfortable home and using the equity to buy investment properties where you have both the rent and tax benefits to help you build a portfolio of properties. Each to their own and you must do what you believe is best.

118　*More Wealth from Residential Property*

Renting while investing

If you are able to rent somewhere cheaply, you could make your first home purchase an investment property. You might be still at home with Mum and Dad, for example, and so be able to take advantage of the cheap rent and free laundry to save a deposit and buy a rental property. Or you might be renting with several others who share the costs. Also, many people in the armed services have relatively cheap accommodation, and are in a great position to buy investment properties for many years before they buy their own home.

Another possibility is to rent from your parents if they have bought an investment property. This could be ideal for both of you. So long as the rent is reasonable, but still at arm's length to legitimise the tax benefits for your parents, you could save a deposit and borrow to buy an investment property for yourself. Your parents would have the satisfaction of getting an excellent tenant — that's you — as they proceed on their road to a comfortable retirement.

A variation on this theme is to buy a property and take in boarders who pay you rent. Many young people already do this but sometimes go to great lengths to conceal the rent from the tax office. What they don't realise is that they may be better off declaring the income and claiming a portion of the interest as a tax deduction, thereby getting a tax refund. For example, if you had three boarders, you could claim three-quarters of the interest bill, electricity, phone, rates, insurance and maintenance, etc, as well as the depreciation on fittings within the house. The only drawback is that the property is no longer free of Capital Gains Tax. This may not be too much of a concern because the tax saved in the interim may far exceed the potential CGT in the future, which you only pay if you sell.

In most cases, you'll need a small deposit to buy your first property in this manner, the same as you would if it were your own home. Despite losing the tax benefits, it's advisable to pay off the loan as fast as you can, so you can use this property as a stepping stone to buy more and more. One way for you to buy a rental property, or any property, without a deposit is if your parents are willing to help by allowing you to use their own property as security for a loan. Then you can borrow the full amount for an investment property without having the cash.

The only problem I see in making your first property an investment is that you need to be disciplined to make sure your surplus cash is invested and not wasted. However, at least the loan repayments should provide a form of commitment so you'll be more likely to save first and spend later. Let's work through an example and I'll explain the difference between living in and renting out your first property.

Chapter 11: Getting Started — Your Own Home 119

Let's consider two scenarios for a $160,000 property bought with 10% deposit: living in it as your home; and renting it out while investing. So that you can see where the discussion is heading, I should tell you that the basic difference is the tax refund you receive on the investment property.

Living in own home

Suppose a young couple decides to buy and *live* in their first property. With a $16,000 deposit, the loan would be $146,500 (including purchasing and borrowing costs of $2,500). With interest at 8.5%, the Principal and Interest loan payments would be $14,156 each year for 25 years. In the first year, the costs, including rates, etc, of $1,600, would look like this:

Costs of buying own home	
Home expenses	$1,600
Home loan costs	$14,156
Net cost = $15,756	

Renting while investing

Suppose a young couple decide to buy and *rent out* their first property for $10,400 a year, while they themselves rent an identical place for the same rent. With a $16,000 deposit, the loan would be $150,000 (including purchasing and borrowing costs of $6,000, as investment property costs are more). At 8.5%, the annual loan payments would be $14,494 for 25 years, at which time they would own the investment property outright. Their property related income and expenses for both properties would be:

Costs of renting + investing		Income from rented property	
Rent payable	$10,400	Rent received	$10,400
Investment prop expenses	$2,600	Tax refund	$3,112
Investment loan costs	$14,494		
Total costs	**$27,494**	**Total income**	**$13,512**
Net cost = $13,982			

The difference between the two cases is $1,774 ($15,756 less $13,982), mostly due to the $3,112 tax refund received as a result of owning the negatively geared investment. However, with extra expenses for the rental property (eg management fees) and higher loan payments as a result of borrowing more, the real saving is just $1,774 not $3,112.

Clearly, the *real* benefits come if you can rent somewhere for much less than $10,400, and these options were discussed earlier. The benefits could then be as high as $10,000 a year and buying an investment property before buying your own home would be a definite financial advantage. You don't have to wait 25 years, though, before buying your own home and you could even move into one of your rental properties at some stage.

120 *More Wealth from Residential Property*

Is one property enough?

Too many people don't buy any more property once they have paid off their own home, believing that they have done enough to retire financially independent. I even heard one elderly couple comment, 'Why would we want to buy another property? We'd only have to pay more rates and more insurance!' To say they are missing the point would be an understatement!

When you retire, if you only have one property, what other assets will you have to produce sufficient income to support your favoured lifestyle? The age pension may not exist and the SGC will not be enough. You could move into a tent and rent out your home. But that's unrealistic. Or you could sell with a view to downgrading.

In some cases, as we have just discussed, many people have enormous equity in their own home as a result of continually adding value and/or moving upmarket. They believe that when the time comes to retire, they can downgrade to a more modest property and release the built up equity to provide additional retirement income. However, most retired people don't want to move and the idea that all older people move to either retirement villages or nursing homes the day after they turn 65 is a furphy.

According to Justin Healey, editor of *Issues in Society: Our Ageing Nation*, 93.1% of people aged over 65 did not move house, and of those who did, 5.4% had to move because of a disability. Furthermore, with almost two thirds of retired people living in homes with three or more bedrooms, it's obvious that most of them prefer to live in larger homes and don't want to downsize. Even among those over 85, over half (51%) of couples live in dwellings with three or more bedrooms. The ABS social report, *Older People Australia,* suggests:

Older people tend to live in homes which are much larger than their household size may appear to need. Many factors contribute to this pattern, including the emotional significance of the family home to older people, the need to have more space when their family visits, attachment to their neighbourhood, and the costs and difficulties associated with moving.

The conclusion? Don't plan your retirement income around the release of equity from your valuable family home. Statistics tell us that it simply doesn't happen. By all means, plan to live in your dream home, but don't do it to the exclusion of further investment. While you are building your wealth, life is a balance between living in a mansion with no other assets, and, as I say in my seminars, living in a tent with 50 rental properties. I believe that if you maintain a good balance, you could well retire with both your mansion *and* your investment properties.

12
More Wealth from Residential Property

My friend Jean is a real expert at making fruit cakes. She has followed the same basic recipe for many years, and her cakes are always perfect. But although the basic recipe is still the same, many things have changed with time. Some of the ingredients have altered slightly: the dried fruit is a different brand and is sold pre-diced; the eggs now come from the local supermarket instead of from her own backyard hens; and her oven is not the same — she now has a new fan-forced oven instead of her cherished old wood stove.

With each change, Jean baked her fruit cake with a little trepidation, wondering if it would turn out to be the same — only to find that the basic fruit cake recipe still worked, no matter what brand of ingredient she used, no matter where the ingredients came from and no matter what kind of oven she baked her cakes in.

You must be wondering by now what making fruit cakes has got to do with investing in property. In principle, everything. Good recipes just keep on working no matter what. My previous books *Building Wealth through Investment Property* and *Building Wealth in Changing Times* were based on a simple recipe for an early, wealthy retirement that involved borrowing, buying and keeping residential investment property for the long term. The ultimate aim was to balance the debt and retire on the rental income, enabling a financially independent retirement, free of government handouts.

The recipe I proposed in those books was not new; I certainly didn't invent it and neither did I have a franchise on it. In fact, an earlier book of mine, *Building Wealth Story by Story,* related many instances where people had successfully followed the recipe for many years *before* Ian and I began using it ourselves almost thirty years ago. The only problem is that this recipe of borrowing to buy and accumulate rental properties is *so simple* that most people overlook it.

122 *More Wealth from Residential Property*

Since the nineties, when my books were written, many changes have taken place. There is a growing awareness in the community of the huge problems our governments face in funding future age pensions, with the result that social attitudes to self reliance in retirement are changing. This has occurred simultaneously with a changing investment climate that has brought with it the lowest inflation levels *and* the lowest interest rates in decades. So at a time when people are *thinking* about the possibility of investing for their future, they are also *wondering* if the simple age-old recipe still works in these changing times.

I believe that this recipe for building wealth through investment in residential property is just as valid today as it was yesterday, as it will be tomorrow. In the next few pages I will explain why I believe this recipe is just as good, despite the changes to some of the ingredients.

Inflation rates, interest rates, growth rates, tax rates, vacancy rates, and most other rates that you could possibly think of have changed in the past few years and yet these changes do not affect the basic recipe for building wealth. In this chapter, I'll explain the recipe again, nevertheless, using different figures, so that you will be reassured and able to see for yourself that the recipe still works today. To do this, we will follow the lives of a couple, Bill and Mary, from the time they enter the workforce at age 21.

We go through the steps of how they save a deposit and buy their first home. Then we see how they buy their first investment property, before looking at how it would be possible for them to build a large portfolio of properties. Eventually, we discuss ways of how they could retire in their mid-forties and live financially independent on the rent for the rest of their lives. While the plan in my previous books is similar, the figures reflect how things are today. These changes, as you will see, have no effect on the goal of becoming financially independent.

All the calculations were done using the Property Investment Analysis (PIA) software described in Appendix B on page 249, so it's really not necessary for you to be able to reproduce every step by hand when you can use a computer to do it easily and instantly. All the same, I have included detailed explanations of the steps so you will understand the basis for the calculations.

Bill and Mary are not real, and the following story never happened. But it could have and it still can, because the recipe they follow is a simple 'fruit cake' recipe that *you* can use yourself by varying the ingredients to suit. The recipe for success is outlined on the opposite page. You should read it, copy it, pin it up and read it again and again so that you firmly understand the principle of building wealth through residential property. Then you will be ready to follow Bill and Mary on their journey to wealth.

Recipe for success

Step 1: *Begin with your first home*

Begin with a goal: Decide when you would like to retire. Work out the assets you will need to give you the income you require for a more than comfortable retirement.

Bank your savings: Start saving as early as possible, so that when you buy your first home, you'll already have a large deposit.

Buy your first home: Borrow to buy your first home (P&I loan). Make sure it is within your means. All the mod cons come later.

Build equity in your own home: Pay off your home loan as quickly as possible, although there is no need to completely pay it off before you start the next step.

Step 2: *Buy an investment property*

Borrow against your equity: Use your own home as collateral to borrow the entire amount for your first investment property, plus the associated costs. Ideally, the loan should be fixed-rate, interest-only.

Buy your first investment property: As a general guide, look for median-priced property, in a reasonable location and in a region with long-term sustainable growth (normally a large city or town).

Step 3: *Build a property portfolio*

Buy more properties: As cash flows increase, refinance to buy more and more properties using the growing equity as collateral. Apply for a tax variation to enhance cash flows.

Be careful: Be prepared for 'Murphy'. Budget carefully and learn to handle large sums of money. Set up access to credit lines. Keep some cash on hand. Fix the interest rate for at least three years. Take out insurances. Set reasonable rents. Maintain the property.

Be patient: Stay committed and disciplined as you wait for cash flows and values to rise. Don't fall into the trap of thinking the grass is greener elsewhere. Don't sell just to see how much you have made.

Step 4: *Balance the debt on retirement*

Balance the debt: When you retire, rents become your main source of income. Manipulate the debt levels by selling one or more properties to reduce the loan so that you now have a positive cash flow.

Buy luxuries: Enjoy your retirement. Buy any luxuries you want.

124　*More Wealth from Residential Property*

Begin with your first home

Back in 1991, when Bill and Mary were both 21, they started work with incomes of $25,000 and $19,000 respectively, the average for their age at the time (ABS Cat. 4101). Looking into the property market, they noted that a suitable house would cost about $116,000, well out of their reach at that point. So, like most young couples, they decided to rent while saving for a deposit. They also wanted to travel and enjoy things they'd missed out on while studying, so they allocated about a quarter of their income to fulfilling their dreams. Their spending and saving pattern over the next five years is illustrated in the table below.

Saving for a Deposit in 5 Years

Start of year	1991	1992	1993	1994	1995
Age	21	22	23	24	25
Bill's wage	25,000	27,039	29,245	31,630	34,210
Mary's wage	19,000	20,532	22,187	23,977	25,910
Joint wage	44,000	47,571	51,432	55,607	60,120
Property value	116,000	121,294	126,830	132,618	138,671
End of year					
Tax	7,902	8,955	10,303	11,785	13,387
Net wages	36,098	38,616	41,129	43,822	46,733
Withdrawals	32,000	34,381	36,772	39,172	41,581
Living expenses	16,000	16,381	16,772	17,172	17,581
Travel, etc	10,000	11,000	12,000	13,000	14,000
Rent	6,000	7,000	8,000	9,000	10,000
Savings	4,098	4,235	4,358	4,650	5,152
Savings + interest	4,159	8,520	13,071	17,987	**23,487**
Property value	121,294	126,830	132,618	138,671	145,000

During the first year, Bill and Mary paid their net wages of $36,098 ($44,000 less $7,902 in tax) into a savings account. Withdrawals included $16,000 for living expenses, $10,000 on travel, etc, and $6,000 on rent, leaving savings of $4,098, which with interest accrued to $4,159 by the end of the year. Over the next four years with wages rising at around 8%, the average at that time for young adults (ABS Cat. 4102), and expenses rising in line with inflation at just over 2%, they saved $23,487. This was enough for a deposit of $15,000, or about 10%, on their first home, which by then would cost them $145,000 after growth of around 4.5% each year for the five years. From their savings, they could also cover the cost of the stamp duty and legals, and buy some inexpensive furniture. After signing a contract, all they needed was a loan of $130,000.

Chapter 12: More Wealth from Residential Property 125

Bill and Mary borrowed the money using a credit line at 8%. Their net wages after tax were paid into the account and expenses were withdrawn when needed, the difference between these deposits and redraws remaining in the account. Having spent the previous five years globe-trotting, they trimmed back on travel, leaving more money in the account. By the end of five years, Bill and Mary had repaid the entire loan of $130,000, by which stage their house was worth $180,000. In just 10 years they had been able to save a deposit and pay off their own home — all the while maintaining a lifestyle that did not constrain them to a diet of bread and vegemite. This is something anyone can do once they put their mind to it and the table below, produced by the PIA software, shows how Bill and Mary did it.

Paying off the Loan in 5 Years

Start of year	1996	1997	1998	1999	2000	2001
Age	26	27	28	29	30	31
Bill's wage	37,000	38,813	40,716	42,711	44,804	47,000
Mary's wage	28,000	29,373	30,811	32,322	33,906	20,000
Joint wage	65,000	68,186	71,527	75,033	78,710	67,000
Property value	145,000	151,408	158,099	165,086	172,382	180,000
Deposit	15,000					
Loan at start	130,000	109,685	86,250	59,394	28,792	0
End of year						
Tax	15,119	16,323	17,681	19,104	20,599	
Net wages	49,881	51,863	53,846	55,929	58,111	
Living expenses	18,000	18,383	18,775	19,175	19,583	
Travel, etc	5,000	4,000	3,000	2,000	1,000	
Loan payment	26,881	29,479	32,071	34,754	37,528	
Loan at end	112,901	91,687	64,024	35,449	**0**	
Property value	151,408	158,099	165,086	172,382	180,000	
Net worth	41,723	71,849	105,692	143,590	180,000	

During the first year, their net wages of $49,881 ($65,000 less taxes of $15,119) were paid directly into the credit line. Redraws totalled $23,000 (living expenses of $18,000 plus travel, etc, of $5,000), leaving $26,881 in the account, even though their loan commitment was just $11,447. After one year, their loan of $130,000 had been reduced to $112,901. Over the next four years, with wages increasing at almost 5%, the average for their age at the time (ABS Cat. 4102), and expenses rising with inflation of around 2%, they managed to pay off their entire loan. At the beginning of 2001, Bill was earning $47,000 per year, the average adult male wage, and Mary, who had decided to work part-time, was earning $20,000, half the adult female wage (ABS Cat. 6302). They were ready for their next step.

126 *More Wealth from Residential Property*

Buy an investment property

To buy an investment property, it was not necessary for Bill and Mary to have paid out their home loan completely. However, for simplicity in explaining the next steps, we will assume this to be the case. Later in this section, we'll see how they could have started investing in property much sooner while still having a loan on their own home.

Bill and Mary, now both aged 31, decided to set a goal to be financially independent by age 45 with a million dollars in today's dollars. They had already looked at their options and knew that normal superannuation would be too little too late, as they wanted access to their money long before the statutory 55 years of age. They were also well aware that investing in shares would mean dealing with a volatile market, limiting their borrowing capacity. Gearing into residential property, they decided, was the fastest and safest way to build wealth. Their plan was to borrow and buy as many properties as they could in the next 15 years, then retire on the rent.

Bill and Mary were conservative people and so, having made up their own minds about property, they decided to talk to others. Recognising the limitations of financial advisors, they consulted several lending institutions until they found a bank manager willing to listen to their ideas. He soon ascertained that with a joint income of $67,000 and a home worth around $180,000 free of debt, they could afford to borrow $500,000 — enough for three properties worth around $160,000 each, plus costs. Knowing that Bill and Mary were cautious, he recommended that two thirds of the loan be a fixed-rate interest-only loan at 8.5% for three years. The remaining third would be set up as a variable rate credit line at 8.5%, with the flexibility to pay just the interest, or pay it down, or draw on it if needed.

And no, Bill and Mary didn't freak out at the idea of borrowing half a million dollars. They had already come to terms with the fact that a debt of this size was much better than a loan one tenth of the size for a new car.

Next they found an accountant who owned investment property and was well versed in the subject. He suggested that, to maximise the tax benefits, the properties should be bought in Bill's name only, and that as soon as he had signed a contract he should apply to the Taxation Office for a reduction in his regular PAYG tax, as allowed under Section 15-15 of the Tax Act.

Bill and Mary also found a real estate agent who specialised in property investment, and settled on three similar properties each worth $160,000. The details of one of these and the loan are summarised on the following page. I will refer to this property from now on as the 'example property', but I must point out that it is in no way intended to represent the perfect investment. Nor is the loan meant to be the ideal loan.

Example Property

$160,000

Property Description

New, three-bedroom, low-set brick house.

Property Details		Loan Details	
Purchasing costs		**Borrowing costs**	
Stamp duty (NSW)	$4,090	Establishment fee	$415
Conveyancing fees	$310	Mortgage stamp duty	$664
Registration title	$100	Mortgage insurance	$0
Total	**$4,500**	Bank's solicitor's fees	$0
Depreciation/building		Valuation fees	$150
Construction cost	$80,000	Registration mortgage	$100
Tax claim (2.5%)	**$2,000**	Search fees	$100
Depreciation/fittings		Other costs	$71
Value of fittings	$15,000	**Total**	**$1,500**
Effective life items	$3,000	Tax claim (1st of 3yr)	$500
Low-value pool	$12,000	**Loans**	
Tax claim (1st yr)	**$2,700**	Total loan	$166,000
Property expenses		Interest only (IO)	$110,000
Agents fees	$1,058	Interest rate (IO)	8.5%
Rates/insurance	$1,030	Credit line (CL)	$56,000
Maintenance, etc	$512	Interest rate (CL)	8.5%
Total (1st yr)	**$2,600**	**Loan payment**	
Rent details		Interest payment	$14,110
Gross rent (1st yr)	**$10,400**	Principal payment	$0
Net rent (1st yr)	**$7,800**	**Total**	**$14,110**

Please note that this example is in no way intended to represent a perfect investment property or an ideal loan. This particular example is the one that has been used throughout this book.

128 *More Wealth from Residential Property*

Borrow the money

How did Bill and Mary manage to borrow the entire amount, not only for the three properties, but for the purchasing and borrowing costs as well? There are two aspects to consider. First, the lender needs security for the loan and an LVR, which stands for Loan to Value Ratio, will be used to calculate this. The lender also needs evidence that Bill and Mary have the ability to repay, or service their loan, and a DSR, or Debt Service Ratio, will determine this. (LVRs and DSRs are defined on page 165 and are also discussed in greater detail in Chapter 14.) For peace of mind, Bill and Mary also need to confirm for themselves if they can afford the loan so I have included their own cash budget. First let's examine the security, or collateral, offered by Bill and Mary to the lender.

Security calculated using LVR

In Bill and Mary's case, having no cash deposit, they needed to borrow $498,000 to cover the cost of the three properties worth $480,000 plus the purchasing and borrowing costs of $18,000. They were able to borrow all this by using the equity in their own home together with that of their three investment properties. This gave them an overall LVR of 75% that was worked out as follows:

LVR for Bill and Mary

Loan for three investment properties

Total property price	=	$480,000
Total purchasing costs	=	$13,500
Total borrowing costs	=	$4,500
Total loan	=	**$498,000**

Value of three investment properties plus own home

Total value of investment properties	=	$480,000
Value of own home	=	$180,000
Total value of properties mortgaged	=	**$660,000**
LVR (Loan to value ratio)	=	**$498,000**
		$660,000
	=	**75.45%**

Bill and Mary had more than enough security to borrow to buy the three investment properties, and with an LVR of 75%, would have no mortgage insurance to pay, as this usually applies to LVRs of over 80%. More often than not, it is the DSR rather than the LVR that stops people from borrowing to invest. How did Bill and Mary find out if *their* DSR was OK; ie if they would be able to afford, or service, the loan?

Chapter 12: More Wealth from Residential Property   129

Serviceability calculated using DSR

The lender will want to be reassured that Bill and Mary can afford the loan payments, or as they say in the finance industry, 'service the debt'. This will depend on both the size of the loan payments and Bill and Mary's total income, including the rents from the investment properties. While all lenders will use these figures in their appraisals, the actual formula they use varies, as does the name they give to it. You may come across names like Net Surplus Ratio, Affordability Ratio, Cash Flow Indicator or Debt Qualifier, to name just a few. However, the one I prefer is the DSR or Debt Service Ratio.

In our example, DSR will be calculated by dividing loan payments by 'eligible' income, expressed as a percentage. Loan payments include those from all loans, even the home loan; and 'eligible' income is restricted to 30% of total wages plus 80% of gross rents. If the DSR exceeds 100%, the loan proposition is deemed to be unviable and is rejected; if 100% or less, the application is acceptable, subject to other criteria such as the LVR. Bill and Mary's initial DSR of 94% was calculated as follows.

DSR for Bill and Mary

Loan payments

Home loan	=	0
Car loan	=	0
Personal loan	=	0
Other loan	=	0
Investment property (interest-only)	=	$42,330
Total loan payments	=	**$42,330**

Eligible income

30% of wages (30% of $67,000)	=	$20,100
80% of rent (80% of 3 x $10,400)	=	$24,960
Total eligible income	=	**$45,060**
DSR (Debt service ratio)	=	**Loan payments**
		Eligible income
	=	**$42,330**
		$45,060
	=	**93.94%**

With a DSR of less than 94%, Bill and Mary would qualify for the loan. Notice how the lender does not take into account any tax refund. Nor do they acknowledge that most, if not all, of a second wage can go towards a loan. Let's see how it looks through the eyes of Bill and Mary.

130 *More Wealth from Residential Property*

Serviceability calculated using a budget

Bill and Mary's budget, based on income and expenditure, is difficult to work out by hand, mostly because of the tax implications of the negatively geared properties. However, using a computer it can be done easily and quickly, and the results of this PIA computer analysis are set out below.

Total income

Rental income was $31,200 ($10,400 per property), while personal income included annual wages of $47,000 for Bill and $20,000 for Mary. This gave them a total income of $98,200 for the first year.

Personal and Property Income (1st yr)

Rental income		**$31,200**
Personal income		
Bill's wage	$47,000	
Mary's wage	$20,000	
Total personal income		**$67,000**
TOTAL INCOME		**$98,200**

Total expenditure

Bill and Mary's expenditure for the first year included rental expenses, loan payments, tax and living expenses, and these are set out below.

Personal and Property Expenditure (1st yr)

Rental expenses (25% of $31,200)	$7,800	**$7,800**
Loan payment (8.5% of $498,000)	$42,330	**$42,330**
Bill's new tax situation		
New income ($47,000 + $31,200)	**$78,200**	
Rental deductions		
Interest	$42,330	
Property expenses	$7,800	
Depreciation on buildings (non-cash)	$6,000	
Depreciation on fittings (non-cash)	$8,100	
Borrowing costs (non-cash)	$1,500	
Total deductions	**$65,730**	
New taxable income ($78,200 - $65,730)	**$12,470**	
Tax on $12,470	**$1,100**	**$1,100**
Mary's tax (unchanged)		**$2,680**
Living expenses		**$20,000**
TOTAL EXPENDITURE		**$73,910**

Chapter 12: More Wealth from Residential Property 131

The first steps they took to work out their expenditure were easy. They budgeted $7,800 (25% of gross rent) for expenses, a little more than the lender allowed to cover themselves, and $42,330 for their interest-only loan payments ($14,110 per property or 8.5% of $498,000). Any spare money, they decided, would go towards that part of the loan set up as a credit line.

Calculating their new tax as a result of the negative gearing benefits was more involved. Soon after signing the contracts, Bill applied to the Australian Tax Office (ATO) for a reduction in his regular tax instalments, as allowed under Section 15-15. His application included the following.

Bill's new income was $78,200, the sum of his wages ($47,000) and rents ($31,200). Rental deductions included interest ($42,330), property expenses ($7,800), depreciation on the buildings ($6,000), depreciation on the fittings ($8,100) and borrowing costs ($1,500). These amounted to $65,730, which, when offset against Bill's total income, resulted in a new taxable income of $12,470 ($78,200 - $65,730), on which he was only required to pay $1,100 in tax, instead of $11,185.

Mary's tax of $2,680 remained unchanged because the properties were not in her name. Had she not been working, she could have earned extra income from Bill by taking care of the financial aspects of his properties. This would have given Bill a tax deduction at a higher marginal rate than Mary would be paying in tax on her additional income.

Bill and Mary then prepared a personal budget for their day to day living expenses and found they would need about $20,000 per year for food, etc. Their total personal and property expenditure came to $73,910.

Calculating the savings

The final step for Bill and Mary was to look at the overall picture as shown in the table below. You can see that even with three investment properties, they had $24,290 ($98,200 - $73,910) to spare. In fact, using the Investment Capacity Calculator in the PIA software, they worked out that instead of putting these savings towards their credit line, they could have easily afforded a total of six investment properties!

Bill and Mary's Budget (1st Yr)

Income		Expenditure	
Rental income	$31,200	Rental expenses	$7,800
		Loan payment	$42,330
Bill's wage	$47,000	Bill's new tax	$1,100
Mary's wage	$20,000	Mary's tax	$2,680
		Living expenses	$20,000
Total income	**$98,200**	**Total expenditure**	**$73,910**
Savings = Total income - Total expenditure = $24,290			

132 *More Wealth from Residential Property*

Build a property portfolio

Now you know the broad strategies involved in buying your very first investment property. What are the next steps towards building a portfolio of properties? Let's continue to follow the progress of Bill and Mary. They now have three properties, so we'll go through the figures to see how they can buy another one about every two years or so, building a net worth of more than a million dollars (in today's dollars) over the 15 years.

I liken the strategy to a fruit cake recipe that you can alter to suit your tastes, but some of you might prefer to think of it as a car trip between Sydney and Melbourne. The map indicates that if you follow a particular route, the distance will be exactly 900 kilometres, so if you drive at 90 kilometres an hour, you will take exactly 10 hours to get there. Now we all know that this is highly improbable — you won't travel at the same speed all the way. There'll be stop signs, slow cars, fast food and a host of other reasons why you won't arrive in exactly 10 hours. No matter how you do it, you do get there. And so it is with investing in property. As you would with the car journey — set a destination, draw a map and enjoy the trip, but take your own time. Now let's get back to Bill and Mary.

Over the page, I'll construct a spreadsheet with all the relevant financial information about Bill and Mary (such as wages, rents, property values and living expenses, etc) and project these values over the next 15 years. You will see how, when rents and wages rise with time, the couple will be able to borrow more and more money, to buy more and more properties to build more and more wealth. First we need to decide what inflation rates are appropriate for calculating the projected values over time

In my previous books *Building Wealth through Investment Property* and *Building Wealth in Changing Times* I produced a similar spreadsheet using the average inflation rates at those times. Likewise, in this new scenario, I have used a set of inflation rates based on the averages over the past decade. These rates are shown in the table below, together with the rates used in my two earlier books. Using these assumptions, we are then ready to build a spreadsheet with projections over the next 15 years, to see what might be possible for Bill and Mary.

Yearly Rates of Increase in Spreadsheet Projections

	Building Wealth through Investment Property	*Building Wealth in Changing Times*	*More Wealth from Residential Property*
Wages	9.5%	6.0%	3.5%
Inflation	8.0%	5.0%	2.0%
Cap grth	11.0%	7.5%	4.5%

Chapter 12: More Wealth from Residential Property 133

If Bill and Mary continued to build their portfolio as outlined in the spreadsheet constructed using these assumptions, they would own property valued at $2,018,860 after 10 years. With loans of $1,008,463, their net worth would then be more than one million dollars — $1,010,397!

After 15 years, with properties worth $3,135,158 and loans of around $1,345,575, their net worth would be $1,789,583. Being realistic, and subtracting the value of their own home worth $348,351 at that stage, this represents a net investment equity of about $1,441,232. In today's dollars, this is roughly one million dollars! Before you go ploughing through the figures, though, let's look at the big picture depicted in the graph below.

It took Bill and Mary ten years to save a deposit, pay off their home, and build a net worth of $180,000. Yet in the next ten years, their net worth had grown to one million dollars! And in another ten years to three million dollars and ... It's easy to see why getting started and buying your first home is the hardest step. From then on, borrowing to buy more rental properties can send your net worth soaring. Perhaps you might like to compare this graph with the one on page 20 to see the alternative!

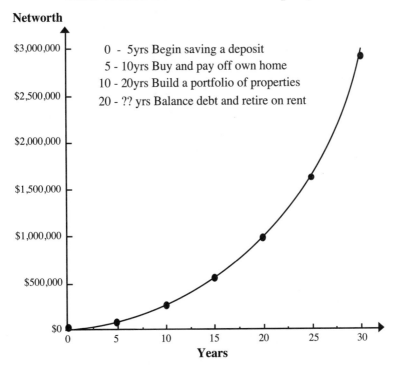

More Wealth from Residential Property

Start of year	2001	1yr	2yr	3yr	4yr	5yr	6yr	7yr	8yr	9yr	10yr	11yr	12yr	13yr	14yr	15yr
1 Home value	4.50%	180,000	188,100	196,565	205,410	214,653	224,313	234,407	244,955	255,978	267,497	279,534	292,114	305,259	318,995	333,350
2 Home loan balance		0	0	0	0	0	0	0	0	0	0	0	0	0	0	0
3 Inv. Property value	4.50%	160,000	167,200	174,724	182,587	190,803	199,389	208,362	217,738	227,536	237,775	248,475	259,656	271,341	283,551	296,311
4 **Total inv. Properties**		**3**	**4**	**4**	**5**	**5**	**5**	**6**	**6**	**7**	**7**	**8**	**8**	**9**	**9**	**9**
5 Total loans		498,000	646,234	622,401	783,683	758,261	728,607	911,373	880,202	1.080m	1.047m	1.266m	1.232m	1.472m	1.437m	1.394m
6 Total value		660,000	856,900	895,461	1.118m	1.169m	1.221m	1.485m	1.551m	1.849m	1.932m	2.267m	2.369m	2.747m	2.871m	3.000m
7 **Loan value ratio**	**LVR**	**75%**	**75%**	**70%**	**70%**	**65%**	**60%**	**61%**	**57%**	**58%**	**54%**	**56%**	**52%**	**54%**	**50%**	**46%**
8 Rental income	2.00%	31,200	42,432	43,281	55,183	56,286	57,412	70,273	71,678	85,297	87,003	101,420	103,449	118,707	121,082	123,503
9 Current net income	3.50%	67,000	69,345	71,772	74,284	76,884	79,575	82,360	85,243	88,226	91,314	94,510	97,818	101,242	104,785	108,453
10 Total income		98,200	111,777	115,053	129,467	133,171	136,987	152,633	156,921	173,523	178,317	195,930	201,267	219,949	225,867	231,956
11 Property expenses	2.00%	7,800	10,608	10,820	13,796	14,072	14,353	17,568	17,919	21,324	21,751	25,355	25,862	29,677	30,270	30,876
12 Living expenses	2.00%	20,000	20,400	20,808	21,224	21,649	22,082	22,523	22,974	23,433	23,902	24,380	24,867	25,365	25,872	26,390
13 New tax		3,780	2,901	3,425	3,365	4,456	6,464	5,072	6,509	4,948	6,608	5,267	6,489	5,900	6,488	9,148
14 Loan payments		42,330	54,930	52,904	66,613	64,452	61,932	77,467	74,817	91,818	88,993	107,632	104,691	125,145	122,154	118,526
15 Total expenditure		73,910	88,838	87,957	104,998	104,629	104,830	122,630	122,219	141,524	141,253	162,634	161,910	186,086	184,784	184,939
16 Cash savings		24,290	22,939	27,096	24,469	28,542	32,157	30,002	34,702	31,999	37,063	33,297	39,357	33,863	41,082	47,017
17 **Debt service ratio**	**DSR**	**94%**	**100%**	**94%**	**100%**	**95%**	**89%**	**96%**	**90%**	**97%**	**92%**	**98%**	**93%**	**100%**	**95%**	**90%**
End of year																
18 Total value	180,000	689,700	895,461	935,756	1.169m	1.221m	1.276m	1.551m	1.621m	1.932m	2.019m	2.369m	2.476m	2.871m	3.000m	3.135m
19 Total loans	0	472,764	622,401	594,250	758,261	728,607	695,197	880,202	844,148	1.047m	1.008m	1.232m	1.191m	1.437m	1.394m	1.346m
20 Net worth	180,000	216,936	273,059	341,506	410,407	492,651	581,017	671,181	777,047	884,953	**1.010m**	1.138m	1.285m	1.434m	1.606m	**1.790m**
21 Investment equity	0	28,836	76,495	136,097	195,754	268,338	346,611	426,226	521,069	617,456	730,862	845,589	979,956	1.115m	1.272m	1.441m
22 Inv. equity (2001 $'s)	0	28,271	73,524	128,247	180,846	243,042	307,780	371,055	444,727	516,659	599,561	680,076	772,689	861,820	964,303	**1.071m**

This table has been produced using the PIA software (see p249). Note that the figures are hypothetical and individual circumstances will differ.

Chapter 12: More Wealth from Residential Property 135

Notes on building wealth table

The spreadsheet was produced using the Property Investment Analysis software (PIA page 249) using variables unique to our imaginary couple, Bill and Mary. As I have stressed, though, your pathway to wealth will probably be different. What is important is that the principle of building wealth by borrowing to buy and keep residential investment property for the long term is exactly the same, no matter what the 'road conditions'.

The two key indicators used to determine when Bill and Mary can buy more property are called the Loan to Value Ratio, or LVR, and Debt Service Ratio, or DSR. Properties were only acquired if the LVR remained at or below 80% and the DSR at or below 100%, complying with most lending institutions' requirements.

For simplicity, the spreadsheet depicts regular annual rates of increase, but it is more likely that the increases will be 'ad hoc' with values such as rents stagnating in some years and increasing by more than the average in others. This may mean that, while you should be able to afford another property every few years, you may buy none in five years, or four in one.

Start of year (Items 1 to 17)

Each year has a start (Items 1 to 17) and end (Items 18 to 22) to make it easy to see the year's progress. For example, at the start of year 1, Item 5 is total loans of $498,000 and Item 6 is total value of $660,000, giving an LVR of 75%. With capital growth and loan reduction, the end of year results are reflected in Item 18, with total value at $689,700, and Item 19, with total loans of $472,764. Net worth (Item 20) is then $216,936. To complete the picture, investment equity (net worth less the home value) of $28,836 is at Item 21, and again at Item 22, as $28,271 in today's dollars.

1. Home value

Bill and Mary's own home was initially worth $180,000 and increased each year at 4.5%. In your case, you may not have a home of your own, and your first property might be an investment property.

2. Home loan balance

Bill and Mary had completely paid off their home loan in this example, but in fact it's possible to start buying rental properties long before this. There is no set amount of equity that determines when more property can be purchased as this depends on the DSR more so than the LVR. Someone on a high income may well be able to purchase investment property with very little equity in their home and a large home loan. Whereas someone on a lower income may need to wait until the equity is large and the amount owing small. Then the lower loan payments would improve the DSR quite considerably.

136 *More Wealth from Residential Property*

3. Investment property value

In our example, Bill and Mary initially bought three rental properties for $160,000 each, and the growth rate was assumed to be 4.5% per year. They could, however, have bought a mixture of both low and high value properties. A point worth noting is that the rate of capital growth usually does not determine the rate of purchase. If property values doubled overnight, you would still only be able to buy more property if your cash flow, and consequently your DSR, allowed it.

4. Total investment properties

This is the total number of investment properties being held. In the first year Bill and Mary bought three, and in the second year after buying one more, the total is four. It's up to you to manipulate the number of properties so that the DSR remains at or below 100%, the LVR at or below 80%, and the cash savings positive.

5. Total loans (including own home)

Loans include existing loans, new loans, and the home loan (if any). All loans include both the borrowing and purchasing costs, which in this case, amounted to 3.75% of the property value.

6. Total value (including own home)

The total value of all Bill and Mary's properties included all investment properties plus the value of the home, which primarily enabled the initial no-deposit borrowing by lowering the LVR.

7. Loan to Value Ratio (LVR)

The LVR is the total loan divided by the total value of all properties held as security for the loan. Bill and Mary's LVR at the time of purchasing their three investment properties was 75%. For the first seven or so years while the property portfolio was being established, it remained above 60%, enabling the wealth building process to be kick started. Over time, with increasing equity as a result of debt reduction and capital growth, the LVR slowly fell towards 50% where it hovered until Bill and Mary made a decision on whether to retire. (See page 165 for more details on LVR.)

8. Rental income

Initial rent was $200 per week ($10,400 per year), representing a gross yield of 6.5% ($10,400/$160,000). Gross rent for the first three rental properties was $31,200 per year and was assumed to rise with inflation at 2%. In your case, however, the rent would depend on many factors such as the property, the city and the market. Yields also may vary according to whether the building is new or old, a house or unit, is in outer or inner suburbia, or is on a large or small block of land.

Chapter 12: More Wealth from Residential Property   137

9. Current net income

By the time Bill and Mary were ready to buy investment property their initial annual joint income was $67,000 and was assumed to rise by 3.5% per year. It consisted of Bill's income of $47,000 and Mary's of $20,000 from part-time work. A lower income simply means it may take a little longer to build a portfolio; a higher income may accelerate the process. But as we'll see later in Item 12 for living expenses, the level of income is no more important than how you spend it.

10. Total income

Bill and Mary's total income was the sum of their salaried incomes and the gross rent from all of their investment properties. In the first year, this was $98,200 ($67,000 plus $31,200).

11. Property expenses

In Bill and Mary's situation, the rental property expenses such as rates, insurances, agent's fees and maintenance, etc, were 25% of the gross rent but in practice, this would vary. In the first year, expenses were $2,600 per rental property, or $7,800 for the three. Inflation increased both rents and expenses by 2% per year, but the increases would most likely be irregular. This affects the cash flows, which will determine the frequency of acquiring additional properties. To be conservative, expenses were set at 25%, however, 20% was used for the DSRs.

12. Living expenses

Bill and Mary's personal living expenses were initially $20,000 per year and increased by 2.0% per year in line with inflation. These expenses included their day to day living costs such as food, clothes, holidays and electricity, etc, for their own home. They would not have been limited to this amount as they could well have used their cash savings each year to boost their living expenses if they chose. This is one of the biggest factors that determines how quickly you build wealth.

Unfortunately for many people, living expenses include the cost of personal loans on furniture, cars, kitchens, not to mention credit cards. It's often the case that a battler's budget shows bare essentials of just $10,000 a year while personal debt repayments of $20,000 bring their living expenses to $30,000, precluding them from borrowing money for even their own home. Budgeting is not about going without, it is about setting priorities. Bill and Mary would not have been condemned to a life of destitution for the relatively short time they were borrowing to buy investment properties. And neither would you be. However, a few years of setting priorities ensures many years of enjoying prosperity.

He is richest whose pleasures are cheapest.

138 *More Wealth from Residential Property*

13. New tax

To simplify the explanations it was assumed that all properties were purchased in Bill's name only, as he was the highest income earner. The total new tax payable of $3,780 was the result of Bill's new tax of $1,100 (instead of $11,185) plus Mary's tax of $2,680, which remained unchanged. Also, as allowed under Section 15-15 of the Tax Act, the tax benefits were accounted for in the year in which they were accrued, not the following year, which would normally occur with a tax refund. Furthermore, tax for the 15 years was calculated using the current tax scales, assuming no changes in future year.

Tax benefits depend not only on the total income, but also on how the income is split. Under the present tax system, for example, the total tax for two people on $47,000 and $20,000 would be less than the tax on a single income of $67,000. This is important with respect to the name(s) in which the property is registered. Property bought in joint names means that both the income and deductions are split equally, but this may be of no real advantage if the spouse is not working.

In fact, it would have been better if Bill and Mary had purchased all of the properties as tenants-in-common, with Bill owning 90% of each property and Mary 10%. And it would have been equally effective for Bill to have purchased about 90% of the properties, or eight of the nine properties, and Mary just one. The net worth after 15 years would then have been about $20,000 more in each case.

14. Loan payments

Bill and Mary took a combination of interest-only loans and a credit line. The rate in both cases was assumed to be 8.5% for the 15 years, with payments in the first year amounting to $42,330. You would more than likely encounter a variety of interest rates, which would affect the rate of further property purchases. I have used a combination of loans here, with two thirds being a fixed-rate interest-only and one third being a variable rate credit line. You might prefer the entire loan to be fixed-rate interest-only and use the cash savings to reduce the debt at each refinance, thus giving yourself the equivalent of a 'fixed-rate loan' with you retaining control over the principal repayments. Or, you could simply obtain a standard P&I loan. Over a term of 25 years or more, the monthly payment is not significantly higher.

15. Total expenditure

Total expenditure for Bill and Mary was the sum of the tax payable, the rental property expenses, the interest on the loan (both principal and interest payments if a P&I loan) and their personal living expenses. In the first year, total expenditure was $73,910.

Chapter 12: More Wealth from Residential Property   139

16. Cash savings

Bill and Mary's savings ($24,290) was the difference between total income and total expenditure, and this money effectively reduced the loan by remaining in the credit line. Instead, the cash savings could be invested in an account in the name of the lowest income earner to minimise tax, but I believe the credit line option is best. The size of the savings can also indicate how soon more properties can be bought.

17. Debt Service Ratio (DSR)

The DSR was the key in determining when Bill and Mary could buy again, a percentage of 100% or less being acceptable. In my view, if your cash savings are positive but your DSR is more than 100% — in other words, if *you* know you can borrow more but the *lender* thinks you can't — you should still apply for a loan. By their own budget, Bill and Mary knew they could have afforded six properties at the start, even with a DSR of 121%. (See page 165 for more details on DSR.)

End of Year (Items 18 to 22)

At the end of each year, Bill and Mary calculated their net worth and their investment equity to make sure they were on track.

18. Total value.

The value of the properties at the end of each year reflected the capital growth of 4.5%. In the first year, the total value of their own home and three investment properties had grown from $660,000 to $689,700.

19. Total loans

During each year, their loan was reduced by leaving the cash savings in their credit line. In the first year, cash savings of $24,290 reduced their initial loan of $498,000 to $472,764, with the benefit of less interest.

20. Net worth

Bill and Mary's net worth in the first year was $216,936, but by the 10th year, their *net worth* including the value of their own home would have been more than *one million dollars*!

21. Investment equity

The investment equity was Bill and Mary's net worth less the value of the family home. In the first year it was just $28,836, but by the 10th year it had reached $730,862 and by the 15th year it was $1,441,232.

22. Net investment equity (in terms of today's dollars)

Using the compounding inflation rate each year, the net investment equity can be calculated in today's dollars. By the 15th year, Bill and Mary's *net investment equity* had surpassed *one million dollars*!

140 *More Wealth from Residential Property*

Balance the debt on retirement

After 15 years of investing, with nine rental properties, Bill and Mary's investment equity would have been $1,070,857 in today's dollars. They would then need to balance the debt so that the rent was greater than their expenses, providing them with a positive cash flow. After all, this was the aim of their whole wealth building exercise. How would it have been possible for them to achieve this? Below are a few of the options they could consider when they decide to retire.

Work part time

Bill and Mary could have ceased full-time work well before 15 years, working only part-time in the years before they retired. This would have put them in wind-down mode for how ever long they so desired. With no further property acquisitions, the rents and wages would gradually overtake the interest, providing them with more and more income independent of their work. This might sidestep the need to sell any properties at all. For people who still love their work, but want more time to do other things, this might be a possible solution.

Sell some properties

Had Bill and Mary retired completely after 15 years they would need to reduce the debt so that the rent became their sole source of income. This might incur CGT, which could be minimised if the properties were sold in a staggered process over a few years. They could also set up a credit line against their properties to 'eat into the capital' while they waited for an appropriate time to sell.

Aim for higher yielding properties

In the scenario just described, net rental yields would have fallen to about 3.5% over the 15 years, as would be expected with property values increasing faster than rents. Bill and Mary could have made a choice during the 15 years. Instead of buying properties with average growth and yield as described, they could have purchased properties with much higher yields but potentially lower capital growth. With rents likely to be higher than the interest, there might not be the need to sell any properties at the end.

Work part-time and wait for super

During the entire wealth building process, Bill and Mary's employer would have been contributing to the Superannuation Guarantee Charge on their behalf. While this would never be enough to enable a comfortable retirement, it could be used to reduce the debt when they turned 55. If they worked part-time until then, it might also alleviate the need to sell any properties.

Part VI

Financing the Project

13
Sources of Finance

Where's the best place to borrow money for investment properties? In recent years, financial deregulation has somewhat levelled the playing field. While we may see little difference in interest rates between the players, the criteria and conditions can vary widely, and no doubt you *will* encounter many brick walls in your endeavour to find a lender.

You must not be disillusioned by a 'no'. Getting a loan involves the same process as buying a pair of shoes, except that most people don't make the connection. Think what would happen if you walked into your local shoe shop looking for a pair of leather work boots. The shop may stock them, or not. If they don't, you'll probably get a 'No, sorry', and understand immediately that this really means 'No, sorry, we don't have work boots'. Then you'll move on and try somewhere else, knowing you were simply in the wrong shop and that there's every chance the next one will have your boots.

Yet when people approach a lender looking for a loan for an investment property, and are told 'No, sorry', they often take it to mean that they've been refused credit and that they'll never ever get a loan from *any* lender. A 'no' really means 'Sorry, we specialise in this type, not that type of loan, so why don't you try somewhere else?' One of the problems with lenders is that they don't hang a sign on the door advertising the loan criteria they prefer.

Will they take security over commercial property, land, acreage, studio apartments, company title or community title? Is all the income from self-employed persons, overtime, pensions, overseas investments, family allowance, child maintenance, partners or spouses taken into account? Do they prefer to lend to owner-occupiers, businesses, investors, non-residents, or owner-builders? Are the loans interest-only, principal and interest, credit line or second mortgage?

The list is endless so it's important to realise that lenders are all very different, and the only way to achieve your goal is to keep looking for one that suits your particular needs. How much will a 'no' cost you if you stop looking? Let's now review who the lenders are.

144   *More Wealth from Residential Property*

Traditional banks

eg ANZ, Commonwealth, National, Westpac

Until about a decade ago, significant differences existed between the 'big four' and other lending institutions, so much so, that you could easily find a loan with an interest rate of up to 3% lower. Today, though, the lending scene has changed dramatically. Competition resulting from the emergence of mortgage originators and mortgage brokers has helped to narrow the gap. In the past, the 'big four' favoured big business via their trading divisions, and first home buyers through their savings divisions. At long last, however, they recognise the security in lending to residential property investors and have become very competitive.

Smaller banks

eg Bank of Queensland, Bendigo Bank, St George, Suncorp Metway

These banks have evolved from building societies and are a first rate source of finance for first home buyers and property investors alike because of their traditional origins in property finance. My experience has been that they seem to have down-to-earth philosophies and very approachable managers. The borrowing costs and interest rates are quite reasonable, and they offer a good middle-of-the-road type loan. Their biggest plus is that they will lend money on fairly high LVRs of up to 95%.

Other banks

eg Macquarie Bank

These tend to be specialist banks with aggressive lending tactics aimed at entrepreneurs. Some specialise in margin lending for the share market.

Building societies and credit unions

eg Credit Union of Australia, Heritage, The Rock

These are excellent for both first home buyers and property investors. Their rates of interest are competitive and they have acceptable upfront charges. But they have strict rules applying to incomes and are not usually flexible if you don't fit their guidelines — even though you can well afford the loan. It's up to you to present your special case.

Mortgage originators

eg Aussie, Collins Securities, RAMS, RESI, Wizard

These 'new banks on the block', or 'non-banks', as they prefer to be called, source their funds from the wholesale market, even other banks, and on-sell to the consumer. They have taken the lending market by storm and the resulting fierce competition has produced a levelling of interest rates across the board. Remember, money is a very marketable commodity and as such, can be bought and sold by registered dealers who then add their margin.

Chapter 13: Sources of Finance 145

Trustee companies
eg ANZ Trustees, Permanent Custodians, Perpetual Trustees

Ten years ago, their interest rates were 2% -3% below the going market rate from banks. Today the difference has narrowed to less than 1% and you would need to consider whether this was worth the higher upfront fees that usually accompany their loans. Mortgages from this source can be inflexible and often a good deal of collateral and income is required, with LVRs of around 65% and conservative DSRs being preferred. Despite these drawbacks, I believe this kind of company can be a great source of finance for experienced long-term property investors.

Finance companies
eg AGC, Esanda

In general, finance companies have almost non-existent upfront fees, but very high interest rates. As a rule, this facility has limited use for long-term property investors; an exception could be if you had opted for a quick and easy interim loan en route to finding something cheaper and more permanent. The high interest rates may not be such a problem for developers and property traders, who often require short-term loans of less than a year. There are a few small finance companies that are exceptions, tending to be more like trustee companies with strict lending procedures.

Insurance companies, etc
eg AMP, AXA, ING, GIO, National Mutual

It is possible to borrow money through insurance, life, superannuation or other fund management companies, as some of their funds are invested in first mortgages. They can be an excellent source of finance, similar to that offered by trustee companies: low interest rates, but usually requiring low LVRs. It is also possible to borrow against the value of your own funds deposited with such companies. Some insurance companies will lend you up to 90% of the amount you have placed with them, and usually at competitive interest rates.

Overseas finance
eg directly obtained from overseas banks

Loans with very low interest rates are often available if you borrow from overseas lenders, but I believe they are extremely risky because of the fluctuating dollar. If the principal of your loan is in a foreign currency, the debt can rise dramatically if the Aussie dollar falls. You could see yourself going backwards and finish up owing more than you borrowed. So unless you are prepared to pay the extra cost of hedging against a drop in the Aussie dollar, stay well clear. Many an investor has been caught in this trap. It may seem very attractive on the way in, but you might find it costly on the way out.

146　*More Wealth from Residential Property*

International banks

eg Chase Manhattan, Citibank, Hongkongbank of Australia

Overseas banks operating within Australia usually offer innovative investment loans that are quite attractive, possibly because they are more experienced in 'marketing money' than their Australian counterparts. They can be a good source of finance, particularly if they are innovative enough to appreciate your needs as a property investor.

Private finance

eg family members, solicitors' trust accounts

Before financial deregulation made access to money much easier, it was standard practice to borrow funds from accountants and solicitors who acted as a go-between for their clients and the public. This method is still used to a limited degree, and may be useful for short-term loans. Family, too, can be a good source of finance, but be wary — misunderstandings and disputes over money can cause disharmony and may not be worth it.

Vendor finance

Vendor finance is almost non-existent in Australia. In a few cases, the vendor will carry back a first or second mortgage, but often a lower interest rate is coupled with a higher purchase price. Currently in Australia, less than 1% of loans are vendor financed and they usually apply to commercial properties. However, a form of vendor financing called a wrap loan (see page 161) has been introduced by some entrepreneurial property investors who on-sell property with the loan in place.

Mortgage brokers

eg Mortgage Choice, Mortgage Force, Mortgage Masters

Mortgage brokers don't originate loans but as the name implies, broker a deal between you and a lender. Ten years ago, mortgage brokers suffered from an identity crisis, being regarded as the place you went to when you couldn't get a loan from anywhere else; and you often paid up to 3% in fees for the privilege. Mind you, they were experts in ferreting out loans from obscure sources. Today, all that has changed.

Mortgage brokers now play a prominent role, selling almost 19% of all residential mortgages, and moving quickly in the direction of their overseas counterparts who initiate 70% of all loans in the United States and Great Britain. Not only have the high fees disappeared, but they can often find you a better loan than you could by yourself. This new breed of mortgage broker should relieve much of the tedium usually involved with sourcing finance as most of them have access to the specific lending criteria required by lenders at their fingertips. As a matter of interest, on a recent visit to a mortgage broker, when I presented a particular scenario, it was accepted by half the lenders on their books and rejected by the rest.

14
How Much Money Can You Borrow?

Most people are excited by the prospect of determining their own future financial independence by borrowing and buying property, and they usually want to get started straight away. Choosing a property is reasonably easy as most of us are familiar with building construction and have a good idea of what we are looking for, even before seeing a real estate agent. Yet, borrowing money can be daunting as most people are not familiar with financial formulas and usually have no idea how to work out the basics of what to do before talking to a lender. They want to know:

How much money can I borrow?

How many properties can I buy?

How much deposit will I need?

How much equity will I need in my home?

How long before I can buy another property?

How much income will I need?

In this chapter, we'll go step by step through the process of working out how much money you can borrow. Nobody needs to be a financial genius to do this. You only need to be able to work out a few sums and percentages. The three steps I will detail are the three criteria common to all lending institutions. They are:

Status: Are you a stable person in the community?

Security: What can the bank keep to ensure that you repay the loan?

Serviceability: Will your income cover the loan payments?

Usually the rules that lenders set are very conservative to accommodate first-home buyers and first-time property investors. So if you're well on your way with a few properties already, you may need to shop around for a lender with a set of rules and guidelines that best suits your situation. Let's now look at these three criteria in detail.

Status

First and foremost, if the bank is going to lend you a lot of money they will need to know about your personal status before they even look at your finances. Don't be frightened or put off by the detail required. Apart from the usual name, address and phone number, they will want to know some other personal details including:

Are you a resident or non-resident of Australia?

How long have you lived at your present address?

How long did you live at your last address?

Are you self employed?

If so, for how long?

How long have you been in your present employment?

What is the address of your current employment?

How long were you in your last employment?

Do you have a partner?

Does your partner work?

How many dependent children do you have?

Have you ever been bankrupt?

How many credit cards do you have?

Lenders first try to determine whether or not you are a good risk as they prefer people who have stable employment and who have lived at the same address for a reasonable time. There are no hard and fast rules as to what constitutes a good client, but if you have five kids, have been unemployed for six years and have lived at four different addresses during that time, you might struggle to get a loan of any kind. On the other hand, I have known lenders to go out of their way to assist businesses dealing with the oldest profession in the world, simply through having had a stable address for many years and a very high predictable, you might say guaranteed, income.

The self-employed can find themselves in a Catch 22 situation, with lenders treating them cautiously. For tax purposes, it is desirable for them to show minimum income with maximum expenses. However, they often find that their tax returns distinctly disadvantage them in applying for a loan, despite pleas like, 'But I *really* earn more than what's showing there' and 'I don't *really* have that many expenses'.

You can see why it's so important to prepare a loan application with information that presents you in a good light, for no one has any legal obligation to approve a loan. Not even if your financial details fit the lender's guidelines.

Security

Have you ever been to a service station, put $50 of petrol in the tank, then found you've left your wallet behind? The attendant doesn't want to let you drive home to get it, even though you've promised you'll return. So not wanting to drag your partner away from work to pay the bill, you offer to leave your Rolex watch as a security to ensure your return. In effect, you have just arranged a short-term loan from the attendant using your Rolex as security. Leaving a $5,000 watch to secure a $50 loan would be overkill, as you may have achieved the same result by leaving your $200 gold wedding ring. If you'd offered the $10 football that your son left in the boot of the car, I'm sure you wouldn't have succeeded.

Lending institutions work the same way. If you borrow a large sum of money to buy an investment property, you need to supply something as a security to ensure you stay committed to repaying the loan. There is a relationship between the value of the security lender's need and the loan they are willing to advance; it is called the Loan to Value Ratio or LVR. In the above case, the LVR in each situation would be:

$$\frac{\text{Loan}}{\text{Rolex watch}} = \frac{\$50}{\$5,000} = 1\%$$

$$\frac{\text{Loan}}{\text{Wedding ring}} = \frac{\$50}{\$200} = 25\%$$

$$\frac{\text{Loan}}{\text{Son's football}} = \frac{\$50}{\$10} = 500\%$$

Obviously the watch with an LVR of 1% is excessive security, and the football with an LVR of 500% is insufficient, while the ring with an LVR of 25% would probably be about right in this situation.

Lending institutions regard residential property as one of the best forms of security with most going to an LVR of 95% for owner occupiers and 80% for investors, or more with mortgage insurance. Ironically, while property is often referred to as a security for a loan, it must *not* be confused with the term 'securities' as defined by ASIC, which refers to managed funds and shares, etc, sold by investment advisors. Perhaps that's why property is often referred to as collateral, instead of security, for a loan.

LVR is the key to borrowing to buy investment properties with no money of your own. However, it is a concept foreign to many investors. In the beginning, I did not understand this principle, and even when it was explained to me by an astute real estate agent more than twenty years ago, I didn't believe it was possible. Like most people, I thought that the only way to borrow to buy property was to save a deposit before you could get a loan. In fact, no-deposit borrowing using the LVR to advantage is the key to building wealth through residential property, as I'll explain.

150 *More Wealth from Residential Property*

Loan to Value Ratio (LVR)

To understand how the LVR works, let's go through three situations involving our couple Bill and Mary — first, when they buy their own home using a cash deposit; second, when they buy three rental properties using their own home as security; and third, when they buy three rental properties before having paid off their own home loan.

1. LVR with cash deposit for own home

In 1996, Bill and Mary used $15,000 as a deposit on their home worth $145,000, borrowing $130,000. Their LVR would be calculated like this:

Loan for own home	=	**$130,000**
Value of own home	=	**$145,000**
LVR (Loan to value ratio)	=	**$130,000**
		$145,000
	=	**89.65%**

With an LVR of just under 90%, the next step is to assess their debt serviceability — can they afford the repayments — which we'll do in the next section on DSR on page 153. Lenders are more willing to lend to owner occupiers with a high LVR than to property investors because they consider that the risk of defaulting on a loan on a place where you live is lower. Ironically, it's harder to keep up the payments on your own home!

2. LVR with no-deposit; home loan paid off

By the time Bill and Mary had paid out their own home it was worth $180,000 and they were in a position to buy three investment properties each valued at $160,000. By using their own home as security, they did not need a cash deposit. Here is what their LVR looked like.

Total loan for three investment properties

Total property value	=	$480,000
Total purchasing costs	=	$13,500
Total borrowing costs	=	$4,500
Total loan for three properties	=	**$498,000**

Total value of three investment properties plus own home

Total value of investment properties	=	$480,000
Value of own home	=	$180,000
Total value of properties mortgaged	=	**$660,000**
LVR (Loan to value ratio)	=	**$498,000**
		$660,000
	=	**75.45%**

An LVR of 75% is very acceptable, provided the DSR is OK. We will do the calculations for this later in the section on DSR on page 154.

Chapter 14: How Much Money Can You Borrow? 151

3. LVR with no-deposit; home loan NOT paid off

A burning question with many people is:

'How much equity do I need to have in my own home before I can start borrowing to buy investment properties?'

Unfortunately there is no fixed amount, but it helps a lot to understand how the LVR works when it concerns a home loan. Let's look at Bill and Mary again and suppose they had not completely paid off their home loan at the time they wanted to buy their three investment properties. We'll suppose there was a debt of $30,000 remaining, leaving equity of $150,000 in their $180,000 home to be used as the additional security. Here is what the LVR would look like then.

Total loan for three investment properties plus own home

Total property price	=	$480,000
Total purchase costs	=	$13,500
Total borrowing costs	=	$4,500
Total loan for three properties	=	$498,000
Loan on own home	=	$30,000
Total loans	**=**	**$528,000**

Total value of three investment properties plus own home

Value of three investment properties	=	$480,000
Value of own home	=	$180,000
Total value of properties mortgaged	=	**$660,000**
LVR (Loan to value ratio)	=	**$528,000**
		$660,000
	=	80%

As before, this LVR of 80% would be accepted with no requirement to pay mortgage insurance, and the loan application would proceed to the next step of determining serviceability, which we'll calculate on page 155. As the table shows, what's important is the size of the home loan in relation to the value of the home, not the amount of equity Bill and Mary have.

For instance, if Bill and Mary still had $150,000 equity but their home was valued at $580,000 and their home loan was $430,000, their overall LVR would have been 87.5%. In this case, they probably wouldn't qualify for a loan, mostly because their capacity to service it would be severely affected by the large repayments on their home loan. On the other hand, for a very high income earner whose DSR is OK, qualifying might be possible if they are prepared to pay a premium for mortgage insurance.

152 *More Wealth from Residential Property*

Serviceability

How can the lender be sure that you are able to make the loan payments required? Once your personal profile has been approved and it is clear that your LVR is acceptable, working out your 'serviceability' is the next step. Below is the simple information needed for calculating this.

Information for Calculating Serviceability

Income:
- Personal income of investor
- Personal income of partner
- Other income
- Future rental income

Expenses:
- Personal living expenses
- Current loan payments
- Future property expenses
- Future property loan payments

Incorporating this information, a formula is then applied to determine your eligibility for a loan. This formula may vary according to the lender. Indeed, I have seen at least 17 methods of manipulating the data to produce serviceability tests. Names for the formulas include Affordability Index, Cash Flow Test, Net Surplus Ratio, Gearing Ratio, Debt Qualifier, Net Income Test, Uncommitted Monthly Income Test, and Debt Service Ratio. Different formulas may even have the same name. However, they are all variations on the same theme and break down to something like this:

30% Total wages + 80% Total rent > Total loan payments

In words, 30% of your all wages plus 80% of all rents must be greater than all your loan payments. The many formulas built around this data vary in the rates used for each component, with wages ranging from 25% to 35% and rents varying between 70% and 80%. They can even factor in a percentage point or more to allow for possible future interest rate rises. Two assumptions, though, are common to all. The first is that an average couple can afford to commit about one third of their total income to loan payments, which includes their home, car and so on, another third to living expenses, and the remaining third to tax. The second assumption is that about 80% of rent will be net, allowing 20% for expenses.

Looking at it critically, using 30% of salary does not suit all investors. The argument does not account for tax benefits, and also it assumes that someone earning $300,000 a year has an annual grocery bill of $90,000! Whatever the guidelines, it is important to do your own homework and to present your own scenario. I suggest you prepare your own budget the same as Bill and Mary did, which is shown on page 130. However, here I will show you how most lenders will calculate your serviceability using Debt Service Ratio, or DSR, so you will know what to expect when you apply for a loan.

Chapter 14: How Much Money Can You Borrow? 153

Debt Service Ratio (DSR)

Lending institutions calculate DSR in many different ways. I have elected to use a method that bears resemblance to the LVR formula. This is:

DSR (Debt service ratio) $= \dfrac{\text{Loan payments} \quad x \quad 100\%}{\text{Eligible income}}$

$\qquad\qquad\qquad\qquad\qquad\qquad = \dfrac{\text{Loan payments} \quad x \quad 100\%}{30\% \text{ income} + 80\% \text{ Rent}}$

Loan payments are the total of all payments including home, car, boat, investment, etc, and eligible income is 30% of total wages plus 80% of all rent. If this ratio is 100% or less, the loan proposition is considered to be acceptable. Let's go back to Bill and Mary so that you can see step by step how their DSR was calculated in each of the three situations for which we calculated the LVR in the previous section.

1. DSR with cash deposit for own home

When Bill and Mary bought their home for $145,000 in 1996, they had a deposit of $15,000. If they borrowed the $130,000 using a credit line at 8%, they would initially be committed to annual payments of $12,040, based on a P&I loan over 25 years. At that stage, Bill's annual salary was $37,000 and Mary's $28,000, making a total of $65,000. Their DSR would then be calculated like this:

Loan payments

Home loan payments	=	$12,040
Other loans	=	0
Total loan payments	=	$12,040

Eligible income

30% of wages (30% of $65,000)	=	$19,500
Other income	=	0
Total eligible income	=	$19,500

DSR

DSR (Debt service ratio) $= \dfrac{\text{Loan payments}}{\text{Eligible income}}$

$\qquad\qquad\qquad\qquad\qquad = \dfrac{\$12,040}{\$19,500}$

$\qquad\qquad\qquad\qquad\qquad = 61.74\%$

With an LVR of 90%, calculated previously, and a DSR of 62%, Bill and Mary were able to borrow to buy their very first home. The next two scenarios are for when they have paid out their home loan completely, and for when they still have some debt.

154   *More Wealth from Residential Property*

2. DSR with no-deposit; home loan paid out

Let's suppose that Bill and Mary have paid out their $130,000 home loan and are ready to purchase three investment properties, each valued at $160,000 and renting for $10,400. If you recall from Chapter 12 (p.127), the committed loan payments, which is the interest only, totalled $42,330 for the three properties.   At this stage, Bill and Mary's wages were $47,000 and $20,000 respectively, Mary having decided to work part-time.

Loan payments for three investment properties

Home loan payments	=	0
Car loan payments	=	0
Personal loan payments	=	0
Other loan payments	=	0
Investment property payments	=	$42,330
Total loan payments	=	$42,330

Eligible income from wages and rent

30% of wages (30% of $67,000)	=	$20,100
80% of rent (80% of 3 x $10,400)	=	$24,960
Total eligible income	=	$45,060

DSR

$$\text{DSR (Debt service ratio)} = \frac{\text{Loan payments}}{\text{Eligible income}}$$

$$= \frac{\$42,330}{\$45,060}$$

$$= 93.94\%$$

A DSR of 94% is well below the acceptable limit of 100% and coupled with the LVR of 75% calculated previously, would easily qualify Bill and Mary for the loan.

By this method of determining the DSR, Bill and Mary would not have qualified for a fourth investment property: the DSR would have been 106%. Estimating their serviceability on four properties by another method, however, reveals that they would have qualified with at least three out of twenty lenders, and for five properties with one out of twenty.   So while the DSR is a good guide, it should not be used as a black and white decision making tool. I suggest that you do your own budget calculations as well as using the method used here to demonstrate to yourself that you are capable of servicing the loan, and to lenders too, who may be willing to use different serviceability criteria.   As I have said before, don't let a 'no' get in your way.   Remember that borrowing money is just like buying a pair of boots: keep trying until you find a shop that can provide you with what you need.

Chapter 14: How Much Money Can You Borrow? 155

3. DSR with no-deposit; home loan NOT paid out

The most common situation is when people want to start buying rental properties before they have paid out their home loan. Let's pick up on Bill and Mary's scenario reflecting this, doing a third DSR calculation. We'll assume they have a $30,000 home loan with annual payments of $12,040. These payments were based on the original $130,000 loan at 8%, however. So the first thing they should do is refinance their home loan to minimise their committed loan payments, which would then drop to just the interest payment of $2,400. Otherwise their DSR will be adversely affected. It is still possible — and highly advisable — for Bill and Mary to continue paying large amounts into their home loan, but from the point of view of the lender, they are not committed to doing so.

Assuming that Bill and Mary buy the same three investment properties with payments of $42,330 per year in addition to home loan payments of $2,400, the DSR calculation is as follows:

Loan payments

Home loan payments (interest-only)	=	$2,400
Car loan payments	=	0
Personal loan payments	=	0
Other loan payments	=	0
Investment property payments	=	$42,330
Total loan payments	=	$44,730

Eligible income

30% of wages (30% of $67,000)	=	$20,100
80% of rent (80% of 3 x $10,400)	=	$24,960
Total eligible income	=	$45,060

DSR

$$\text{DSR (Debt Service Ratio)} = \frac{\text{Loan payments}}{\text{Eligible income}}$$

$$= \frac{\mathbf{\$44{,}730}}{\mathbf{\$45{,}060}}$$

$$= \mathbf{99.26\%}$$

With an LVR of 80%, as calculated previously, and DSR of 100%, Bill and Mary would qualify with most lenders.

If their home loan had been very large, with high payments, they might only be able to buy one investment property to start with. But hey, who cares. The important thing is to have started. As Ian always says:

A journey of a thousand miles begins with the first step.

156 *More Wealth from Residential Property*

Tips to help you qualify for a loan

What can you do to improve your chances of qualifying for a loan?

Improve your image

You can score many brownie points with good presentation when you apply for a loan. I know a handyman who hopped on a train in a hired suit with a borrowed leather brief case and travelled 400 kilometres to see a bank manager. He left with a half million dollar loan to buy rental properties. He not only looked like a VIP, but he had a folder of his personal finances.

- Dress like you're already worth a million dollars. I know you really shouldn't judge a book by its cover but many bank managers still do.
- Prepare a detailed financial report including your assets and liabilities, proposed purchases, income and expenditure statements, and a budget.

Lower your LVR

Your LVR can be important in determining how many properties you need to mortgage and if you need to pay mortgage insurance — the higher the valuation, the lower the LVR. Graft and corruption aside, there are many things you can do to influence a valuation.

- Make a property look its best with cheap cosmetic improvements such as cleaning and mowing.
- Do your homework and prepare a list of similar properties that have recently sold in the area at good prices. Valuers are often not aware of the latest sales as it takes months for them to settle and be registered.
- Try to be on site during a valuation so you can 'talk up' the property, pointing out the features that make it special.
- Be aware that valuations vary greatly according to the purpose. For example, a property may be valued lower if the valuation is requested by a lender for security, or higher if requested by you for an 'in-house' sale to your partner as a negatively geared rental property. Don't worry if the property doesn't 'value up'. A valuer would rather be persecuted by you for undervaluing, than prosecuted by the lender for overvaluing!

Decrease your DSR

There's not a lot you can do to improve the income side of the DSR equation. There's much you can do to decrease the loan payments.

- Consolidate personal loans with high repayments into your home loan.
- Extend the term of your home loan to 25 or 30 years or even to interest only to minimise the monthly payments.
- Throw away your credit cards as about 5% of the limit will be deemed to be a loan payment — even if you pay them out on time.

Where to next? It's time to see which type of loan is best.

15
Which Loan Is Best?

In previous chapters, we followed the steps that Bill and Mary took to borrow and buy three investment properties using their own home as extra security. And we saw how they could use interest-only loans and lines of credit to build a portfolio of investment properties. We also looked at how they would qualify for those loans using LVR and DSR criteria. What we have not focused on in any great detail is the types of loans that were available to them and why they chose the particular ones they did. Are all loans equal? Or are some more equal than others?

I first heard the term 'interest-only' loan almost a decade after we began investing in property. I remember having difficulty in comprehending the difference between 'interest-only' and 'interest-free', but on reading up on it, I began to realise that an 'interest-only' loan seemed to be the answer to our cash flow constraints. Until that time, all of our properties had been financed with standard principal and interest loans over a short term — a very, very short term, I might add; some for only 10 years. However, in my haste to refinance our loans to interest-only, I missed the fact that this new lender charged a myriad of other fees. It was almost a case of out of the frying pan and into the fire.

I learnt a lot in those early years. Now, after much experience, I find I spend more time considering how to organise the finance and deciding which loan is best than looking for the next property. I'll make a lot of phone calls, look up the internet and play around with our assets and liabilities statement to work out the best way to arrange, and sometimes rearrange the loans.

There's certainly a lot more to borrowing money than just mortgaging property, so it's time to look into the pros and cons of each type of loan. Is interest-only better than principal and interest? What about a credit line? Should there be one loan or two? From one lender or more? Is a second mortgage needed? I'll also explain some loan terminology. What is the difference between interest-only and interest-free; deposit bond and deposit; and interest in arrears and advance. Then we'll look at some of the more interesting and thought provoking ways of arranging loans.

Loan types

Loan types vary as a rule, depending on the security or the way in which the interest is paid. Some common types of loans include:

Principal and interest loan

Familiar to most people is the traditional principal and interest or P&I loan, where the principal represents the amount of money borrowed. The regular (usually monthly) repayment consists of two components. One part is the interest on the loan and the second is a contribution towards the principal, so that in time the loan is completely repaid. For example, a P&I loan of $166,000 over 25 years at an interest rate of 8.5% would require monthly payments of $1,337 totalling $16,040 per year for the term of the loan. The two components at years 1, 5 and 25 are shown in the table below.

$166,000 P&I loan at 8.5% over 25 years

	1yr	5yrs	25yrs
Principal component	$2,007	$2,816	$15,325
Interest component	$14,033	$13,224	$715
Principal and interest payment	$16,040	$16,040	$16,040

Notice how the proportion of principal to interest changes over time. Interest is only charged on the amount outstanding so, whilst the total loan payment is constant, the proportion going towards the interest reduces over time and the principal component increases.

P&I loans are great for owner occupiers with a home loan, but they have several disadvantages for property investors:

- The part of the repayment towards the principal is not tax deductible.

- The reducing principal lowers the interest and therefore the tax benefits.

- The larger repayment may lessen your ability to fund further properties.

These reasons make me prefer an interest-only loan, as described in the next section; however most lending institutions seem to stick with old fashioned policies and like to see loans being reduced over time, rather than standing still. That's why P&I loans are more prevalent and why you'll probably have a hard time finding interest-only. P&I loans are OK if the term of the loan is 25 years or more, particularly if the interest rate can be fixed for at least the first five years. As you can see from the P&I table, the principal component is not large enough to have an impact on your DSR during the first five years or so. Also on the upside, a P&I loan can offer peace of mind to those who can't quite come to grips with an interest-only loan. We'll examine this next.

Chapter 15: Which Loan Is Best? 159

Interest-only loan

Interest-only loans mean that you only need to pay the interest on the loan, with no principal contribution. Referring to our example property on page 127, for a $166,000 loan at 8.5% on an interest-only basis, the payments would be $14,110 per year. (Note that the interest in the first year of a P&I loan is only $14,033 as the principal would have been gradually reduced over the year.) Usually the loan contract states that you must repay the loan in full at maturity, which is a period from 1 to 10 years, but it's normal for lenders to refinance the loan at whatever rate is appropriate at the time.

Don't be confused between interest-only and interest-free. Interest-free usually refers to those gimmicky loans offered by retailers selling goods at top prices, on terms where no interest is payable — at least for the first two or so years. You can be sure that the interest you don't pay is either built into the price at the start or in the higher interest rate that kicks in two years later, or in the penalties for not paying on time.

Interest-only loans maximise your cash flow and allow you to service the loans on many more properties. Although the amount borrowed with an interest-only loan remains constant, it will be declining in terms of the dollar value. You can build net worth much faster with capital growth on several properties bought with interest-only, than by building up equity in just one and paying principal and interest.

Consider if you'd bought a house in Brisbane 25 years ago for $23,500, like we did then, and you borrowed the entire amount as an interest-only loan — like we didn't, but should have. You always own the property despite having a 'never-ending' loan. Today, with this interest-only loan, you would still owe that same $23,500, but the property would probably be worth around $140,000, like ours is now. The loan is in 'yesterday's' dollars, but the property increases in value in 'today's' dollars. The equity build up and increased rent should be your ultimate aim. So if you sold on retirement, the loan would simply be repaid from the proceeds of the sale; or alternatively, the rent should have overtaken the interest payments and the property should produce a positive cash flow.

Suppose the interest on the initial loan of $23,500 was 10% or $2,350 per year and the initial rent was $1,350 per year. Obviously the interest payments exceed the rent and you would need to fund the shortfall. But consider the situation today. Even if the interest rate was still 10%, with identical interest payments of $2,350, the rent could well be $9,000 per year, providing a cash surplus sufficient to fund many more properties over that 25 years. If all your money had gone into repaying the initial loan of $23,500 as a P&I loan, the extra payments would have reduced your cash flow and severely curtailed your opportunity to buy more properties.

160 *More Wealth from Residential Property*

Credit line

I'm happy to say at the start: I think credit lines are the best thing since deregulation — and sliced bread. They go by a variety of names such as mortgage power, smarter mortgage, mortgage manager and equity access loans, to name a few. I prefer to think of them as yoyo loans because of the way they work. The bank takes your property as security and gives you a credit facility to a predetermined upper limit. You can redraw and repay at will, but you only pay interest on the outstanding balance.

As an example, consider an owner-occupied property worth $180,000 with an existing home loan of $30,000. In conjunction with the home loan, it would be possible to set up a credit line for investment with a limit of $114,000, creating an overall LVR of 80% calculated as follows:

$$\textbf{LVR} = \frac{\$30,000 + \$114,000}{\$180,000} = \frac{\$144,000}{\$180,000} = 80\%$$

The original home loan of $30,000 could also be set up as a credit line if desired, replacing the traditional P&I loan. Keeping the two credit line accounts separate is absolutely imperative so that the tax deductible and non-tax deductible interest don't get tangled.

How does this $114,000 credit line work? Suppose monthly income of $5,000 is placed in the account, reducing it to $109,000. At the end of the month, $2,000 might be redrawn to pay out your credit card which you used for expenses, utilising the interest-free period. This increases the loan to $111,000; however, the interest will be less for that month. And so on. While this saves some interest (about $30), the *real* benefit comes from leaving $3,000 in the account permanently, rather than $5,000 temporarily.

Once the loan has been substantially lowered, it can be drawn on over and over again to the limit of $114,000. You might use it as a deposit on another property with the intention of borrowing the rest from a different lender, or for council rates or even renovations. It could also be used to pick up bargain-priced investment properties with a cash contract, giving you time to refinance to a less flexible, less expensive, fixed-interest loan at your leisure. In calculating DSRs for future loans, however, the full credit limit, not the amount actually drawn, is used.

For property investors, credit lines are a must and I strongly recommend you include them in your strategy as a ready source of cash. It's cheaper than having money sitting in dead bank accounts. But they shouldn't be used as the sole type of investment loan, as their interest rates are variable and you could be left vulnerable to rising rates. You should also take care not to use them to buy consumer items, or you will find that your pool, car, boat or Christmas presents bought 'on the house' will quickly erode your net worth and undermine your wealth building plans.

Chapter 15: Which Loan Is Best? 161

Assumable loan

An assumable loan is one where the mortgage is 'tied' to the property. In other words you can sell the property together with a mortgage and it usually only requires a simple name change on the mortgage document. If the mortgage has a low fixed-interest rate with a long term remaining, the property may be highly attractive to potential purchasers. In the United States, many property sales involve assumable mortgages, in contrast to Australia where they are rare. As a result, many American books on the subject of property investment are about creatively manipulating finance, not price! So if you read books written for America, learn from their ideas, but remember that assumable loans are not the norm here.

Wrap loan

Until recently wraps, or wrap-around mortgages, were unheard of in Australia, but some innovative investors have attempted to initiate them here. Wraps involve selling a property to a home buyer with either a 'rent now, buy later' or 'instalment' contract. Under the 'rent now, buy later' scheme, the vendor retains ownership of the property and the original loan, and the would-be home buyer is contracted to buy the property after renting it for a set time. With an 'instalment contract' the property is sold with vendor financing in place and the home buyer takes immediate possession. Wraps are supposed to be a win-win situation that enables a person to buy a home with finance they may not otherwise be able to get. It also gives the investor the opportunity to profit from the lending arrangement and the sale of the property. This sounds good in principle but there are risks for investors in conforming to the credit code act and for purchasers if something happens midway through the deal.

Second mortgage

The possibility of having a second mortgage often conjures ideas of being on the brink of insolvency. This is not necessarily the case. Second mortgages can be less expensive than paying mortgage insurance and nowadays, the interest rate is often the same as a first mortgage. You can even take it as a credit line.

Personal loan

This is just a short-term P&I loan, often with a high interest rate, in which property is not used as a security. Instead, the lender relies solely on your personal credibility to advance the loan. Personal loans are usually used by people wanting to buy consumer items when they don't have the cash. However, I do know of a young engineer who desperately wanted to buy his own home as soon as he graduated. He got a personal loan for the deposit, his high income enabling him to repay it very quickly. Unless personal loans are used in special circumstances like this, steer well clear.

162   *More Wealth from Residential Property*

Loan terminology

To be a successful property investor, you don't need to learn all the jargon associated with finance. But you will find a few names helpful to know to avoid confusion and these are listed below.

Deposits

Cash deposits are not necessary if other property can be used as security for the loan. Saving for a deposit may be the time-honoured method of buying your first home but it is not necessarily the best way to acquire investment property. As saving involves accumulating cash in a bank account, for every dollar you earn in interest you give up to half back in tax. So for two steps forward, you go one step back. It can take a long time to save a deposit at this rate and by the time you have enough money, property values may have increased.

No-deposit borrowing

When other properties are available as security for a loan it may be possible to borrow the entire purchase price, the purchasing and borrowing costs and some extra cash as a reserve. You can even borrow enough for the deposit on the next property, or to prepay the interest upfront; or for renovations, rates or management fees. Providing you have the security and serviceability for the loan, you can usually borrow any amount you require. Lenders don't really care what you do with the money — so the emphasis is on your ability to repay, rather than on what you buy. One point to note. While the lender mightn't care two hoots about what you do with the money, if you wish to claim the interest as a tax deduction, the Tax Office does; the onus is on you to justify the purpose of the loan.

Deposit bonds

Quite often, when you buy a property off the plan, the developer will want a significant deposit paid on signing the contract, even though the settlement date may be a year away. While it is possible to provide a cash deposit which can then be invested for that time (who gets the interest can be negotiable), it may be better to use a deposit bond, sometimes called a deposit guarantee. This is a certificate given to the developer in lieu of cash to guarantee the money will be handed over on request. There are two ways of securing a deposit bond. Firstly, you can obtain one from a lender who'll want security over some property. Or secondly, you can buy one from an insurance company for a nominated amount. Either way, on settlement, you will be required to pay the full purchase price including the deposit. If you default, the vendor can claim the amount of the deposit from your lender, who is holding your property as security and can sell it if required, or from the insurance company who has taken the risk.

Chapter 15: Which Loan Is Best? 163

Purpose of the loan

For tax purposes, it is not the asset *mortgaged* that is relevant, but the *purpose* of the loan. It is possible for the interest on a loan against your principal place of residence to be tax deductible. Normally, home loans are not tax deductible. However, if the funds are invested in a rental property, the interest should be tax deductible. As distinct from this, you can not use money borrowed against a rental property to buy a new kitchen for your home, and still expect the interest to be tax deductible.

This distinction is very important when people who own their own home, decide to go upmarket to their dream home. Many will decide to keep their existing home for investment (because they have seen just how good an investment it has been), and borrow against it to build their new home. They then have an investment property with a mortgage — but the loan is not tax deductible, because the *purpose* of the loan was to build their new home and not to buy the rental property.

One solution might be to sell the first home, put the proceeds towards the new one, then remortgage it to borrow to buy a rental property. With the purpose of the loan now being for investment, the interest on the loan would be tax deductible. However, it may not be necessary to sell to an outsider. Depending on ownership, it might be possible to sell from one partner to the other, or vice versa, at least providing a partial answer to the problem.

With more property purchases in mind, a couple might consider buying their own home in the name of the lower income earner only. Then, in future, when they wish to move upmarket, the property could be sold to the highest income earner who then borrows the money to buy it as a negatively geared rental property. The proceeds from the sale could then be used to buy the new home.

Because change of ownership means paying stamp duty and legals, the tax benefits may not always outweigh the costs, so do the sums carefully to decide on the overall benefits, not just the tax advantages. And before you attempt any 'in-house' family transactions it's a good idea to check with your accountant.

Name on the mortgage

Many lenders require both partners' names on a mortgage document, even though the title to the property is in one name only. However, this does not present a problem with the ATO, as they are more concerned with the name on the title. In the above scenario, the ATO would assume that the money has been lent to both partners, one of whom then lends it at the same interest rate to the partner who is the purchaser, so the overall tax position of the non-owning partner is neutral.

164 *More Wealth from Residential Property*

Name on the title

Properties with a negative cash flow offer more tax benefits if bought in the name of the highest income earner than if bought in joint names. Conversely, property with a positive cash flow should be bought in the name of the lowest income earner, to minimise the tax liability. You should check with your accountant to ascertain if the property should be in joint names, and if so, whether as Tenants in Common or Joint Tenants. As Tenants in Common, it is easier to apportion unequal percentages in ownership and it may be possible to nominate the equity/debt sharing arrangements. For example, one owner might pay cash, receiving income and paying tax, while the other(s) could borrow and receive tax benefits.

Properties bought in a company name warrant special mention. The main reasons for buying properties in a company name are associated with preservation legalities, not financial benefits. If you want to protect your assets from either warring children or libellous creditors, you could set up a limited liability company — although far more financial advantages are available to individuals than companies.

Firstly, the initial set up and yearly compliance costs of a company can be expensive. Also, the company tax rate of 30% is much less than the top personal rate of 47%, so more tax is saved by an individual through negative gearing; and company losses can only be offset if there is other income, otherwise they are simply carried forward. If the property is cash positive, the 30% company rate applies from the first dollar earned with no tax-free threshold and no concessional marginal rates. Furthermore, if a property is sold, the 50% discount for Capital Gains Tax is not available.

Properties bought by family trusts do provide tax advantages if there is income to be distributed to the members. However, with both major political parties vowing to treat trusts the same way as companies, you would want to have some special reasons for buying properties in the name of a trust. In general, trusts are useful only when you are retired and wish to be tax-effective in using the profits.

Unencumbered property

An unencumbered property is one that it is not mortgaged. For tax purposes, it may have a loan (mortgaged to another property), but it is free to be used as security for further property acquisition. As an example, an investment property purchased by mortgaging *only* your home would be unencumbered. Your home *would* be encumbered (mortgaged); but the reason for the loan was to buy the rental property so therefore the interest on it would be tax-deductible. Try to keep at least one of your properties unencumbered to maintain some flexibility, though this may be difficult in the early stages of building a property portfolio.

Chapter 15: Which Loan Is Best? 165

Loan to Value Ratio (LVR)

As explained earlier, the Loan to Value Ratio, or LVR, is the ratio of the total loans given to a borrower to the total value of security held by the lender. The normal method of calculating the LVR is as follows:

LVR (Loan to value ratio) = $\dfrac{\text{Total loans} \times 100\%}{\text{Total value}}$

Most lenders will go to LVRs of 80% for residential property without incurring mortgage insurance (see page 173). In Bill and Mary's situation, in borrowing $498,000 to buy three rental properties worth $480,000 in total, plus $18,000 in costs, their LVR by mortgaging *just* these three properties would have been 104% ($498,000/$480,000). However, by mortgaging their $180,000 home *as well*, their overall LVR was reduced to 75% ($498,000/$660,000), well within the acceptable limit.

It's a good idea to get maximum mileage from LVRs by mortgaging the least amount of property for the maximum amount of loan. That is, don't give the financial institution any more security than it needs. This allows you to keep future investment options open by having as many unencumbered properties as possible.

A word of warning, though, on what to expect from valuations! We saw on page 156 that properties are generally valued on a 'needs' basis. Sometimes lenders use 'in-house' valuers who can be instructed to value at 80% of *market* value. In such cases, even though the lender may say they go to LVRs of 80%, 80% of 80% is an LVR of just 64%. So valuations for the purpose of mortgage finance may not come up to expectations, mostly because lenders and valuers are understandably conservative and partly because we all tend to overvalue our own properties. This can mean getting a much smaller loan than anticipated, having to pay mortgage insurance, or needing to use more property as security.

Debt Service Ratio (DSR)

On page 152, we defined Debt Service Ratio, or DSR, as one of many names given to a formula that determines your ability to service a loan. It is worked out on the basis of various combinations of income, rents and loan payments. This book uses the following DSR formula:

DSR (Debt service ratio) = $\dfrac{\text{Loan payments} \times 100\%}{\text{Eligible income}}$

= $\dfrac{\text{Loan payments} \times 100\%}{30\% \text{ income} + 80\% \text{ rent}}$

It pays to prepare your own budget rather than relying solely on the DSR that a lending institution is using, since it can be calculated in so many different ways that your loan application might be approved by some lenders but disallowed by others.

166   *More Wealth from Residential Property*

Penalty costs

If you repay a fixed-rate, fixed-term loan before the due date, you could be charged a penalty, or as the lender calls it, a fee for the economic cost. There are many ways of calculating this fee. It can be a set amount, or is more likely to be dependent on market interest rates at the time. According to one major lending institution's terms and conditions:

The economic cost is the Bank's reasonable estimate of its loss, if any, from the early termination of the loan or a prepayment. It is calculated by the Bank as the difference between the Bank's cost of funds at the start of the relevant fixed interest rate period and its cost of funds at the date of termination or prepayment, over the remainder of the period. This is then discounted back to the net present value at the rate equivalent to the Bank's cost of funds at that date.

Let me simplify this for you. Suppose you fixed the interest rate on a $100,000 loan at 15% for three years and after one year, rates drop to 8% and you decide to refinance to take advantage of the lower rate. The economic cost to the bank, or the penalty cost to you, depending on which way you look at it, would be very approximately 7% (15% less 8%) of $100,000 for two years, or $14,000.

While I believe that at least two thirds of all loans should have fixed interest rates, I think that in some circumstances it may be worthwhile paying the penalty to refinance. If your DSR is preventing you from borrowing to buy more properties, for example, paying the penalty and changing to a lower interest rate might lower your DSR enough to enable you to borrow more. I see a penalty as the insurance you pay to protect against interest rate rises, and since the costs are deductible, think of it as paying the extra interest in advance.

Deed of variation of loan

When property values rise, you could consider a 'deed of variation of loan'. This involves having the properties revalued so that you can then borrow against the increased equity to buy more property on the same mortgage. You may be up for valuation and solicitors' fees, but you should only have to pay stamp duty on the amount of loan variation.

Cash contracts

With a cash contract, a property is bought with no 'subject to finance' clause. There may be a loan involved, but it has been 'teed up' before, using other property or the prospective property as security to have finance pre-approved. Vendors find cash contracts attractive and this could help you gain a price advantage of many thousands of dollars. I'd advise against signing a contract 'subject to finance' if you think it's a way out of the sale, as finance is relatively easy to obtain these days.

Chapter 15: Which Loan Is Best? 167

Loan arrangement

Here are some ways that Bill and Mary might arrange their loans when they purchase three $160,000 properties while still having a $30,000 loan on their $180,000 home. The lending institutions being considered are called X, Y and Z and we'll call the investment properties 1, 2 and 3. Looking at the options for borrowing the $498,000, the DSR would not change in any situation but their LVR would need to be calculated each time. Here are some possibilities.

Option 1. One lending institution, two loans

- Retain the $30,000 home loan with X. Refinance to a credit line with minimum repayments to lower the DSR.
- Take fixed-rate interest-only loan with same lender X for $498,000.

Result: One credit line and one fixed-rate interest-only loan with X.

Option 2. One lending institution, three loans

- Retain the $30,000 home loan with X. Refinance to credit line with minimum repayments to lower DSR.
- Take second credit line with X for $114,000 bringing total LVR on own home to 80% calculated as ($30,000+$114,000)/$180,000.
- Take fixed-rate interest-only loan with same lender X for $384,000. The LVR with X for the fixed-rate interest-only loan will be 80% calculated as $384,000/$480,000.

Result: Two credit lines and one fixed-rate interest-only loan with X.

Option 3. Two lending institutions, three loans

- Retain the $30,000 home loan with X. Refinance to credit line with minimum repayments to lower DSR.
- Take second credit line with X for $114,000 bringing total LVR on own home to 80% calculated as ($30,000+$114,000)/$180,000.
- Use money from second credit line as a deposit for borrowing $384,000 for the 3 investment properties with Y at a fixed-rate, interest-only. The LVR with Y will be 80% calculated as $384,000/$480,000.

Result: Two credit lines with X and one fixed-rate loan with Y.

Option 4. Three lending institutions, three loans

- Retain the $30,000 home loan with X. Refinance to credit line with minimum repayments to lower DSR.
- Take second credit line with X for $114,000 giving LVR of 80%.
- Use $38,000 from second credit line with X as deposit for 1 and borrow a fixed-rate interest-only loan for the remaining $128,000 with Y.
- Use $76,000 from second credit line with X as deposit for 2 and 3 and borrow $256,000 as a fixed-rate interest-only loan from Z.

Result: One credit line with X; one fixed-rate interest-only loan with Y: one fixed-rate interest-only loan with Z.

168 *More Wealth from Residential Property*

As you can see, there are many ways to solve this problem and these few samples of the many that are possible should give you plenty of food for thought as to how you can creatively arrange your own loans. I would probably lean towards Option 2 or 3 over Option 1 or 4 because I believe it's a good idea to have about two-thirds of loans as fixed-rate interest-only, with the rest as a variable-rate credit line, and three lenders is a bit messy. This would give you the safety of having the major portion of your loans fixed, while still giving you the ability to pay down a loan in the form of a credit line if you want to. Whether or not you use one, two or more lenders would depend on the terms available to you at the time.

One further point needs clarifying. I often state that my preference is for having two thirds of the loan at a fixed-rate interest-only, but there is very little difference between this and a fixed-rate P&I loan over a term of 25 years or more, at least for the first five years. So don't be dismayed by my constant use of this phrase, particularly when there is a predominance of P&I loans in the market place, with lending institutions still stuck in 'must-pay-out-the-loan' mode. Also, you will probably find that most lenders will fix the interest rate for the P&I loan for only a nominated number of years, such as five, insisting that it revert to variable there after. However, five years is a long time in a lender's life and I would think you'd be able to renegotiate with them after that time.

Don't leave it to a lender to decide how to arrange your loans. They'll choose the option that is easiest for them but not necessarily best for you and furthermore, they will take as much security as they can possibly get. It's common to find people with loans of around $15,000 from a lender holding properties worth several hundred thousand dollars as security!

Creative use of mortgages can greatly improve the returns from your property investment portfolio and allow you to be less restricted in your wealth building plans. It's most important to realise that you don't need large amounts of cash upfront to invest in property and that there's always more than one way to finance or refinance property. The manner in which your assets are used as security is just as important as where you borrow money and this becomes more and more important after you've purchased a few properties.

If you have not set up your finance appropriately early on, it may prove costly to rearrange later because of the refinance charges that could amount to several thousands of dollars. Whenever I am about to purchase property, I should remind you that I may spend several weeks sorting through the options available to me to arrange the loans, and several days looking for the property. Be flexible, think laterally. As my friend Robyn says:

Simple strategies you may never have dreamed of, for situations you may never have imagined.

16
The Costs of Borrowing

We all like a bargain, but be very careful when shopping for money. Simple comparisons between interest rates offered by the various lenders can not only be confusing, but downright misleading.

A few years ago, when interest rates for property were around 16.5%, a friend rang and asked what I thought about taking a loan at an interest rate of 12.5%. It sounded too good to be true, he said. My instant reaction was that there is no such thing as a free lunch and so I gave my friend a list of questions to ask relating to other less obvious borrowing costs.

Sure enough, in the midst of a whole host of 'other charges', was an establishment fee of 3%, mortgagee's solicitors' charges of $2,500, and compulsory mortgage insurance, all of which suddenly made the loan much less attractive. The effective rate of interest over 3 years was 17%! This was a fairly exceptional case, but it proves the point that there is more to shopping for money than simply comparing interest rates.

Many investors go to great lengths to ensure they purchase properties at bargain basement prices. They may spend many months agonising and haggling over prices, and travel hundreds of kilometres looking at different properties. Yet when it comes to financing the property, they spend a few hours deciding where and how to borrow the money. The right finance can far surpass the apparent gains of buying property at bargain prices.

However, don't do a 'ring around' of all the lending institutions and simply ask for the current interest rate — this is quite meaningless. I'm sure you wouldn't dream of ringing up your local electrical shop to ask for the price of just any TV. To get a comparison between shops, you'd need to find out about the size, style, warranty and all other relevant aspects.

Buying, or borrowing, money is the same. You will need information about both the interest rate and other borrowing charges before the real cost of a loan becomes clear. There have been some moves in the industry to enforce the disclosure of the effective rate of interest; however, this has not been universally accepted so you still must do your own homework. The following points should help.

170 *More Wealth from Residential Property*

How is the interest charged?

Interest is the 'rent' you pay on borrowed money. But the ways of calculating interest can be so different that you might be comparing apples and oranges. Here are some of the factors you need to be familiar with.

Fixed or variable

Interest rates can be fixed for as little as 90 days to as long as 10 years or more. Whether you take a loan with a variable or a fixed interest rate depends on your perception of the money market at the time, something on which even economists can not agree, and your financial muscle — can your budget withstand an upward movement in interest rates? I strongly recommend fixed interest rates for at least two thirds of all loans. Cash flow budgets are important to property investors and fixed rates allow for better budgeting and peace of mind. Some of the fixed rates I have had have been as high as 16.5%, while others were as low as 6.5%. If interest rates go up, I'm protected. If they go down, I still manage to smile.

Usually, three to five years is a desirable term to fix the interest, but if you come across a particularly attractive rate, it may be worthwhile fixing the rate for a longer term. As you might expect, fixed interest rates are more stable than either variable rates or short-term bank bills. The figures over the last 20 years illustrate this well.

Property investment loan rates (1980 – 2000)

Fixed 3-year rates	7 – 17%
Variable rates	6 – 19%
90-day bank bills	5 – 21%

Capitalised interest

Capitalising the interest simply means adding the interest bill to the principal. So if you had a loan for $166,000 at 8.5% or $14,110, you would not need to pay the interest from your cash flow; but after one year the loan would be $180,110, and so on. Although this technique has been used by businesses for years, under Tax Ruling TR 98/22 the ATO has ruled that capitalised interest will not be allowed as a tax deduction in the case of linked or split loans that have been structured to link payments between private and investment loans. Linked loans involve capitalising the interest on an investment loan, freeing up an investor's cash flow so they can pay off a private loan, usually their own home loan. While you can still set up linked loans and capitalise the interest on the investment loan, you now don't get the tax benefits beyond a 'fair and reasonable apportionment' — ie you can no longer claim the capitalised interest as a tax deduction. If all this sounds very confusing, it is — so check with your accountant first.

Chapter 16: The Costs of Borrowing 171

Arrears or advance

Interest paid in advance is dearer than in arrears. The difference is the interest on the interest for the time you have the use of the money, before the interest is due. So the difference between 8% monthly in arrears and monthly advance is 0.08 x 0.08 x (1/12), or around 0.05%, making 8% in arrears the equivalent to about 7.95% in advance.

Yearly in advance

Paying the interest in advance can be an extremely useful strategy for reducing a tax liability that you suddenly become aware of near the end of a financial year. For instance, you can pay a whole year's interest in advance in May, and claim that expense in your June tax return, regardless of how little rent you have earned. This has the effect of deferring tax for a full year. You could even receive a tax refund within one month of purchasing a property if you bought it in May and settled in June.

However, for the 'interest paid in advance' to qualify as a legitimate tax deduction, the ATO deems that you must receive a commercial advantage other than just a tax saving. This can be achieved by getting a reduced rate of interest on the loan. In the above example, interest at 8% monthly in arrears would be the equivalent of 7.36% (8% less 0.08 x 0.08) yearly in advance, so you would need to acquire a loan at a marginally better rate than this.

If you're considering paying the interest in advance, be wary of bank bills. Although the money, including the interest, is 'loaned' in advance, the interest is paid when the loan is due and can not be claimed in advance.

Frequency of interest calculations

With investment loans, unlike your first-home loan, there is little or no incentive to make additional payments. However, if you have a P&I loan and wish to pay extra, be aware that daily calculations are better than monthly. If you make a lump sum repayment at the start of the month on a loan where the interest is calculated monthly, you would effectively be giving the bank the loan of your money for a full month, free of interest.

Frequency of payments

If you have an interest-only loan, some lending institutions may be prepared to be flexible on the frequency of interest payments (ie monthly, quarterly or yearly). Consider the reverse situation: would you prefer to receive interest monthly, and get interest on your interest, or yearly? So too with borrowing money, and 8% interest paid quarterly in arrears is cheaper than 8% paid yearly in advance. A rule of thumb is that the sooner you make repayments on a loan, the lower the interest rate should be to account for the time the lender is holding your money.

172   *More Wealth from Residential Property*

What are the borrowing costs?

It costs money to set up a loan and these expenses are usually referred to as borrowing or loan costs. Loans with very high interest rates and no borrowing costs might be suitable for the short term (which you probably don't want), but a low interest rate loan with higher borrowing costs might be more attractive for long-term investors (hopefully, that's you). The following list should help you sort out the borrowing costs.

Establishment fees

This refers to the initial upfront fee and it can be charged at a flat rate or as a percentage of the loan. The amount varies from nil to 4% or more of the loan and sometimes other costs such as solicitor's fees and valuation fees are included. It is important that you know all the components so that you can make comparisons between loans.

Application fees

Most of the time, the establishment fee and application fee are one and the same. But some lenders may charge a non-refundable application fee of a few hundred dollars when you first apply for a loan, and a second fee called the establishment fee when you go ahead. Lending institutions are in the business of 'selling' money so these fees are really a commission you pay to someone for arranging the loan.

Valuation fees

Some institutions charge nothing for valuations, but the standard fee is approximately $1.50 per $1,000. This can vary depending on location, number of properties and whether or not it's a revaluation.

Mortgagee's solicitor's fees

Solicitors acting for the lender (the mortgagee's solicitors) charge fees for preparing the mortgage documentation. They may be 'in house' or from an external firm and their fees vary from nil to a few thousand dollars. If the lender uses an external solicitor, those fees will be unavoidable. For although you may decide not to use a solicitor for your conveyancing, you will not be allowed to prepare the mortgage documentation yourself. My experience has been that lenders who use external solicitors and charge you accordingly, generally have lower interest rates.

Search fees

The mortgagee's solicitor usually conducts searches to ensure that your property is free of 'liabilities', such as a resumption order on a part of the land for an impending main road. The lender doesn't want to be holding a property as security if it is likely to be devalued for some reason later. Search fees are charged by various government departments, and these vary.

Chapter 16: The Costs of Borrowing   173

Administration charges

There may be a small ($1–$10) monthly fee and that is quite normal. The ones to watch out for are the yearly charges of $1,000 plus. These charges may add virtually another 1% to the interest rate.

Mortgage insurance

You should not confuse mortgage insurance with 'mortgage repayment insurance' which covers your loan payments if you are ill or lose your job. Unlike this, mortgage insurance purely protects the lender. If you fail to meet your loan obligations, the mortgagee can sell your property and claim any shortfall between the loan and selling price from the mortgage insurer. Lenders often approve a loan 'subject to approval by mortgage insurer' and it can happen that while one will approve, the other will not. Most prefer LVRs of 80% or less and loans over this can incur mortgage insurance of up to 2%.

Life insurance

Life insurance may be compulsory with some loans, and in this case it should be tax deductible. It's a good idea to have it anyway, but be sure you are not coerced into taking additional coverage if it is not needed.

Brokerage fees

A decade ago, the standard brokerage fee was around 1% of the loan, but as I've explained, the new breed of mortgage broker can source finance for you without the large upfront charges and you could well pay less than if you went to the same source yourself. While some brokers still charge extreme fees, most are paid a small commission plus a trailer on the interest from the lender. Brokers may not be independent and may have access to only a limited range of lenders, but, if you are foot weary and mind boggled from looking for the loan, a broker might be an answer.

Penalty costs

With flexible loans, there may be no penalty for early repayment. In other cases, usually where the interest rate is fixed, the penalty may be very high. I don't consider penalties a huge barrier, as they are part and parcel of less flexible, lower-interest loans. (See page 166)

Mortgage transfer

In some cases, a mortgage may be transferred to another property. If you have properties that have substantially increased in value, rearranging a mortgage might unencumber a property. For example, suppose you have a property worth $200,000, carrying a loan of $160,000. If this property increases over time to $500,000, it may be advantageous to transfer the mortgage to a less valuable property. Doing this could free up more equity and give you the flexibility to do other things with your property.

174 *More Wealth from Residential Property*

Mortgage release fees

Each state government charges a mortgage release fee and so may your lender. The fee may be just the cost of releasing the registered mortgage or, if you are trying to release one property from a multi-property mortgage, it may include such costs as the mortgagee's solicitor's fees, rearrangement fees, increased mortgage insurance, and revaluation fees of other properties.

Rollover fees

When you take out a fixed-rate, interest-only loan for a set period, such as three years, rolling over for a further period usually costs money. This fee can be almost nothing, or quite substantial, depending on whether solicitors are involved. It is a real cost and should be taken into account at the beginning when you are seeking the best loan. The size of this fee may also determine whether you rollover your loan with the same lender, or seek another source of finance. Rollover fees do not apply to P&I loans as these loans are continuous for the duration of the term until repaid.

Government charges

The states levy various charges on borrowing. A reasonable guide is:

- Stamp duty on mortgage: about 0.4% of the loan
- Registration of mortgage: about $100
- Stamp duty on mortgage insurance: 5% of premium
- Stamp duty on mortgage release: about $1
- Mortgage release: about $100
- Government debits tax (on redraw facilities) of about .05%

Typical loan costs

If you bought a property for $160,000, with purchase costs of $4,500 and borrowing costs of $1,500, your total loan would be $166,000 if you borrowed the lot. A typical set of borrowing costs for a loan of this size where the LVR is below 80% with no mortgage insurance could be:

Borrowing costs	
Establishment fee (0.25% of loan)	415
Stamp duty on mortgage (0.4%)	664
Mortgage insurance	0
Mortgagee's solicitor's fees	0
Valuation fees	150
Registration of mortgage	100
Search fees	100
Other costs	71
TOTAL	**$1,500**

Part VII

Taxing the Project

17
Typical Tax Deductions

Several years ago at the end of a seminar, a man confessed to me that for the past three years he had not declared the $100 a week he was getting from his rental property for fear of paying tax on his only retirement nest egg. He had a loan of $30,000 on the property with interest at $4,200 per year, and rates, etc, of $800 taking his total expenses to $5,000. So he figured that with an annual rental income of $5,200, he was up for tax of $80 on his profit of $200, taxed at his marginal rate of 40%.

But when *all* the tax deductions were considered, we discovered that he was *owed* a tax refund. He had neglected to take into account the deductions for borrowing costs, depreciation and travel, which were quite substantial as he collected the rent himself each week via a 50 kilometre round trip. All in all, he was entitled to a tax refund of $700 in that one year alone. His fear and lack of understanding of the tax laws had probably cost him a few thousand dollars over the years! So while keeping in mind that tax benefits are not the sole reason for investing in property, you would be crazy not to claim your full entitlements.

The substantiation rules put the onus on you to be able to support your claims by documentation. It also might be a good idea to check with your accountant to satisfy yourself that your investments are structured tax effectively. Accountants may not be experts in showing you how to build wealth through residential property, but they should be able to expertly answer all your questions and prepare your tax returns. But don't simply supply a shoe-box full of receipts and expect the best.

If you want more information about investment properties and tax, the Australian Tax Office (ATO) has published several booklets on the subject. The three you will find most useful are called *Rental Properties*, *Guide to Capital Gains Tax* and *Guide to Depreciation*. They are available at no cost by downloading from the website *(www.ato.gov.au)* or you can have them posted to you by phoning 1300 720 092. In this section, I will summarise and offer a few useful tips on the tax deductions available for rental properties. They fall into two categories: capital costs and revenue costs.

178   *More Wealth from Residential Property*

Capital costs

Capital costs include those for buying and selling, and improvement. I discuss the buying and selling costs in Chapter 19, so here we'll put our finger on what constitutes an improvement. A thin grey line divides what you would like to call a repair, which makes it tax deductible now, from a capital improvement, which is taken into account in the Capital Gains Tax payable if you sell. Repairs are defined as the maintenance that restores the property to its condition at the time you bought it — not to its original condition when built. Capital improvements make the property *better* than when you bought it.

One of the most often asked questions is, 'If I buy a rental property, how long do I have to wait before I can claim the painting as a repair?' Although various well-meaning people provide answers ranging from one to three years, the truth is that the taxation office sets no fixed time for claiming such repairs. For example, if you bought a rental property that needed painting immediately and you held off for one year to paint it, the taxation office could well disallow such a claim on the grounds that the property needed painting at the time of purchase.

However if you bought a property in immaculate condition, and after one day the tenant dismantled a motorcycle in the living room (highly unlikely) necessitating repainting immediately, then the cost of repainting should be tax deductible. This is a case of restoring the property to the condition in which it was bought, even though the repairs were carried out shortly after purchase.

If you buy a property that badly needs painting, don't hold off, hoping that the costs will be tax deductible at a later date. It is far better to paint it straight away, even though the painting in this situation will be classed as an improvement. Not only does it increase the value of the property, but it is also makes the property easier to let, and probably at a higher rent.

There is also a subtlety in doing 'repairs'. For example, if you re-roof an old, rusted iron-roofed house with iron it would probably be considered a repair. But if you were to use tiles, it could be classed as an improvement.

Although you can not claim the cost of improvements immediately, you can borrow the money for them and claim the interest. Also, if you have made substantial improvements to your property since 16 September, 1987, they should qualify for the capital allowance of 2.5%. This means that at least some of the improvement costs are tax deductible. If, for example, you erected a carport costing $10,000 for your rental property, you would be able to claim $250 each year for 40 years. Capital costs are added to the cost base in calculating the Capital Gains Tax. (See page 204)

Chapter 17: Typical Tax Deductions 179

Revenue costs

Revenue costs are the costs of earning rental income and they may be classified as 'cash' or 'non-cash'. Cash deductions, such as interest and expenses, are deductible at the time the cost is incurred. However, non-cash deductions such as depreciation and borrowing costs are claimed over time without necessarily costing you money in that particular year. Over the page is a typical list of tax deductions including both cash and non-cash.

The claims are based on the rental property Bill and Mary bought for $160,000 with a loan of $166,000 (including $4,500 purchasing costs and $1,500 borrowing costs) at an interest rate of 8.5% or $14,110 per year. Rent is $10,400 per year and property expenses are $2,600 per year. It can be very deceiving to calculate the deductions solely on the basis of cash costs. In the example, these would come to $16,710 ($14,110 + $2,600), yet non-cash costs of borrowing and the depreciation on the building, the furniture and the fittings, would add $5,200 to the claims, taking the total claims to $21,910.

Further tax benefits are possible if your family members are involved in managing and maintaining your properties. The items with an asterisk depict those areas where you might consider making payments to family members who have been responsible for tasks such as cleaning, gardening, accounting, managing the property, secretarial bookkeeping, mowing, or even painting. These costs would appear as a deduction on the investor's tax return and as income on the family member's return. If the family member's income was lower than the investor's, the overall tax liability for the family would be less. The investor, however, must substantiate the time, date and payment for the work with appropriate documentation.

While the list is a comprehensive guide to deductions, it is important to note that all of the items do not apply to every property all of the time. For example, in Bill and Mary's property there are no electricity, phone or PABX costs as you might find in a holiday unit. Also, the deductions may change from year to year. In particular, a quantity surveyor's fees would be a one-off cost in the first year, but maintenance might be much higher a few years down the track.

By now, you're probably wondering where the Goods and Services Tax or GST fits into the picture. The fact is that for residential property, it doesn't. Residential rents do not attract GST and therefore, while most of the expenses have a 10% GST component, there is nothing to offset these GST credits against. So they are simply included in the expenses without appearing separately. For commercial property, however, GST does apply to rents, so any GST paid on expenses can be credited against any GST received.

180 *More Wealth from Residential Property*

Typical Tax Deductions

	Deductions	Cash	Non-Cash	
Accounting fee	20	20	0	*
Advertising	10	10	0	
Bank charges	0	0	0	
Body corporate fees	0	0	0	
Borrowing costs	500	0	500	
Cleaning	20	20	0	*
Council rates	900	900	0	
Depreciation – building	2,000	0	2,000	
Depreciation – furniture	2,700	0	2,700	
Electricity/Gas	0	0	0	
Fire levy	72	72	0	
Gardening and mowing	20	20	0	*
Insurance	130	130	0	
Interest on borrowings	14,110	14,110	0	
In-house video/PABX	0	0	0	
Land tax	0	0	0	
Letting fee	200	200	0	*
Legal expenses	0	0	0	
Lease costs	0	0	0	*
Pest control	0	0	0	*
Property agent's fees	858	858	0	*
Quantity surveyor's fees	200	200	0	
Repairs and maintenance	100	100	0	*
Replacement (linen, etc)	0	0	0	
Secretarial fees	20	20	0	*
Security patrol fees	0	0	0	*
Stationery/Postage	20	20	0	
Telephone	10	10	0	
Travelling allowance	20	20	0	*
Workers' compensation	0	0	0	
Your business deductions	0	0	0	
Total deductions	**$21,910**	**$16,710**	**$5,200**	

* These items could be costs incurred by family members who are involved with the management and maintenance of an investment property. Although no cash leaves the household, the costs need to be declared as an expense by the investor, but as income by the family member.

Checklist of tax deductions

Here is a checklist of many of the deductions you can claim against your income-producing investment property, with some useful tips on what to look out for. Perhaps you can think of more that might relate to your own individual situation.

Accounting fees

If you have several properties, you could well include accounting fees in a general business section of the tax return as discussed on page 192. Although it is wise to use a professional accountant to prepare your tax returns, you should keep good records so that you can provide a detailed list of your rental expenses and depreciation schedules. Go armed with a list of questions about everything relating to your rental properties.

Advertising

This may include newspaper advertisements or fliers to obtain tenants or tradesmen. If you advertise and need to buy newspapers regularly to check on market rent levels, or even property prices, you may be able to claim a percentage of newspaper costs as well.

Bank charges

Most of the bank charges will be taken care of in your loan costs. However, if you use a bankcard or cheque book for payment of property expenses you may claim a percentage of your cheque account/bankcard charges according to the amount of rental property use.

Body corporate fees

These fees usually apply to unit complexes and vary greatly depending on both the value and age of the building and the facilities. They consist of an administrative fund and a sinking fund; the latter is usually set aside specifically for the maintenance of the building. If some of the sinking fund has been used for capital improvements, however, it may not be tax deductible. Your accountant should be able to distinguish between a capital cost and revenue cost within the fund.

Borrowing costs

The borrowing costs can be deducted over five years or the term of the loan, whichever is the lesser period. They include all costs associated with the loan, such as establishment fees, valuation fees, mortgage insurance, search fees, mortgagee's solicitor's fees, registration fees, mortgage stamp duty, broker's fees, etc. If you sell a property, but still have unclaimed borrowing costs, you can claim the remainder in that year. And if the property is refinanced or sold, the fees for releasing the mortgage or paying the penalty are fully deductible in that particular year.

182   *More Wealth from Residential Property*

Cleaning

These are the costs of cleaning carpets, cupboards and curtains, etc. Normally the tenant pays for these cleaning costs as agreed to under the lease, but if the property needs to be cleaned on the tenant's departure and you redeem the costs from the bond, they would not be tax deductible.

Council rates and charges

This means all local council charges such as general rates, water rates, garbage collection, sewerage and, if applicable, registration fees for flats, etc. If rental properties are bought in the middle of a rateable period, which is usually the case, the rates are apportioned between the vendor and the purchaser according to the number of days owned. The portion of rates paid by the purchaser on settlement is then tax deductible.

Depreciation on a building

The depreciation on a building, sometimes called a capital allowance or special building write-off, allows for the fact that a building will depreciate over time. It is not based on the cost to the investor, but on the original cost of construction. Investment properties built between 17 July, 1985 and 16 September, 1987 qualify for a 4% depreciation rate, or if constructed after that date, 2.5%. Capital improvements such as garages, kitchens and extensions, etc, that have been built since that date also qualify for the 2.5% allowance. Below is an example of how the claim for the building depreciation is calculated:

Depreciation on building

Property cost (building + fix & fit + land)	=$160,000
Land value	= $65,000
Fixtures & fittings	= $15,000
Building costs	= $80,000
Depreciation on building (2.5% of $80,000) =	$2,000 ea yr for 40yrs

For a property worth $160,000, the building costs — excluding the fixtures and fittings and land — might be $80,000 at time of construction. The deduction would then be $2,000 each year for 40 years, as allowed under Division 43. However, to justify this claim, the ATO states in Tax Determination TD 94/83 that 'an estimate of the cost of construction must be made by a quantity surveyor or other appropriately qualified person' such as the project organiser, supervising architect or builder.

Since 13 May, 1997, in calculating the Capital Gains Tax (CGT) to be paid if the property is sold, the amount claimed for building depreciation during the holding period must be 'written back' and subtracted from the cost base. This is discussed in Chapter 19 on page 204.

Chapter 17: Typical Tax Deductions   183

Depreciation of fixtures and fittings and furniture

Fixtures and fittings in a building gradually reduce in value over time as they approach the end of their useful lives. Assets that lose value in this way are said to depreciate and in recognition of this fact by the ATO, the cost can be written off over a period of time. The 'cost' of an item includes the original price paid, the architectural fees apportioned at about 7%, the builder's overheads apportioned at about 9%, transportation costs, installation costs, customs duty and relocation costs. For example, after including all associated costs, a hot water system purchased for $500 might well be depreciated from an opening written down value of $950.

Although it is not required by law to have a quantity surveyor prepare a Division 42 depreciation schedule for fixtures and fittings, I think it's a worthwhile idea. There are many items such as kitchen cupboards, mirrors and toilet roll holders that we might assume are depreciable but they may constitute part of the building; and a quantity surveyor should know the difference. They are also up to date with tax rulings, can often find items you would never think of, and are better qualified to establish the value of fixtures and fittings in older buildings, something you might have trouble with if you can't get the original owner's depreciation schedule.

Since 1 July, 2000, the depreciation rates for items have been based on their effective life. According to the ATO, for each item this is:

... the estimated period over which it can be used to produce income if it is maintained in good order and condition and subject to normal wear and tear.

Effective life can then be used to calculate depreciation rates by using either the diminishing value or prime cost method, the taxpayer making the choice. These rates are calculated like this:

$$\text{Prime Cost (PC)} = \frac{100\%}{\text{Effective life (yrs)}}$$

$$\text{Diminishing Value (DV)} = \frac{150\%}{\text{Effective life (yrs)}}$$

For example, if the effective life of an asset is 20 years, its depreciation rate using prime cost would be 5% and by diminishing value, it would be 7.5%. And for an item with an effective life of 10 years, its depreciation rate using prime cost would be 10% and by diminishing value, it would be 15%. Obviously, the shorter the effective life, the higher its depreciation rate. You can make your own estimate of the effective life of assets or adopt the effective life as determined by the ATO.

The next two pages provide a list of depreciable items associated with an investment property together with the ATO's suggested effective life. It is by no means comprehensive but it should give you a good guide.

Depreciation Rates for Common Items

	Effective Life	Prime Cost	Dimin Value
Air conditioning units – central	15	6.7%	10.0%
Air conditioning units – room	10	10.0%	15.0%
Alarm systems	20	5.0%	7.5%
Blinds	20	5.0%	7.5%
Carpets, lino	10	10.0%	15.0%
Cooktops	20	5.0%	7.5%
Curtains	7	14.3%	21.4%
Dishwashers	7	14.3%	21.4%
Dryers	7	14.3%	21.4%
Exhaust and Range hoods	20	5.0%	7.5%
Electronic security systems	20	5.0%	7.5%
Fans	20	5.0%	7.5%
Fire control systems	20	5.0%	7.5%
Fire alarms	20	5.0%	7.5%
Fluorescent lights	20	5.0%	7.5%
Furniture and fittings	15	6.7%	10.0%
Garbage disposal	7	14.3%	21.4%
Hair dryer	10	10.0%	15.0%
Heaters	10	10.0%	15.0%
Hot water systems	20	5.0%	7.5%
Lawn mowers	7	14.3%	21.4%
Letter box – polycarbonate	15	6.7%	10.0%
Letter box – aluminium	40	2.5%	3.8%
Light fittings	10	10.0%	15.0%
Microwave ovens	7	14.3%	21.4%
PABX	20	5.0%	7.5%
Plants – artificial	13	7.7%	11.5%
Radios	10	10.0%	15.0%
Rain water tanks – galvanised	20	5.0%	7.5%
Rain water tanks – concrete	50	2.0%	3.0%
Refrigerators	15	6.7%	10.0%

Chapter 17: Typical Tax Deductions   185

	Effective Life	Prime Cost	Dimin Value
Reticulation pumps and timers	20	5.0%	7.5%
Roller door motors	20	5.0%	7.5%
Sauna/spa	15	6.7%	10.0%
Smoke alarms	20	5.0%	7.5%
Solar water heaters	20	5.0%	7.5%
Stoves	20	5.0%	7.5%
Swimming pool – above ground	10	10.0%	15.0%
Swimming pool – concrete	50	2.0%	3.0%
Swimming pool – fibreglass	20	5.0%	7.5%
Swimming pool filters	15	6.7%	10.0%
Switchboard/distribution system	20	5.0%	7.5%
Synthetic lawn	10	10.0%	15.0%
Telephone installations	20	5.0%	7.5%
Television antennas – master system	20	5.0%	7.5%
Television sets	10	10.0%	15.0%
Vacuum cleaners	10	10.0%	15.0%
Video recorders	10	10.0%	15.0%
Wall ovens	20	5.0%	7.5%
Washing machines	7	14.3%	21.4%
Water irrigation system	20	5.0%	7.5%
Rental property business			
Answering machine	7	14.3%	21.4%
Computer system	5	20.0%	30.0%
Concrete mixer	10	10.0%	15.0%
Lawn mowers	7	14.3%	21.4%
Power tools	5	20.0%	30.0%
Sewing machines	10	10.0%	15.0%
Trailer	10	10.0%	15.0%
Furniture – home office	15	6.7%	10.0%
Carpet – home office	10	10.0%	15.0%

Note: Bedding, crockery, cutlery, linen, glassware and cooking utensils are claimed as replacement value, not depreciated.

186   *More Wealth from Residential Property*

The tables concur that the shorter the effective life of an item, the higher its depreciation rate, with the diminishing value method having a higher rate than prime cost. I prefer to use the diminishing value method as it confers greater tax advantages in the initial stages. If we look at how a $3,000 carpet depreciates using both methods, you will see why. First, using 15% diminishing value, you can see that the amount claimed is higher in the first year, and then diminishes in the following years when the depreciation is calculated on the declining balance.

Diminishing Value Depreciation of $3,000 Carpet

Year	Opening value	Rate	Claim	Closing value
1	$3,000	15%	$450	$2,550
2	$2,550	15%	$383	$2,167
3	$2,167	15%	$325	$1,842
4	$1,842	15%	$276	$1,566
5	$1,566	15%	$235	$1,331
6	$1,331	15%	$200	$1,131
7	$1,131	15%	$170	$961
8	$961	15%	$144	$817
9	$817	15%	$123	$694
10	$694	15%	$104	$590

Using the prime cost method, as shown below, at a rate of 10%, the amount claimed in the first year (and every year for 10 years) is just $300, significantly less than the $450 claimed by using diminishing value.

Prime Cost Depreciation of $3,000 Carpet

Year	Opening value	Rate	Claim	Closing value
1	$3,000	10%	$300	$2,700
2	$2,700	10%	$300	$2,400
3	$2,400	10%	$300	$2,100
4	$2,100	10%	$300	$1,800
5	$1,800	10%	$300	$1,500
6	$1,500	10%	$300	$1,200
7	$1,200	10%	$300	$900
8	$900	10%	$300	$600
9	$600	10%	$300	$300
10	$300	10%	$300	$0

Chapter 17: Typical Tax Deductions   187

As I've explained, the investor can choose the effective life of particular items, although it may be quite different from the ATO's suggestions. To illustrate this, if an investor bought a holiday unit on the beach front, they could select an effective life for the carpet of 5 years instead of 10 years, knowing that it might experience greater wear and tear.

A more significant — and positive — change to the depreciation rules has been the removal of the 100% write-off for items worth less than $300 and the introduction of a low-value pool for items worth less than $1,000. To complicate matters, the ATO has ruled that this low-value pool is to be written off at half the rate, or 18.75% in the first year and 37.5% from then on. There is no pro-ratering (apportioning the depreciation amount to the number of days owned), so that in the first year the full 18.75% can be claimed, even if the property is bought on June 30th in a particular year.

At first estimation, a drop in the rate for the low-value pool from 100% to 18.75% seemed to disadvantage property investors. But for an average investment property, closer scrutiny reveals that almost all of the depreciable items would fall into this new low-value pool. So the effective life tables really only apply to items valued at more than $1,000.

To show how effective this new rate is, let's look at Bill and Mary's $160,000 investment property that had $15,000 in fixtures and fittings. The carpet was valued at $3,000, the remaining $12,000 being made up of items which were individually valued at less than $1,000 — such as the hot water system at $950. This is how the depreciation schedule for the low-value pool would look over the first five years.

Depreciation of Low-value Pool

Year	Opening value	Rate	Depreciation claim
1	$12,000	18.75%	$2,250
2	$9,750	37.50%	$3,656
3	$6,094	37.50%	$2,285
4	$3,809	37.50%	$1,428
5	$2,381	37.50%	$893

The amount claimed in the first year would be $2,250 and in the second year it would be $3,656. This is significantly higher than with claiming these items using the effective life rates. For example if the hot water system valued at $950 were depreciated using the effective life diminishing value rate of 7.5%, the amounts claimed in the first and second year would be $71 and $66 respectively. However, in the low-value pool the claims become $178 and $289 respectively — a significant difference! You can see how this seemingly adverse change to the depreciation laws has been most beneficial to property investors.

188   *More Wealth from Residential Property*

Electricity/gas

This is usually the tenant's responsibility, but if you pay for it, you can claim it. You can also claim the fees for reconnection where these occur. If you have a home office, a percentage of your own electricity bill can be claimed separately, usually as a general business deduction.

Fire levy

This varies and could be collected by local governments, or could be a separate account levied by the states.

Gardening and mowing

When I go running around the suburbs, I can often tell a tenanted place by the length of the grass. One way to ensure the mowing is done more regularly is to subtly drop someone's business card for lawn maintenance in the letter box. Generally, tenants should be responsible for mowing and the like, but if you pay for it, the costs are tax deductible. The costs of hiring a trailer, mower fuel, gardening tools and such can be claimed in full, or else apportion them if they are sometimes used for private use.

Insurance

Both property and contents insurances are tax deductible. It may also be possible to claim your personal life insurance, but only if your financier insisted on it being part of the loan conditions.

Interest on borrowings

If the loan is fixed-interest, interest-only, the amount claimed each year will be constant. If the loan is P&I, just the interest component of the repayment is tax deductible and, because the principal is being paid off, the annual interest deduction will decline. If you are trying to rent a property and can't, or if you are renovating between tenancies, the interest is a cash cost and should be deductible. However, if you are building an investment property, the interest may be added as a capital cost until it is finished.

In-house video/PABX

Most likely this will be an expense incurred in a managed holiday unit complex where each unit is connected to cable television and has a network of telephone systems, both of which are usually leased on a monthly basis.

Land tax

Land tax varies from state to state but you can often jointly own a few properties between a husband and wife before you exceed the tax-free limits. The family home is usually omitted from the calculations. While this tax applies to a specific property, it is often incurred as a result of holding other investment properties. Consequently, land tax could be spread by claiming it as a general property business deduction.

Chapter 17: Typical Tax Deductions 189

Legal expenses

Some legal expenses are tax deductible, but the majority are not. For example, the costs of evicting tenants are deductible. The lease is usually prepared by the managing agent and hopefully, any dispute that arises over the lease agreement will be sorted out long before legal action is necessary. Legal expenses that are not tax deductible include those of a capital nature that relate to the property, not the tenant. According to the ATO, such expenses might include the 'purchase or disposal of your property, costs of resisting land resumption, and defending your title to the property'. These non-deductible expenses may, however, form part of the Capital Gains Tax calculation if the property is sold.

Lease costs

There are expenses of preparing leases. If you have a property manager, the costs are usually incorporated into the first week's letting fee.

Pest control

Pest control is only a deduction if paid for by the owner. However, managing agents are continually looking for ways in which tenants may contribute more towards the maintenance of the property. Consequently, pest control is often considered to be the responsibility of the tenant who is then required to present a pest control certificate on departure. In such cases, it is not a deduction for the owner.

Property agent's fees and commission

Agents' fees for both letting and managing the rental property are tax deductible and can vary between 5% and 20% of gross rent depending on the agent and if the property is for holiday letting. I believe it is a good idea to use a property manager, though some investors seem to cope very well. When deciding whether to use a property manager, remember that the fee is tax deductible, and that it is based on the rental income, not the property value, and therefore is a small cost compared to fund managers' fees which are a percentage of the total asset value. In Chapter 21, I discuss property management in more detail.

Quantity surveyor's fees

As described in the depreciation sections above, a quantity surveyor can prepare schedules for depreciable fixtures and fittings, and also the building, under Divisions 42 and 43 respectively. Quantity surveyors are usually up with the latest tax laws, rulings and determinations, and have their finger on the pulse regarding common trade practices. They have even been used by architects in commercial situations to suggest tax effective ways of construction. For example, removable stand-alone partitions in an office building can be depreciated but not concrete walls.

190　*More Wealth from Residential Property*

Repairs and maintenance

These include re-wiring, re-fencing, re-tiling, re-roofing — just about anything that can be classed as property maintenance — but check the distinction between repairs and improvements as outlined earlier. It is very tax-effective to have repairs carried out towards the end of the financial year (in say May or June). If you do the repairs yourself, you can claim the costs of the material, but not your time, unless the property is in the name of your partner. If the property is jointly owned and you do the repairs, you can charge your partner half the repair costs including your labour, but the fee must also be added to your income — so it may not be worth your while. I prefer to leave the property manager to handle minor repairs to a nominated value stated in the management agreement, usually to about $100. It's more effective to have someone else make decisions on small things like whether or not to spend $20 getting a new set of keys cut.

Replacement

Holiday houses and units are usually let fully furnished, and items such as crockery and bed linen are claimed at the time of replacement.

Secretarial fees

A friend of mine pays someone to regularly do the bookwork pertaining to her many properties. If you enjoy doing that kind of work, it's a good way of keeping an eye on things; otherwise, get someone else to do the tedium or just leave it to your accountant at the end of the financial year.

Security patrol fees

These days, many housing estates are fully enclosed and have security patrols. Your proportion of the costs for this service is tax deductible.

Stationery/Postage

All writing and office materials can be deducted in proportion to their business/private use. The first item you should buy is a spike or container to hold all those receipts until you get time to file them. You can also claim postage. These days, however, it is possible to pay bills through electronic banking, cutting down on the paperwork.

Telephone

The tenant is responsible for all costs associated with a telephone at the property. However, if there is no phone, and your tenant wants one, you should negotiate to pay a portion of the installation costs — if not all. Some tenants want cable connection for the internet and television, a cost that could also be a shared. For telephone usage from your home, keep a detailed record of all calls for a set period of say three months, and work out the percentage relating to investment properties compared to private use. You can use this ratio for future claims until the situation changes.

Chapter 17: Typical Tax Deductions 191

Travelling allowance

If you collect the rent, do the repairs or simply drive past to check the property, you should be able to claim a car allowance. Below are the per km rates for the 2000/2001 financial year, as allowed by the ATO for business travel up to 5,000 kilometres per year. Under this method, there is no need to substantiate any of the actual expenses.

Car Allowance 2000/2001		
Normal engine	**Rotary engine**	**Rate/km**
Up to 1600 cc	Up to 800 cc	48.9c
1601 to 2600 cc	801 to 1300 cc	58.5c
2601 & over	1301 & over cc	59.5c

If you have many properties and so exceed 5,000 km per year, there are methods other than the 'per km' rate for claiming car expenses. No matter which method you choose, do a three month trial logbook and work out the percentage of travel attributable to your investment property business over the year. This percentage can then be used for future claims.

If you travel interstate for inspections, body corporate meetings or any other reason relating to the management of your properties, you *may* be able to claim your return airfare, accommodation and meal costs. You *may* also be able to apportion these costs between private and business if you stay longer for a holiday. The ATO states:

... if you travel to inspect your rental property and combine this with a holiday, you need to take into account the reasons for your trip. If the main purpose of your trip is to have a holiday and the inspection of your property is incidental to that main purpose, you are not entitled to a deduction for that travel. However, you may be entitled to claim local expenses directly related to the property inspection, and a proportion of accommodation expenses.

So, if your rental property is interstate, you would be wise to travel to it with the specific intention of attending a body corporate meeting, or supervising repairs, and make your holiday incidental to your investment properties needs. Keeping a diary of where you went on what day and who you talked to would help validate your travel expenses.

Workers' compensation

Insurance for workers' compensation will vary from state to state and is usually only a minimal cost, but it is well worthwhile. It covers you in case the handyman, who has neglected to take out workers' compensation, falls off the roof of your rental property and hurts himself. Potentially, he could make a claim back on you.

192　*More Wealth from Residential Property*

Your business deductions

As I have said, owning rental properties is like operating a business. You might, then, have many expenses that you could list under the general heading of business deductions.

Your list might include anything accessed to help you with investment decisions such as newspapers, manuals, books, magazines, videos, tapes, computer software, seminars, consultants, courses, conferences, etc. It also might include items required for property maintenance in general and yet difficult to apportion to a particular property. Such items might be nails, screws, nuts, bolts, glue, filler, putty, sandpaper, paint, paintbrushes, hand tools, whipper-snipper cord, lawn mower fuel, cotton, curtain tape, pins, needles, travel costs, car expenses, postage, stationery, etc. In addition, there could be a separate schedule of depreciable items such as power tools, trailer, lawn mower, wheelbarrow, concrete mixer, mulcher, brush cutter, whipper snipper, sewing machine, camera, and ladder.

When you have items that you use privately as well as for your rental properties, you can still claim a percentage of the depreciation. As a guide, if you have one rental property, the split might be 10% rental and 90% private. By the time you have 15 properties, the split would more likely be 90% rental and 10% private.

You could also have costs associated with a 'home office' or 'place of business' but according to the ATO, there is a subtle difference between the two. Home office costs might include running expenses for heating, lighting, telephone and depreciation on equipment such as a desk, chair, filing cabinet, computer, bookshelves, printer, answering machine, fax machine, photocopier, etc. But if you have a particular place set aside for business so your home becomes a 'place of business', then additional claims for rates, insurances, repairs and interest may be made. Claims are based on the percentage of the floor area used as an office. However, if your home was purchased after September 19, 1985, and you claim the extra costs as a place of business instead of just those for a home office, you may jeopardise your home's status as being free of Capital Gains Tax.

• • •

Phew! This comprehensive list is by no means complete but it should set your mind thinking about what you are entitled to claim for your rental properties. I have found the ATO to be very helpful and always willing to provide information on what you can and can't claim, and I urge you to get their three publications listed at the start of the chapter.

Now it's time to put these tax deductions in perspective and to look at how they translate into a tax benefit for you. Let's see how this works.

18
Negative Gearing

We often hear the term 'negative gearing' used in relation to real estate investment, but what exactly does it mean? In essence it simply means using OPM to buy property. What is OPM? It stands for Other People's Money, and the only way you can use OPM is to borrow it. By borrowing money, you can buy and control a very valuable asset using a relatively small amount of your own money. If the total expenses including interest on this borrowed money exceed the rent, creating a negative cash flow, the property is said to be negatively geared.

So long as the property is producing income and you intend the net cash flow to be positive, legislation allows you to offset the loss against other income. This other income may be from any source such as your salaried job, business, bank deposits or even other properties. The 'loss' usually results in a tax refund that lessens the impact.

But the purpose of owning a negatively geared investment property and making a 'loss' is not simply to get a healthy tax refund. I liken it to growing an apple tree. You plant the seeds, water and nurture them until they sprout, then fertilize them for many years until one day the tree bears apples for you to pick. And year after year your apple tree continues to grow and produce apples that you can pick and enjoy whenever you want.

Borrowing, buying and keeping rental properties works the same way. In the short term, you feed your properties money — *you* have to make up the difference between all the expenses and what the tenant and taxman contribute. Over many years, while you are still working, you continue to direct money into your rental properties. And in the long term you reap the rewards, with the capital gain and the increased rent providing you with a wealthy retirement.

How does negative gearing work and does everyone benefit from it? What if I'm only a low income earner? Do I have to wait long for my tax refund; and have the new GST tax scales affected it? We'll look at these questions and others in this chapter and the answers should give you a better understanding of the concept of negative gearing.

194   *More Wealth from Residential Property*

Tax benefits

Under the present tax scales (see below), the harder you work, the more you earn and the more tax you pay. The really good thing about borrowing to buy rental property is that the harder you work, the more you earn, the more tax you get back. This section shows how this is possible, but keep in mind as you read that the tax benefits are just a bonus, not the be-all and end-all, and definitely not the reason for borrowing money and negatively gearing.

2001/2002 Tax Scales

Income	Marginal Rate
Below $6,000	nil
$6,001 to $20,000	17%
$20,001 to $50,000	30%
$50,001 to $60,000	42%
Over $60,000	47%

Note: Medicare Levy of 1.5% to be added to incomes over $13,550

If you earn more than $60,000, you will pay tax on your 'top' dollars at 48.5% (47% + 1.5% Medicare Levy). Consequently, any tax deductions will result in a tax refund at the same rate of 48.5%. Let's look at the tax benefits for an average income earner like Bill with his salary of $47,000 per year. Assume that we are using Bill's $160,000 investment property with a loan of $166,000. Annual interest of $14,110 plus expenses of $2,600 totals $16,710, and of this, the tenant pays $10,400 (62.2%), the taxman refunds $3,626 (21.7%) and Bill puts in just $2,684 (16.1%).

Who Pays the Cost?

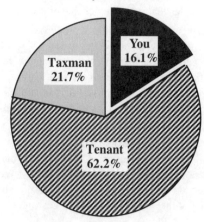

Chapter 18: Negative Gearing   195

Of course, such things as rent, expenses, the interest rate, and most importantly, your marginal tax rate will cause these percentages to vary. While it is quite true that negative gearing assists higher-income earners more, it works no matter what your level of income. I know of many property investors who earn much less than the average wage, yet are well on their way to achieving total financial independence long before their higher-salaried bosses.

The table below shows the tax benefits for the same $160,000 rental property described earlier for taxable incomes of $20,000, $47,000 (the average wage) and $70,000. They have been calculated using the Property Investment Analysis (PIA) software described in the back of this book.

Tax Savings on a $160,000 Rental Property

Current income	$20,000	$47,000	$70,000
Rent	$10,400	$10,400	$10,400
Total income	$30,400	$57,400	$80,400
Rental deductions	$21,910	$21,910	$21,910
New taxable income	$8,490	$35,490	$58,490
Present tax	$2,680	$11,185	$21,330
New tax	$423	$7,559	$15,823
Tax refund	$2,257	$3,626	$5,507

Note: Taxes include Medicare Levy of 1.5%

From these three examples using widely different incomes, you can see that negative gearing favours higher income earners. For someone earning $20,000 per year the tax savings would be $2,257, while for someone on $70,000 with exactly the same property, the same loan and the same rent, the tax refund would be more than three thousand dollars greater at $5,507. This is by no means to suggest that *only* higher-income earners should borrow to buy rental property, but simply to show that the tax benefits are greater. What it does mean therefore, is that there is clearly a financial advantage if negatively geared property is bought solely in the name of the highest income earner.

You can now see why the $160,000 was best bought in Bill's name only, rather than Mary's: his income of $47,000 provided $3,626 in tax benefits but hers of $20,000 would have provided just $2,257. What if the same investment property had been bought in joint names? In this case the tax benefits would have been $2,877 — marginally better than buying in Mary's name, but a long way short of buying in Bill's. Is it possible for low income earners like Mary to still buy negatively geared property? Let's see.

196 *More Wealth from Residential Property*

Negative gearing on low wages

As testament to the ability of low-income earners to buy property, the ABS (Cat. 8711) found that the incomes of the lowest 20% of property investors averaged merely $17,992, as you can see from this table.

Incomes of Lowest and Highest Earners

	Lowest 20%	Highest 20%
Range of incomes	Less than $29,000	More than $85,000
Average income	$17,992	$121,524

Source: Cat. 8711

Not only do people on low incomes invest in property, many of them have *borrowed* to buy. The table below shows the lowest and highest income categories and their average loan on each property.

Loans by Lowest and Highest Earners

	Lowest 20%	Highest 20%
None	53.1%	16.9%
Less than $50,000	17.2%	11.3%
$50,000 to $100,000	16.5%	20.1%
$100,000 to $200,000	8.4%	25.6%
$200,000 or more	nil	17.0%
Not stated	4.8%	9.1%

Source: ABS Cat. 8711

As you would expect, higher income earners borrow more money. But with 33.7% of very low income earners borrowing up to $100,000, and 8.4% borrowing more, negative gearing is attractive to everyone.

Just to prove that indeed it is possible for low income earners to buy investment property, let me show you how a young man earning $15,000 per year could do it. Suppose he borrowed $124,400 to buy a $120,000 rental property, including the costs, using his parents' home as security, so his LVR is OK. If the interest was $10,574 (8.5%) with rents of $7,800, his DSR would be calculated like this:

$$\text{DSR (Debt service ratio)} = \frac{\$10,574}{(30\% \text{ of } \$15,000) + (80\% \text{ of } \$7,800)}$$

$$= 98.45\%$$

According to the lender, he should qualify for a loan. But what are his tax benefits and what would it cost each week? With interest of $10,574 and property expenses of $1,950 (allowing for 25%), total outlays would be $12,524. If the tenant paid $7,800, his tax benefits in the first year would be $1,756 and his cost would then be $2,968 or just $57 per week!

Chapter 18: Negative Gearing   197

Negative gearing; positive cash flow

Property investors sometimes encounter a rather strange phenomenon called negative gearing with a positive cash flow. Let's first look at the normal situation where a tax refund occurs because the deductions exceed the rent, and the investor has a negative cash flow because the expenses plus interest are greater than the rent plus the refund, as shown below.

Negatively geared with a negative cash flow

Negative gearing

| Tax deductions | > rent | = tax refund |

Negative cash flow

| Interest + expenses | > rent + refund | = negative cash flow |

The more unusual situation where the investor receives a tax refund, but at the same time has a positive after-tax cash flow would be:

Negatively geared with a positive cash flow

Negative gearing

| Tax deductions | > rent | = tax refund |

Positive cash flow

| Rent + refund | > interest + expenses | = positive cash flow |

This situation usually occurs when significant non-cash tax deductions such as depreciation, are combined with high rent, small expenses or low interest. For example, if Bill and Mary borrowed $166,000 at 6%, instead of 8.5%, they would still be negatively geared and receive a tax refund of $2,318. But instead of having a negative after-tax cash flow of $2,684 in the first year, it would be a positive of $158, as this table shows.

Negative Gearing with a Positive or Negative Cash Flow

	Negatively geared Negative cash flow	Negatively geared Positive cash flow
Interest rate	8.5%	6%
Interest	$14,110	$9,960
Expenses	$2,600	$2,600
Total expenses	**$16,710**	**12,560**
Non-cash deductions	$5,200	$5,200
Total tax deductions	**$21,910**	**$17,760**
Rent	$10,400	$10,400
Tax refund	$3,626	$2,318
Annual cost	**-$2,684**	**+$158**

198 *More Wealth from Residential Property*

Negative gearing and the GST

Now that the Goods and Services Tax or GST is firmly entrenched, you may be wondering how the new tax scales affect negative gearing. The answer in short is yes, of course lower tax scales will reduce the tax refund for most tax payers, as deductions occur at your marginal rate of tax. The pre and post GST marginal tax rates are shown here:

Tax Scales for Pre GST and Post GST

Pre GST	Rate (%)	Post GST	Rate (%)
0 - 5,400	0	0 - 6,000	0
5,401 - 20,700	20	6,000 - 20,000	17
20,701 - 38,000	34	20,001 - 50,000	30
38,001 - 50,000	43	50,001 - 60,000	42
50,001 +	47	60,001 +	47

For average investors earning up to $50,000, the top marginal tax rate has dropped from 43% to 30%, and this must obviously have an impact on the negative gearing tax benefits available. For example, for someone like Bill earning $47,000 per year, the tax benefits on a $160,000 rental property are $3,626 under the post GST scales. But under the old, pre GST scales his tax saving would have been $4,896, or $1,270 more! We need to see this in perspective, however, noting some important points.

First and foremost, I have made it clear several times that the tax refund is not the sole reason for investing in property. Most of the tax benefits arise because of the deductibility of interest on the borrowings. We should not borrow, however, for this tax deduction, but for the leveraging effect of investing very little of our own money while receiving returns on a much larger asset.

Secondly, higher income earners have been largely unaffected as the top marginal rate of 47% has not changed.

Furthermore, even for average investors, bracket creep will ensure that you move gradually into higher tax scales. It has been almost three years since the new tax scales were first mooted. At that stage, Bill's income would have been about $42,000 and his tax refund $4,446, just $820 more, not $1,270 with no bracket creep. In another three years, if he is earning $52,110, his tax refund in similar circumstances would jump to $3,879 and he'd almost be back to where he started at pre GST rates. As if to verify my assertion that bracket creep is real, within days of writing this chapter, *The Weekend Australian* (11-12 August, 2001) reported that:

Bracket creep has already clawed back from middle Australians $3 billion of the $12 billion in personal tax cuts intended to sweeten the GST.

Chapter 18: Negative Gearing   199

Another point to note is that the GST is not a new concept. There are now many countries with a broad based consumption tax that operates in combination with lower marginal tax rates. In fact some countries, such as Great Britain with its Value Added Tax (VAT), have no tax concessions for negative gearing, yet residential property has still been a highly effective investment. Finally, all negatively geared investments whose tax benefits are for the most part determined by the tax scales will be similarly affected, whether they be shares, property or managed funds.

For those most interested in the hip-pocket cost of the investment, let's do the sums so you can see how negative gearing under pre and post GST tax scales might affect you. We'll look at Bill and his $160,000 property, and calculate the cost of the property in the first year and the resultant spare income, as set out in this table.

Pre and Post GST Tax Benefits in First Year

	Pre GST	Post GST	Difference
Income	$47,000	$47,000	0
Tax payable	$13,517	$11,185	
Disposable income	**$33,483**	**$35,815**	**$2,332**
Tax refund	$4,896	$3,626	
Rent	$10,400	$10,400	0
Interest	$14,110	$14,110	0
Expenses	$2,600	$2,600	0
Cost of property 1ˢᵗ yr	**$1,414**	**$2,684**	**$1,270**
Spare income			**$1,062**

You can see that after subtracting the tax payable in each case from Bill's income of $47,000, his disposable after-tax income is $33,483 and $35,815 for pre and post GST tax scales respectively. Taking into account the tax refund in each case, the cost of the investment property would then be $1,414 with pre GST tax scales and $2,684 with post GST tax scales. However, with $2,332 in additional income available to Bill as a result of paying less tax, he would be able to cover the extra cost of $1,270 for the property and still have $1,062 in spare income for any potential increases in other expenses.

Of course there would be other factors to consider, but the point is that the new scales have little impact on the costs of investing in negatively geared property. Besides, I have no doubt that market forces far outweigh the impact of any government legislation. If those who believe they will be adversely affected by the GST invest elsewhere, leaving a shortage in rental properties, the rest of us can only benefit from higher yields.

200　*More Wealth from Residential Property*

Varying your PAYG tax

If you are a PAYG (Pay As You Go) worker and receive tax benefits as a result of negative gearing, you are entitled to a tax refund at the end of the financial year when your true tax situation is assessed. It could be, though, that you'd have to wait many months for a refund cheque. But it is possible to reduce the amount of tax you pay each pay day so that instead of waiting for a tax refund, you pay less tax throughout the year. Ask yourself: if you were owed $3,626 in tax benefits, would you like to wait more than a year for it, or pay $70 less in tax each week? I know what I would rather do. It doesn't make sense to me to be owed money by the ATO for that length of time when it could be put to good use in loans, saving me interest along the way.

A decade ago, all you needed to do was write to the ATO and apply for a tax variation under Section 221D. It was a simple matter. Today, the ability to vary your tax comes under Section 15–15 and the ATO requires you to fill in a 16 page booklet entitled *Application for variation of amounts required to be withheld under PAYG Income Tax Withholding*. You can submit your application on paper or electronically through the internet. While it is time consuming, you can always get your accountant to do it. But it is a worthwhile exercise.

In due course you will receive a letter from the ATO indicating that you only need to pay a certain percentage of your income in tax. With Bill, for example, he is owed $3,626, so all he needs to pay is $7,559 instead of $11,185 in the first year. Part of his letter from the ATO might read:

*The prescribed rate of instalment deductions to be made from your salary and wages has been varied to **16.08%** of gross earnings per pay period. This is in accordance with Section 15–15 of Schedule 1 of the Tax Administration Act 1953.*

The set percentage has nothing to do with marginal rates. It is derived from dividing $7,559 by $47,000 and applying it to Bill's weekly salary, and is simply a convenient way for the ATO to tell you how much tax to pay. Consequently Bill's weekly pay slip might read:

	Pre-variation of PAYG	Post-variation of PAYG
Gross wages	$903.85	$903.85
Tax	$215.07	$145.36
Net wages	$688.78	$758.49

Instead of paying $215.07 in tax each week, Bill gets the benefit of the $69.71 owed by paying tax of only $145.36. There's nothing quite like getting that next pay packet with almost $70 extra in take-home pay.

19
The Costs of Buying and Selling

The costs of buying and selling property are capital costs and should not be confused with the borrowing costs associated with finance. These two kinds of costs have very different tax implications. As we have seen already, borrowing costs provide immediate tax benefits as the costs are tax deductible over the term of the loan or five years — whichever is the lesser period. But buying and selling costs are not directly deductible against income and are only accounted for in calculating the Capital Gains Tax (CGT) payable when, or if the property is sold.

The costs of buying include your solicitor's fees for transferring the property title (conveyancing) as well as state government stamp duty. Selling costs are your solicitor's fees for conveyancing, the real estate agent's commission and any other costs of selling the property. The CGT is indirectly a selling cost and I will discuss it here in detail because it, too, is incurred on the sale of the property.

The largest cost associated with buying property is state government stamp duty. Take a $160,000 investment property in New South Wales, for example. The stamp duty would be $4,090, or 2.5% of the property value. If you'd spent the same money on shares, however, the stamp duty would have been only 0.3% or $480 prior to 1 July, 2001, and after that date, when stamp duty on shares was abolished, it would have been zero. Interestingly, in New Zealand there is no stamp duty on property transfers.

To property investors, stamp duty can seem an unfair and irksome tax, yet it actually has a steadying effect on property values. The high buying costs discourage investors from buying and selling property, which reduces the amount of turnover, causing values to stabilise and minimising the risks. One of the reasons why shares are so volatile is that there is a very high turnover in the market place because of the lower (and now nil) stamp duty; however, there is still Capital Gains Tax. Let's look at the costs involved in buying and selling property.

202 *More Wealth from Residential Property*

Buying costs

Whether or not a rental property is bought with borrowed money, the purchaser incurs buying costs. These costs are government stamp duty, your solicitor's fees, registration on the title and any other costs such as travelling. You can borrow the costs and claim the interest as a tax deduction, but the costs themselves are not immediately tax deductible and will only be taken into account in the CGT calculation if the property is sold. In the ACT, however, the purchase costs are treated as the cost of leasing the land for 100 years, and are deductible in the year of purchase.

Stamp duty on purchase

Your financier will usually insist that the stamp duty be paid before settlement. The rates for stamp duty vary from state to state and with the cost of the property, but as a guide, for a property between $100,000 and $200,000, you will pay from 2% to 3.5%. Owner occupiers usually pay stamp duty at a lower rate than investors.

Your solicitor's fees

Borrowing money and buying property normally involves two different solicitors. Yours does the conveyancing; the other prepares the mortgage documentation for the lender. The fees you pay for conveyancing are part of the purchasing costs while the fees for mortgage preparation are part of the borrowing costs. Since they are deductible over the loan term, the fees for the mortgagee's solicitor are more tax effective than those for your own. You could, nevertheless, apportion some of the latter towards the borrowing costs by arranging for your own solicitor to scrutinise your mortgage documents and conduct searches requested by your financier. Each state has a scale of standard solicitors' conveyancing fees with the rate varying from $200 to $1,500 for a $160,000 property. Some states have 'land brokers' who do conveyancing and are much cheaper, as a rule. It is also possible to do it yourself, but it is very time consuming.

Registration of the title

The title of the property must be registered at the lands department in each state. The cost of this varies, but it should be around $100.

Other costs

At times, buying an investment property can mean a lot of hard yakka. You may travel to and fro, up and down the coast or interstate or inland. It might mean flying thousands of kilometres and staying in hotels. It is worth the effort — but the costs associated with finding and purchasing a rental property are capital costs and can not be included as a tax deductible revenue cost.

Selling costs

Before you contemplate selling a property you should look at all the hidden costs that drain your profits. Depending on how long it takes to sell (usually about three months), there may be an opportunity cost factor of lost rent. This could be high if tenants move out well in advance. If you sell a property within a short time of buying, and do it often enough, you may be classed as a trader. The capital gain would then be classed as income and taxed at your full marginal tax rate with no discount on the profit, as I explain in more detail on the next page in the section on the CGT. If you bought a property for $160,000, renovated it, and sold it within a year for $250,000, the real costs might look like this:

Costs of Buying and Selling

Agent's costs	$7,000
Stamp duty	$4,000
Solicitor's fees	$1,000
Renovation costs	$35,000
Borrowing costs, etc	$2,000
Interest	$17,000
Miscellaneous costs	$4,000
Tax on profits (if classed as trader)	$10,000
Total costs	**$80,000**

The costs arising from selling could even be more than the $80,000 here. Where is the profit? I don't think that $10,000 made on a $160,000 investment is a great return, especially if you've just spent 52 weekends working on it! That's about $9 an hour for your time! You don't want to pay this kind of financial and personal cost every few years, so stick to the plan: buy and keep and build your profits for the long term.

Your solicitor's fees

Selling entails less work than buying, so solicitor's fees are less. The fees may vary from state to state and according to the type of property, but they are usually negotiable. If you do it yourself, it is much easier to handle the conveyancing when you sell than when you buy.

Sales commission

Commission is set on a sliding scale and it varies from state to state. The rate for properties between $100,000 and $200,000 is approximately 3%. You should take this into account when calculating any CGT liability or profits on selling.

204   *More Wealth from Residential Property*

Capital Gains Tax

Capital Gains Tax (CGT) was introduced on 19 September, 1985. Its aim was to discourage short-term profit taking by property speculators, something it did very effectively. For long-term investors, the tax was cushioned, as it was paid only on the gains over and above inflation. Even then, by special averaging provisions, if your other sources of taxable income were low (eg if you were retired or had other negatively geared property), you could have been liable for very little CGT.

New rules for calculating CGT were implemented on 21 September, 1999, based on recommendations from the Ralph Review of Business Taxation *(www.treasurer.gov.au)*. These discard inflation indexing and averaging provisions, and simply calculate the tax liability at 50% of the net capital gain added directly to the taxable income in the year of sale.

Making it complex for investors who bought properties before these new rules were introduced, if they sell in the future, they will have to decide on one method or the other. This isn't as good as it might sound at first because indexation of the cost base was frozen at 30 September, 1999. So if you bought a property in 1995 and sell it in 2005, you'll only be able to index for the first four years if you choose the indexation method. Which method *should* you use if you have pre-Ralph properties? The ATO advises that as a rule of thumb you should consider the following time frames.

Time held	CGT method
3 – 4 yrs	Discount
5 – 7 yrs	Either
8 + yrs	Indexation

While this is a reasonable guide, I strongly urge you to do your own separate calculations to see which method is better in your situation.

For now, let's look at exactly how the new system works, then we'll make some interesting comparisons between the CGT under the old and new systems, noting some subtle differences between the two. While you do need to understand the implications of the CGT, though, you should realise that you only pay it *if* you sell an asset, so the best philosophy is to avoid selling at all.

Calculating the CGT

The CGT analysis in the next few pages focuses on the $160,000 property that Bill bought in 2001, with $15,000 in fixtures and fittings. We'll project that he sells it 10 years later for $248,475, allowing for annual capital growth of 4.5%. We assume inflation to average 2% per year. The CGT has been calculated using the PIA software.

Calculating the property costs

First you need to separate in value the assets being bought and sold, as the ATO requires that the fixtures and fittings purchased with the property be treated as separate assets. To keep our analysis straightforward, we'll assume that the $15,000 worth of fixtures and fittings in Bill's house has been sold at the written down value of $733, hence attracting no CGT. Looking at the 'property only' value, the purchase and selling prices are:

Purchase price

Purchase price	=	$160,000
Fixtures and fittings	=	$15,000 less
Purchase price (property only)		= **$145,000**

Selling price

Selling price (10 yrs @ 4.5% grth)	=	$248,475
Fixtures and fittings	=	$733 less
Selling price (property only)		= **$247,742**

Calculating the cost base

Having established the purchase and selling prices of the property only, we need to calculate the cost base. This begins with the sum of the initial purchase costs, selling costs, any building improvements and other costs that were unclaimed such as the painting that was done soon after purchase.

If we assume that the initial purchase costs are $4,500 (stamp duty of $4,090 + solicitor's fees, etc, of $410) and the selling costs are $8,570 (sales commission $7,328 + solicitor's fees $1,242) and that building improvements and other costs are zero, the preliminary cost base would be $158,070, as shown below.

But we have another step to go. Since 13 May, 1997, any deductions for building depreciation (also called a special building write-off or capital allowance), have had to be written back. Consequently, $20,000 claimed in building depreciation ($2,000 each year for 10 years) must be subtracted, giving a final cost base of $138,070. Here is the entire calculation:

Purchase price (property only)	=	$145,000
Purchase costs	=	$4,500 plus
Selling costs	=	$8,570 plus
Building improvements	=	$0 plus
Other costs	=	$0 plus
Cost base (preliminary)	=	$158,070
Building depreciation	=	$20,000 less
Cost base (final)		= **$138,070**

206 *More Wealth from Residential Property*

Calculating the net capital gain

To calculate the net capital gain, we subtract the cost base of $138,070 from the selling price of the 'property only'. This was $247,742 so the net capital gain is $109,672.

Selling price (property only)	=	$247,742
Cost base	=	$138,070 less
Net capital gain		**= $109,672**

Calculating the discounted capital gain

Under the new system, the CGT liability is based on 50% of the net capital gain. So if the net capital gain is $109,672, 50% of this gives a discounted capital gain of $54,836.

Net capital gain	=	$109,672
Discounted capital gain	=	**$54,836** (50%)

Calculating the Capital Gains Tax

Finally we are ready to calculate the CGT payable in this situation. This is done by adding the discounted capital gain of $54,836 to Bill's total taxable income in the year of sale and working out the CGT at his marginal rates, assuming the sale occurs at the end of the full year. Here are the calculations.

Salary	=	$64,056
Rent	=	$12,429 plus
Deductions	=	$19,407 less
Taxable income	=	$57,078
Tax normally payable on $57,078	=	$15,209
Discounted capital gain	=	$54,836
Income + discounted capital gain	=	$111,914
Tax now payable on $111,914	=	$41,658
Capital Gains Tax	=	**$26,449**

The taxable income in that year is calculated by adding Bill's salary of $64,056 to the rent of $12,429 and subtracting deductions of $19,407, assuming he holds the property for the full year before he sells. This will give him a taxable income of $57,078 on which he would normally pay $15,209 in tax.

If we then add the discounted gain of $54,836 to his taxable income of $57,078 to get his new income of $111,914 ($57,078 + $54,836), the tax on this amount would be $41,658. The difference between his normal tax and the tax now payable is $26,449 ($41,658 less $15,209). This is the amount of Capital Gains Tax payable.

Chapter 19: The Costs of Buying and Selling **207**

CGT – for better or for worse

The above set of calculations probably makes the CGT sound far more complicated than it really is. In fact this new way is simpler than the old. But is it better or worse for property investors? In the examples below, the CGT has been calculated over 5, 10 and 20 years using both indexation and discounted methods. Don't confuse this with the choice of one method or the other for pre-Ralph properties. This is just an exercise to highlight the differences between the two systems — in reality, there is no choice if the property is bought after 30 September, 1999.

For the $160,000 property with capital growth of 4.5% and inflation at 2%, the results for both the old indexed method and the new discounted method are:

CGT with Growth at 4.5% and Inflation at 2%

	5yrs	10yrs	20yrs
New CGT – Discounted	$10,822	$26,449	$63,831
Old CGT – Indexed	$12,106	$36,582	$92,427

As you can see, the new discounted system appears to be better, with less CGT payable over either short or long periods. However, the real test comes when we look at periods of high inflation and high capital growth. Then the story is quite different. For growth of 12% and inflation of 10%, the CGT payable using both methods is:

CGT with Growth at 12% and Inflation at 10%

	5yrs	10yrs	20yrs
New CGT – Discounted	$30,704	$84,889	$335,410
Old CGT – Indexed	$15,715	$54,220	$255,533

It is clear that with high inflation and very capital growth, the CGT under the new system is far worse. When you think about it, it's quite obvious. With very high growth, but no provisions for indexing to take inflation into account, the new discount CGT is calculated on the full capital gain, whereas under the old system, the CGT is calculated only on the gain over and above inflation.

So in times of low growth and low inflation, the new system is better, but in times of high growth and high inflation, the new system is worse. Let me point out again: you only pay CGT if you sell property, not if you keep it. But what happens when it's time to sell the odd property in order to reduce the debt and retire? Let's see how the CGT can be minimised.

208 *More Wealth from Residential Property*

Minimising the CGT

Once you are in a position to retire, you may need to balance the debt such that the rent from your properties becomes your primary source of income. Some properties might need to be sold, in which case you will have to consider the implications of the CGT. For example, if you sell at an inopportune time, such as while you are still working and earning a high income, this tax could be considerable. However, there are many ways you can wind down towards retirement and minimise the cost of the CGT. Below are a few ideas.

Don't sell any properties

- Rather than continue to build the portfolio, with several years before retirement, you could cease to buy properties and allow the rent to gradually overtake the interest. This would create a positive cash flow without the need to sell, although at the same time your tax refund would gradually diminish because of the reduced tax deductions.

- Alternatively, if you have some other cash savings at the time of your retirement, perhaps as the result of a superannuation payout, you could use this lump sum to reduce or pay off the debt.

- Or, if you have a lump sum, rather than pay off the debt, its earnings could be used to supplement your income and help pay the interest bill, while waiting for rents to increase.

- You could also gradually reduce the debt in the years prior to retirement by either taking a principal and interest loan, or keeping an interest only loan in combination with a credit line, making loan reductions as desired.

Sell some properties

- You could sell some properties in a staggered manner instead of all at once. This would spread the CGT over a number of years, and keep most of the taxable capital gain within the lower tax brackets.

- Or you could sell the properties that attract the least CGT, such as those in the name of the lower income earner, or those that have incurred the least capital growth, generally the ones with high yields.

- The properties could be sold when your income is lowest, such as when you retire completely from the workforce.

- Alternatively, while still working, you could create a lower taxable income by paying a year's interest in advance.

Let me conclude with one little anecdote. You should not allow yourself to get bogged down with CGT issues, or you'll find that you spend more time worrying about selling properties than buying them!

Part VIII

Maintaining the Assets

20
Financial Management

Would you hop in the shower without testing the water? I doubt it. Do you cross the road without first following the kindergarten saying of 'Look to the right and look to the left and you'll never ever get run over'? Probably not. And yet many people begin their journey to wealth without taking all precautions necessary to ensure their success. Building wealth through residential property means not only following the right principles, but also preparing for all that might happen *before* it happens. An old English proverb sums it up perfectly:

An ounce of prevention is worth a pound of cure.

Investing in residential property is very affordable, costing the average person only around $50 per week to get started. But this net figure can be the result of large amounts of money flowing in and out of bank accounts, something you need to learn how to manage if you want to retire wealthy. In a previous book, *Building Wealth Story by Story*, I share some detail about a young couple who own a portfolio of properties worth over a million dollars, which costs them around $100 per week.

We pay interest of $70,000 per year and property expenses of $17,000 per year, and we get a tax refund of $7,000 and $75,000 in annual rent. I'm just a clerk for a hardware store in our town and my wife and I have a bigger turnover of money than the store.

This is typical of investors who own many properties. Managing your portfolio needs a business-like approach and you must learn to develop a 'being rich' mentality to cope with the large amounts of money. The lack of this ability is why people who win Lotto, or inherit a fortune, are likely to squander their wealth quickly. A spokesperson for Lotto was quoted in *The Weekend Australian* (10 –11 Feb, 2001) as saying:

People who win lotto are not rich people, but poor people with a lot of money.

This chapter will show you how to develop the mindset of a wealthy person so that you can manage and master your finances and protect your wealth building plan.

212   *More Wealth from Residential Property*

Prepare a budget

It is important to prepare a budget and check it every few months so that you keep an eye on all your incomings and outgoings — don't rely on intuition. C.E. Hoover once said that budgeting is:

Telling your money where to go instead of wondering where it went.

The main reason why many people don't have spare money to invest is that they have committed it all to repaying debt on consumer goods rather than to loans on investment properties. Short-term personal loans and credit cards with high rates push up repayments to a level where the DSR is already at 100%, so you have no capacity to borrow for any investment.

Also, many people don't realise that a multitude of small ticket items end up costing a fortune. I remember a young couple who excitedly told me after a seminar that since they had prepared a budget, they had been easily able to save an extra $60 per week, enough for two more investment properties. They both loved chocolate and always bought a bar with a bottle of mineral water for their ten minute work break, figuring that the water compensated for the calories in the chocolate. But when they did the sums, they found that a seemingly small cost of $3 each time for each person twice a day for five days came to $60 per week!

Fix the interest rate

I am a great advocate of fixing interest rates on loans, no matter how high or low they may seem, as you are able to budget far more effectively. If you can afford to borrow money at the rate offered, fix it for a minimum of three years, or even longer if the rate seems particularly low. It can be a recipe for disaster if you take a variable rate loan. At the time of deciding, you may think that interest rates couldn't possibly go higher. Yet they have no upper limit, as we saw during the 1980s. The investors who lost then were those who were forced to sell because they couldn't keep up with the larger repayments on variable rate loans. My view is that if rates go up and mine are fixed, I'm covered. If they go down, I haven't lost money. With a variable rate, if they go up, I could lose a lot.

Take interest-only loans

An interest-only loan maximises your cash flow and gives you better tax advantages compared to a P&I loan, in which the payment towards the principal is not tax deductible. P&I also increases your loan payments unnecessarily, affecting your DSR and possibly limiting your ability to borrow further. But, if you feel more comfortable with a P&I loan, and it is all that's on offer from the lender of your choice, take it over a long term (preferably 25 to 30 years). Then the loan payment is almost all interest in the first five years.

Set up a credit line

This type of overdraft facility (see page 160) allows you to draw against an approved upper limit and repay the money at your convenience. It's a great sort of loan — not as long-term finance, but for immediate cash access. Your ability to get your hands on money quickly can alleviate temporary crises. Maybe you can't do overtime this month, or your property has become vacant the same week you have to pay school fees, or ... The unexpected always happens when you least expect it.

In fact, with the advent of these readily available credit lines, you no longer need cash reserves, something I always advocated before this facility came into use. I see no point in having large amounts of cash sitting in a dead savings account earning a pittance, when you can park it in a credit line and save the 8% or so on interest payable on the loan. From the time you buy your first investment property it is possible to set up a credit line, if only for a small amount, in conjunction with a fixed rate loan. As these loans are usually variable rate, it's a good idea to aim for about one third of your loans as a credit line with two thirds as a fixed-rate, interest-only loan.

However, don't use your investment property credit line for school fees or kids toys, as the interest won't be tax deductible. It's also worthwhile pointing out again that credit lines can be dangerous in that the money is far too easy to get for people who lack discipline. Finance manager Peter Kidd was reported in *The Weekend Australian* (12-13 Dec, 1998) as saying:

The big risk with a line of credit is that it can be a nightmare for people who can not maintain their budget.

Reduce tax instalments

If you are a PAYG taxpayer, it will help your cash flow if you apply to the tax office for a variation on your regular tax instalments as allowed under Section 15-15. (See page 200.) I see no point in waiting a year or more for a tax refund when your larger pay packet can mean the difference between being comfortable or strapped for cash. You could save hundreds of dollars in interest by placing all your tax savings in your credit line over that time instead of waiting for a one-off tax refund.

Aim for a reasonable LVR

As a guide, you should be aiming to maintain an overall loan to value ratio (LVR) for your portfolio at about 50%. This means that by the time you have a million dollars worth of property, you would be managing a debt of around $500,000. You shouldn't be too concerned if your LVR is more or less — and it probably will be much more early on, like 90% or so when you start. This is just a guide keep your debt in perspective.

214   *More Wealth from Residential Property*

Don't count on unreliable income

Do not commit any unreliable income to loan payments. If you are a two-income family, and one of you is likely to stop work in the very near future (eg to start a family), don't commit both incomes to loan payments. If one member of the family intends working for three or four more years, take advantage of this now, but make sure that the debt is manageable before that person stops work. If you've had regular overtime for the last five years, take this into account, but also take steps to ensure continuity of loan payments if the overtime should suddenly stop. By all means, *plan* what you want to do when rents and wages increase, but never treat 'maybe income' as if it exists. While rents normally rise long term in line with inflation, they may soar in some years and stagnate in others.

Don't speculate

Don't waste your time speculating on what may or may not happen to property values in the future. Slow, steady growth is what makes property investment work; you won't succeed on a roller coaster ride based on rumour and speculation. 'Get in and buy before the GST hits, or prices will be sky high afterwards', I heard many times, when in fact, builders were so overworked before its implementation that they could charge any price they liked. Now that we have the GST, many are lowering their prices to well below previous quotes to attract business. No one has a crystal ball. The best idea is to stick to your plan and invest long term.

Look into rent insurance

You can choose from quite a few innovative insurance policies to cover you for loss of rent. They cost a few hundred dollars, but in some cases, this includes contents insurance for curtains, carpets, etc. The insurance is tax deductible and a most worthy consideration if you are at all concerned by the impact of vacancies on your cash flow.

Check out mortgage repayment insurance

If you have any fears about job security or health, you might consider taking out insurance that will cover your mortgage repayment if you are unable to work. This can be expensive: it is probably cheaper to take other precautions such as setting up a credit line to cover you for such events. But if it means investing or not, do it.

Consider income replacement insurance

For self-employed people, loss of income through a downturn in the economy or some other factor is a justifiable worry. If you are in this position, it is practical to consider an insurance policy that replaces at least part of your income should it cease. These policies can be costly, but offer great protection; and the payment should be tax deductible.

Chapter 20: Financial Management 215

Take out term life and disability insurance

There's always that morbid chance that you will die or become severely incapacitated leaving your loved ones with properties that you have heavily negatively geared, and no income. It is quite inexpensive to take out life insurance for death and disability. Don't forget to insure your partner. Too often it's the male who takes life insurance, with no cover for the partner. This can cause untold hardship to the widower left to care for school-age children, with the housekeeping and childminding fees. Act before the unthinkable happens and don't skimp on life insurance. The cost of peace of mind can be very small.

Invest in health insurance

What do I mean by 'investing in health insurance'? Many people spend thousands of dollars each year on health insurance, more because of fear tactics used by governments and insurance companies than sound economic reasoning. According to a report in *The Courier Mail* (20 May, 2000):

Healthy young Australians could save themselves thousands of dollars by self-insuring instead of being scared into private health insurance.

The report quoted Ian McAuley, a lecturer in public sector finance at the University of Canberra, as saying:

Consumers who invested $1,000 a year from the age of 31 would be $200,000 better off by the time they retired. There is a good public hospital system and you can save for elective surgery through what you would have put into health premiums.

I have long believed that you are financially better off investing your would-be insurance premiums into property so that if you need elective surgery, you can use your own funds to pay for it. Again, it is just a matter of having that line of credit in place.

Get property insurance

Don't skimp on property insurance. It's important to minimise risks, and being inadequately insured can put a big hole in your finances. Make sure you take out insurance on the day you sign the contract, because if anything happens to the building between signing and settlement day, it's your loss. Insurance should cover replacement value as well as lost rent, demolition fees, architect's fees, etc, with the value being a good 20% over what you think is just building cost.

Contents insurance, which is usually taken out separately, should cover curtains, carpets, blinds, etc, if the property is otherwise unfurnished. Some insurance packages are especially suited to investors, covering both building and the basic contents. Also, as a courtesy, remind your tenants to insure their own items.

216   *More Wealth from Residential Property*

Avoid external partnerships

Avoid partnerships outside the family if you can. Business deals with friends can be a good way to lose them. I've seen many friendships torn apart by joint ventures into property investment. One wants to use an agent, the other wants to manage it. One wants it repainted now, the other can't afford to. One loses his job and wants to sell because he has no cash reserves, the other wants to buy him out and they can't agree on price. If a partnership is the only way you can get into property investment, do it, but be wary of the pitfalls.

Make a will

It's such a simple exercise to make a will, yet many people fail to do so. Perhaps we don't like to be pessimistic, however, a ten minute exercise can avoid untold hardship if the inconceivable ever happens. It's amazing how many relatives turn up when you die intestate (without a will). Your family will not want to have an entire property portfolio left in the hands of someone else, such as the public trustee, for a lengthy term.

Gain more knowledge

Financial fear is often caused by being uninformed. Keep up with the pursuit of knowledge: talk to as many other property investors as you can, read as much as you can and learn by your own experiences. Financial management is easy. The trick is to build a safety net beneath you so that if you ever falter, you don't go into free fall.

Don't get too greedy

One final warning. Don't get too greedy. I have known many people who have acquired considerable wealth by steadily investing in property, only to lose the lot by throwing money into risky business ventures. In *Building Wealth Story by Story*, I wrote about Jett and Tina who expanded their car spare parts business into an area they knew little about using their many investment properties as security. They told me afterwards:

Our biggest mistake was that we got sidetracked. I think I'll be honest and say we got greedy. We were convinced we were going to make more millions overnight for our children, even though we knew it had taken us thirty years to make our first million.

Our next biggest mistake was that we put our properties at risk by mortgaging them for a business venture we hadn't investigated thoroughly. We relied solely on the hype of a relative. Our properties had got us to where we were, yet we mistakenly believed that something else would be a better investment.

What more can I say? Stick to what you know best and don't put all at risk by being too greedy.

21
Property Management

Building wealth through residential property gives you complete control over the management of your investment — but don't confuse management with involvement! Unfortunately, some investors feel that they must be actively involved in everything that happens to their property, which often results in them selling. The ABS (Cat. 8711) found that 15.5% of property investors who sold in the five years prior to a 1997 survey, did so because they believed their rental property was 'too much worry'. These people think they must save every last dollar to make their rental property work; they personally fix the washers, paint the walls, and collect the rent.

You don't have to be personally responsible for every little incident. Do-it-yourself investment in residential property does *not* mean do it *all* yourself! The returns from property can be so good that you can afford to pay a specialist to do the maintenance and management, yet still achieve great results. For my part, I prefer to forgo a *fantastic* return in favour of a *great* return by delegating the things I either don't enjoy, or don't have time for, to someone else. It's a matter of putting a value on your own time.

One aspect of property management I prefer to leave to others is dealing with the tenants. It is difficult to distance yourself and too easy to fall into the trap of becoming emotionally involved. I remember vividly the tenants in our very first investment property. In the early stages, the rent remained static, until, eventually, it fell so far behind market rates that it needed a 50% rise to bring it back into line. I didn't feel comfortable doing this, particularly since the tenants were struggling to keep up (mostly due to all their hire purchase commitments).

Every year that passed, for ten years, I might add, I resolved that when these tenants left, I would raise the rent. But this was not to be. The tenants were firmly entrenched and had no intention of moving — and indeed *could not afford* to move. Catch 22! After this experience, I prefer to use a professional property manager. Whether you use a professional manager or not, you should consider the following points to maximise your returns and minimise the fuss.

218   *More Wealth from Residential Property*

Keep an eye on maintenance

Remember that you are running a superannuation fund: don't let your property become run down or you'll find it affects your payout at the end. Tenants understandably dislike miserly landlords, especially those who collect the rent in a Porsche, yet refuse to fix a leaking roof. Good tenants are attracted to a property kept in good condition — and your repair bills are tax deductible anyway. Well maintained properties are much easier to rent, an especially important factor in times of high vacancies. Just a reminder. Unless you enjoy being a handyman, don't try to do everything yourself. You'll find the property becomes an albatross around your neck, when it should be a great vehicle for building wealth.

Distinguish between maintenance and improvements

Don't make the mistake of over-capitalising your property. If you want to add a third bedroom, work out the cost and judge whether it is justified in terms of the additional rent and recovery on sale. The most effective additions are outdoor living areas. Pergolas are inexpensive, increase the living area, and make the property more appealing to tenants. Likewise adding a carport is generally more cost effective than a garage.

Screen your tenants

Contrary to popular belief, people with young children and pets often make good tenants. It has been my experience that, providing there is a clause in the contract for pets to be kept outside, tenants with pets can be just as fastidious as those without. Rather than try to choose tenants on the basis of such things as children, pets or marital status, it is far more important to select them according to their cleanliness and ability to pay. A reference from a previous landlord or employer, and a quick look at the last place of residence, may be all you need. Or you may want to run a credit check through one of the recognised credit agencies. Better still, get a good property manager to do the tenant screening for you.

Set a reasonable rent

The rent can be collected directly, deposited in an account, or mailed to you, or an agent can do the same. Rent should be maintained at, or close to, the prevailing market rate, which is something with which an agent should be much more familiar. Don't fall into the trap of only increasing the rent after the tenants have left. They'll probably never leave if they're on such a good wicket, so you never get the chance to put the rent up. If there is a temporary over-supply of rental property, a slightly lower rent may mean fewer vacancies and appeal to a larger number of tenants from whom you can choose. Personally, I prefer to have fewer vacancies and a lower rent (80% of something is better than 100% of nothing).

Prepare a sound lease

A lease protects both you and the tenant. A minimum of six months is standard and additional clauses can be added. The Real Estate Institute (REI) in your state has standard leases for use by real estate agents, or you can obtain your own lease from a stationer.

Follow up quickly on arrears

Even though you may retrieve some money from the bond, prevention is better than cure and good tenant selection is critical. If a tenant is a long way behind in rent, approach them tactfully; court action can be costly and you still may not recoup any rent (if they don't have it, they can't pay).

Prepare ahead for change of tenants

Placing an advertisement in the local or metropolitan newspaper at least three to four weeks in advance will usually get a good response. Describe the property in an appealing way and be prepared to negotiate on the rent.

Minimise the vacancy rate

According to BIS Shrapnel, a vacancy rate of about 3% provides a good balance between supply and demand. This means that at any one time, 3% of rentable properties are vacant, or that a property is vacant for almost two weeks per year. Too many investors expect 100% occupancy and become dismayed if a property lies vacant for more than a week. Remember that 30% of the population rent and that this percentage is increasing. So there will still be tenants around, but they can often afford to be choosy.

Clean, well maintained properties in handy locations, with reasonable rent, should normally have low vacancies. Lowering the rent is another simple strategy to attract tenants. Simply by following these few rules, you'll find tenants attracted to your property, who will be inclined to stay longer. A good property manager can advise on how to reduce vacancies, and they can have a new tenant lined up, just as one leaves.

Make sure you have a bond

This is usually four weeks' rent, and legislation in most states requires the bond to be placed with a Rental Bond Authority. Disputed bonds are probably the most frequent cause of concern for both landlords and tenants. Quite often the dispute arises from a simple misunderstanding that should have been clearly spelled out in the lease in the first place.

Keep a business relationship with tenants

Good property management is often about good people management. Tenants are an integral part of property investment and need to be treated with respect, not as second-class citizens. It is surprising how positively people respond to a little attention. But always maintain the relationship as one of professional courtesy.

220 *More Wealth from Residential Property*

Do regular inspections

These should be at least six-monthly, but it certainly doesn't hurt to see your property more frequently. Even if your property is interstate and managed by an agent, it pays to show an interest, if only by telephone. Agents are much more responsive when they have direct contact with the landlord. Besides, if you do have to travel quite a distance to check on your property, the cost should be a legitimate tax deduction.

Seek professional property management

If you decide to use a professional property manager instead of doing it yourself, you should take the trouble of finding a good one. This means finding a real estate agent who runs their rent roll as a business — not just as a sideline to their real estate sales. If need be, a property manager can do so much more than just collect the rent, organise the tradesmen and pay the rates and insurances. I have known my own property manager to dig a ditch to drain water away during a torrential downpour because he couldn't get anyone else at the time! The best property managers are usually very good people managers. Let me give you a sample of the many reasons for using a professional property manager.

First and foremost, they provide the all important buffer between you and the tenant. Secondly, they are best placed to assess the appropriate rent and can ensure that it remains at market levels. In many cases they can find tenants more quickly and of a better quality than you can. They may not have to advertise, as they have a lot of 'walk in' enquiries and can personally screen the tenant. In times of high vacancies, a good property manager can 'sell' a property to a tenant by pointing out its advantages.

Good property managers do more than just sign up the tenant on the dotted line. They take care to remind the tenant of their commitments as they are often so eager to move in that they don't fully take in the extent of their obligations. This often prevents potential disputes.

As in all other professions, property managers develop their own tricks of the trade. This is a tactic one of my own property managers practises. He avails himself of every opportunity to check on the tenants without being too intrusive. So, if a tenant rings up about a 'spot of trouble', he responds *immediately* as this gives him the perfect opportunity to see the property 'as is', without the tenant doing a massive clean-up prior to a formal inspection. The tenant thinks he's great because the problem has been seen to instantly, and the landlord thinks he's great, knowing that the property is being properly managed.

Never underestimate how important a good property manager can be to the success of your wealth building plans! We have even bought rental properties in an area with a particular property manager in mind.

22
Understanding
the 'What Ifs'

I could easily write another book answering the 'what ifs' that people unnecessarily worry about when investing in property. It's good to be cautious but some people become so obsessed with 'what ifs' that they do nothing. They worry if interest rates go up — it's too late to buy property now; they worry if they go down — there's a recession coming. Even if they've already bought a property, they worry that it's not the perfect one. The yield is too high — it won't last forever; the yield is too low — there must be something wrong. And when these 'what ifs' have been logically answered for people, they find a few more to worry about. What if there's too many investors? What if there's too few tenants? What if, what if ...?

More than fifty years ago, Norman Vincent Peale wrote about worry in his now famous book *The Power of Positive Thinking*. He said:

Worry is simply an unhealthy and destructive mental habit.

He had a simple strategy for overcoming the worry habit. He believed in conquering each worry one by one, and he likened it to cutting down a tree on his farm.

Men came with a motor-driven saw, and I expected them to start by cutting through the main trunk near the ground. Instead, they put up ladders and began snipping off the small branches, then the larger ones, and finally the top of the tree. Then all that remained was the huge central trunk, and in a few short moments, my tree lay neatly stacked, as though it had not spent fifty years in growing.

'If we had cut the tree down before trimming off the branches, it would have broken nearby trees in falling. It is easier to handle a tree the smaller you can make it,' so explained the tree man.

In this chapter, I'll go through some of the more common 'what ifs' one by one, step by step, so you can ease your worries by understanding that there are logical answers to most questions. Then you'll be able to concentrate on building more wealth through residential property.

What if the population declines?

Up to a point, capital growth depends on continued demand for land. In turn, this requires increasing numbers of people. In the past 100 years, Australia's population has increased from 3.4 million in 1901 to a present population of more than 19 million, a rate of 1.7% compound annually. If it continues to increase at the expected yearly rate of 1.5% (ABS: Cat. 3102), we will reach almost 24 million by the year 2021. Of more importance to property investors is the prediction by the ABS (Cat. 3236) that by then, the number of households will have increased by as much as 46%, much greater than the population growth of 24% over the same period. Clearly, demand for housing will continue to grow. Let me expand on this.

Calls have been made from several quarters to reduce immigration from overseas and so some property investors may start to worry, fearing a decline in the population, reduced housing needs, stagnant capital growth and falling rental yields. Now I don't want to get too deeply involved in a debate on the issue of immigration, but I can offer some food for thought to help you make up your own mind on the possibility of a declining population.

According to a report in *The Weekend Australian* (3-4 April, 1999) there is a 'need to bring in more productive workers' and also to resolve the problem of the 'youth bulges in African countries, Pakistan, Mexico and The Philippines'. The report states:

Both will challenge our current population and immigration policies.

Another factor is world-wide unrest that is seeing refugees on the move in ever rising numbers. Recent events have shown Australia to be a prime target, with thousands of boat people arriving on our shores. This was anticipated in an article in *The Courier Mail* in July, 1993. Considering how likely Australia was to receive enormous influxes of dispossessed people, the article explains:

The United Nations warned Australia to be prepared for a flood of refugees and migrants as the world population explodes. Population and environmental pressures would lead to unprecedented numbers seeking new homes and improved lifestyles in relatively wealthy countries.

On the home front, remembering Australia's ageing population, one solution is to encourage immigration of younger, able workers. Although controversial, Germany is already doing this to boost the tax base and Australia could well follow suit.

Aspects such as these support the figures projected for the continued growth of the population. Indeed, being realistic about it, we can virtually anticipate unprecedented demands on housing.

Chapter 22: Understanding the 'What Ifs' 223

What if there's too few tenants?

An important question for many property investors is whether there will be a continuing supply of tenants in the future to fill the investment properties they have bought. You would think, with the vision in front of them of what is happening to our ageing population, that surely more and more young people would get started in buying their own homes as soon as possible — particularly with interest rates the lowest they have been in 30 years. Not so, according to Dr Judith Yates, author of *Decomposing Australia's Home Ownership Trend, 1975-1994,* a report that delves deeply into the subject. Her study leaves little doubt that the Great Australian Dream is under threat.

While statistics from the ABS (Cat. 4130) indicate that home ownership has stayed relatively steady at around 70% over the last few decades, Yates found a disturbing trend within these superficially stable figures. Twenty years ago, 32% owned their homes outright and 38% had a loan and were in the process of buying. Today, 43% are outright owners with only 26% paying off a loan — a 12% decline in people buying their own home!

Yates also found that the trend was a direct result of more and more young people choosing to rent. In 1975, 58% of households under 35 had a mortgage, but by 1994, this had fallen to 43%. In other words, in years to come, with fewer home owners in the pipeline, the overall rate of home ownership will decline significantly, with an associated increase in tenants from 30% to 40%, according to Yates.

Many reasons have been suggested for this decline in home ownership, with delayed purchase and lack of affordability being the dominant ones. Let's look at these, because, if we understand why people are choosing to rent, we can allay our fears about a continuing supply of tenants.

Delayed purchase

There is a trend for people to stay in the education system longer, stay at home longer, marry later and have children later, all of which may delay home ownership. Also, with a decade of corporate downsizing and a trend to casual and contractual employment, lower job security could result in people holding off purchasing their own home until their employment prospects are more stable. Yet another factor may be that people prefer to rent while investing elsewhere, delaying the purchase of their own home until they have built up an asset base in a tax favoured investment.

However, while delaying the purchase of a home might impact on the figures in the short term, buying at a later date should not affect the trends long term. There must be other reasons why more and more people are choosing to rent, and being unable to afford to buy is an obvious one.

224 *More Wealth from Residential Property*

Affordability

A number of factors might result in people having less money to buy a home. For instance, disposable income is potentially reduced by payments for the Higher Education Contribution Scheme and wage rises could be slowed by the SGC. Even so, home ownership is at its most affordable in decades. Measured by expressing mortgage payments as a percentage of full-time adult earnings, home loan affordability indices have halved in most capital cities since 1990, as shown in the table below. (Note that a lower index equates to property being more affordable.)

Home Loan Affordability Indices

	Syd	Mel	Bri	Ade	Per	Hob	Can
1990	71.4	58.0	43.4	40.6	39.5	34.6	46.6
2000	38.3	30.9	19.9	17.1	20.3	15.7	21.6

Source: BIS Shrapnel Residential Property Prospects, 2000 to 2003

Why is the percentage of renters rising, then, if some people are simply delaying the purchase of their home and affordability is close to its best? I believe the biggest factor is lifestyle. My experience is that people increasingly want to rent quality accommodation that is much nicer than they could afford to buy; then they furnish it with items they can only afford on credit. Credit card debt in Australia has burgeoned to almost $20 billion. While some of this debt is the result of people making the most use of their interest free days, over half is the result of cards with 'no free days'. *The Australian Financial Review* (21 Nov, 2000) reported:

The no free day account was clearly being used as a personal lending product by card holders as distinct from a transactional payment device.

With the first home owner's grant in full swing, one might wonder how it might affect tenant numbers. While 147,000 couples have taken up the offer, this is only 7.5% above the underlying demand for new dwellings (BIS Shrapnel), so it is not likely to have a significant long term impact. Furthermore, anecdotal evidence from agents suggests that while many of these couples had been on good incomes for many years, they still had not saved any money — a recipe for poor spending patterns carrying over, with the potential for a spate of 'mortgagee in possessions', I was told.

There might be immediate social and economic benefits in renting, but the future holds little hope for tenants who favour short-term gratification over long-term financial security. Ironically, this trend can only be good for property investors. Badcock and Beer, authors of *Home Truths*, state:

A likely decline in the home ownership rate, together with downsizing of the public rental sector, will put increasing pressure on the private rental market.

What if there's too many investors?

Once people realise that property is a great investment, many fear that the word will spread and that too many investors will jump on the band wagon, decreasing the returns. This could not be further from the truth. There are many who want to invest in property but just can't get started. They attend every seminar and read all the books, and believe property to be the best investment — but they just can't take that first step. There are also those who start but never stay. They are always looking for greener grass, or simply don't follow the golden rules. Let's see why most people never start, while others never stay.

Some people never start

In his book *Riches from Real Estate* (1979), Fred Johnson made this observation about why people do not invest in property:

The answer is human nature: apathy — inertia — laziness — lack of time — lack of confidence in one's own ability to make decisions. 90% of the world's wealth is in the hands of 10% of the people — those 10% being the ones who overcome inertia or lack of confidence and go and do something about it. Of those who read this book, no more than 10% will take some positive step towards real estate profits after today. Not even 10% who are convinced will embark on some more profitable course of real estate investment in the future. That's just the nature of people and the reason why everybody isn't doing it.

Fred Johnson knew what he was talking about when he figured that only 10% of people would become involved in investment property. The ABS (Cat. 8711) found that only 6.5% of households invest in residential property, changing little from 6% in 1993 when interest rates were much higher. Why do so few people do it? I could fill another book, but some of the reasons given to me over the years are:

- *We don't seem to be able to find a good investment property.*
  (These people went to their first seminar four years earlier.)
- *My wife's father doesn't think it's a good idea to borrow money.*
  (The wife's father was on the pension.)
- *I'm waiting for my wife to go back to work so we'll have extra money.*
  (He was earning $65,000 per year.)

The most common reason why people never get started in investment property is 'I can't afford to', like the gentleman who was waiting for his wife to go back to work. But poor spending habits are so entrenched that they will *never* be able to afford to. *Income makes little difference to your ability to invest in property — it's what you do with what you earn that counts.*

226　*More Wealth from Residential Property*

Most people who *think* they can't afford to buy property, spend their money on 'living for today'. They are the 'better buyers' who think:

I can't be bothered cooking tonight — better buy take-away.	$31
We've got friends coming — better buy some new towels.	$52
I'm going to a disco tonight — better buy some new shoes.	$77
I've just joined the tennis club — better buy a new tracksuit.	$170

The odd take-away or new tracksuit won't send you bankrupt. But this kind of thinking then extends to big ticket items, and before you know it, you've taken out a personal loan to buy a leather lounge, a new kitchen, a boat or a four wheel drive. The table below reveals what it would cost to buy these items with a personal loan at 12% over 5 years.

The Cost of Buying Consumables on Credit

Consumables bought on credit	Value	Weekly cost
New leather lounge	$6,000	$31
New kitchen	$10,000	$52
New boat	$14,000	$77
New four wheel drive	$33,000	$170

Most people live for today, believing they can not afford an investment property. I have heard many a person say they think that the real estate salesman is 'pulling their leg' when he tells them how little it really costs to buy a rental property. But the table below (for an investor on $47,000 per year) graphically confirms that this is true.

The Cost of Borrowing to Buy an Investment Property

Property bought with loan	Value	Weekly cost
Small two-bedroom unit	$120,000	$31
Average three-bedroom house	$160,000	$52
Large four-bedroom house	$200,000	$77
Three average three-bedroom houses	$480,000	$170

This table is not a guide to the cost of particular properties. The aim is to show you that the weekly cost of borrowing to buy a small unit can be no more than the weekly cost of a leather lounge — $31; and the weekly cost of a large house can be the same as a new boat — $77. (See page 69 to recall why a property can cost an investor so little). Even if you have paid off the boat, or whatever, after five years, it is probably worth much less than what you paid for it. While the equity you would have if you had borrowed to buy an investment property would put you well on your way to an early, wealthy retirement.

Some people never stay

In spite of getting started on buying investment property, many, sadly, do not see it through. We have already seen on page 107 that while 79.8% of people buy property with the intention of keeping it for the long term, about 50% either sold, or intended selling within a seven year period. So you see, many people do not understand the principle of 'buy and keep' property for the long term. How long is long? I believe a minimum of 10 years and preferably longer — at least until retirement.

Furthermore, among those who do keep their first investment property, very few go on to buy more, as this table confirms.

Number of Investment Properties Owned

Rental properties	% of People
1	5.0%
2	1.0%
3 or more	0.5%
TOTAL	**6.5%**

Source: ABS Cat. 8711

Of the 6.5% who own investment property, 5.0% own just one, 1.0% own two, and only 0.5% own three or more. Perhaps those with a single property are not committed, but 'accidental' investors, with no intention of buying more. The ABS reported that 25.6% of 'one only' investors were renting out their previous home, while 3.8% had inherited it. So almost a third had acquired their investment property through circumstances other than a carefully planned strategy. There's nothing wrong in starting out this way, as I know from experience — after an 'accidental' start we rented out three homes before moving on and buying again. But you need to keep the momentum going and buy more and more afterwards.

Further investment in residential property is a commitment requiring financial discipline, something that many people don't have. Lack of discipline and commitment are two of the reasons why most people fail at anything they attempt, whether it be for their wealth or their health. I have already pointed out that only 4.7% of couples retire on $50,000 per year or more. Rosemary Stanton in her book *The Diet Dilemma* suggests that only 1% of people succeed in dieting. And KRS Edstrom in *Healthy, Wealthy, and Wise* said of people on diets:

... only 1 in 200 will keep the weight off for more than five years.

No matter what aspect of life we refer to, only a small percentage of people have the patience and discipline to be successful. So the next time you worry if there are too many investors, try to remember just how few will ever last the distance, despite my efforts to convince them otherwise.

What if negative gearing dies?

It has been said many times before, but it is worth repeating here. Two things in life are inevitable: the first is that one day you will die, and the second is that you will continue to pay taxes until you die. Not many people enjoy paying taxes, probably because they don't think they get value for money. Certainly no one likes paying too much tax. Some people will go to extremes to pay the absolute minimum in tax; and towards the end of every financial year, we see the promotion of various tax advantaged investment products, some of which are little more than a scam. With this kind of attitude towards tax prevalent amongst investors, it is not surprising to find that many see the negative gearing tax concessions as the sole reason for investing in property, as events of the mid 1980s proved.

In 1985, the then Labor Government abolished the right to offset the interest on money borrowed for investment against other income. (All other expenses were still deductible, and losses could be carried forward to when the property was cash positive.) It was seen as a way of getting rid of property *speculators* and in doing so, saving the government money by reducing the size of the tax refund owing to property *investors*.

At the time, the government must have been aware that it needed to offer an alternative incentive to investors so that they would continue to invest. So they simultaneously introduced a capital allowance, or building depreciation, of 4% on the construction cost of new buildings, which could be directly offset against income. By encouraging investors to buy new properties, the building depreciation had the potential to also stimulate the housing industry. The policy planners, however, had completely misread the psychology of the investor. Despite the seemingly attractive 4% depreciation on new buildings, investors shied away from buying property.

Unfortunately for the government, the people most affected by these tax changes were not investors, but tenants. The lack of property investors caused a shortage of rental properties and rents skyrocketed. In some of the capital cities, rents almost doubled and the tenant backlash was much greater than any analysts had anticipated.

In New South Wales alone, the number of people on the waiting list for public housing increased by almost 40% between 1985 and 1987. Suddenly the government became acutely aware that taxation benefits may play an extremely important role in assisting with the provision of housing to a large section of the population. It turns out that giving tax incentives to investors to buy investment properties is a cheaper way for governments to house the disadvantaged in our society.

So great was the effect on tenants that the legislation was reversed two years later, in 1987, with full deductibility restored to investors. The government's stated reasons for this about face were that the Capital Gains Tax (CGT) was now acting as a sufficient deterrent to property speculators and that the cost of giving tax refunds to negatively geared investors would be offset by the CGT. With the negative gearing deduction reinstated, investors were once again lured into property investment. The chart below graphically shows the rise and fall in the number of people on the public housing waiting list in New South Wales, with the time of increase and decrease in numbers clearly coinciding with the abolition and reintroduction of negative gearing.

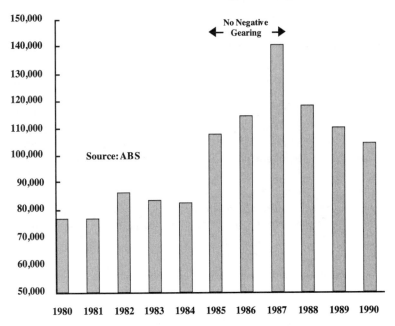

Additions to Public Housing Waiting List in NSW

An overseas comparison helps illuminate the role of negative gearing. Most Western countries subsidise the costs of housing people who are socially disadvantaged. They do it either by direct rental assistance, or by providing government owned housing, or by subsidising the purchase of property, or by giving tax incentives to the private sector. Most European countries, particularly the socialist ones, fund their public housing directly, rather than relying on tax incentives to the private sector. Consequently, more than 20% of their populations rely on government owned and rented accommodation.

230   More Wealth from Residential Property

Now consider Australia. Here, about 30% of the population rent and the government assistance comes mostly in the form of tax incentives to the private sector. Less than 8% of the population rely on public housing, while the remaining 22% rent privately. Australia has a great need for rental accommodation, but it would require huge capital outlays, money that governments do not have, to reverse the method of subsidy. The legislators have apparently rationalised that it is cheaper and more effective to subsidise the private sector to provide rental housing.

Now you know the rationale for having and retaining the negative gearing laws. Would any government try to repeal them again? Both major political parties have stated that they are 'committed to the retention of negative gearing in its present form'. Yet the promises of politicians are often victims of political expediency. Let's consider what *could* happen if the right to claim losses from rental properties against other income were withdrawn. In other words, suppose that tax refunds from investment properties were non-existent as of now. What would you do?

If you were to do like most investors did between 1985 and 87, you'd most likely look around for some non-property investment that offered more attractive tax advantages. Perhaps films? And do you know what would happen then? Just as in the 80s, there would probably be a rental property shortage followed by massive hikes in rent due to the changing supply and demand ratio created by more tenants chasing fewer properties. (After negative gearing was abolished in 1985, rental yields were very high, averaging 12% in Sydney.)

If we analysed this situation, you would see the folly of believing that tax deductibility of interest is the cornerstone of property investment. The overall long-term rate of return from investment property may not be significantly affected because the loss of tax benefits would probably be compensated for by the increase in rental yields.

One further point needs mentioning. In the event that any government tampered with the negative gearing laws, they would be highly unlikely to be made retrospective (the laws were not made retrospective in 1985). So anyone who already owned negatively geared property would still be able to continue with their existing claims.

If negative gearing were to be abolished today, it would make little difference to our own investment strategy of buying investment properties. Between 1985 and 1987, when this scenario last occurred, we continued to borrow to buy property as though nothing had happened, with the added advantage that the properties were mostly positively geared, as rents were significantly higher than the interest.

Chapter 22: Understanding the 'What Ifs' 231

What if the inflation rate changes?

Inflation rates have plummeted since the early 1990s, with politicians hailing this as an economic saviour. But not everyone thinks it's the best thing since sliced bread. One dismayed group is the retirees who were receiving significant incomes from high interest on bank deposits in the late 80s, but who now have now seen their incomes significantly reduced with inflation induced low interest rates.

Another group are those property investors who believe high inflation, and therefore high capital growth, is the 'be all and end all' of property investment. Their shaky confidence would not have been helped by the financial commentators who saw the lower inflation rates of the 90s as an obituary for property investors. Headlines appeared along the lines:

Low inflation removes much of the cream from property investing!

Negative gearing is dead!

Property investors have been murdered!

Influenced by the upward spiral in property values, particularly during the latter half of the 1980s, these commentators created their own fuzzy logic about the relationship between inflation, capital growth, interest rates and property investment. It was based on the following assumptions.

The fuzzy logic of how inflation affects capital growth

High inflation=   High capital growth   = Good for property

Low Inflation =   Low capital growth   = Bad for property

This fuzzy logic was carried over to negative gearing, with a new set of assumptions.

The fuzzy logic of how inflation affects negative gearing

High inflation= High interest =High tax refund =   -ve gearing is great

Low inflation = Low interest =Low tax refund =   -ve gearing is dead

Although the commentators were certainly correct in concluding that lower inflation would undoubtedly lead to lower capital growth and lower tax refunds, a more thorough analysis shows that low inflation does *not* kill property as an investment, and that negative gearing is *not* dead. In fact, as I will show in depth, the long-term returns from property are excellent over the entire range of inflation rates that Australia has experienced.

Before we begin this analysis, we need to look at the nature of the relationship between inflation, capital growth, and interest rates so we can then make some meaningful comparisons.

232　*More Wealth from Residential Property*

Links between inflation, growth and interest

Is it possible to have low inflation yet high capital growth? Or high interest rates with low inflation? What about high capital growth with low interest rates? To gain a better insight into these relationships, let's look at each of the past four decades, since they have provided a wide range of economic conditions.

Property in the 60s, 70s, 80s and 90s

What exactly did happen to residential property over the past forty years? Everyone old enough remembers the boom times for growth in the late eighties. Some may not be old enough to remember the rampant inflation of the Whitlam era in the early seventies. Even fewer will remember the sixties with their very low interest rates. Let's take a closer look at capital growth, inflation and interest rates over those decades.

Comparing the Past Four Decades

	1960s	1970s	1980s	1990s
Inflation (CPI)	3.0%	11.0%	8.0%	2.1%
Capital growth	6.5%	14.5%	11.5%	4.7%
Interest rate	4.5%	7.5%	13.5%	8.5%

Sources: Reserve Bank, ABS, BIS Shrapnel, and REIA

In the 1960s, average inflation was 3%, while growth was 6.5% and interest rates were between the two at 4.5%. The 70s saw much higher inflation at 11% but, again, it was exceeded by capital growth at 14.5%. Ironically, interest rates did not keep pace with inflation and were low at 7.5%. The 60s and 70s produced a unique opportunity for investors. In those decades, with interest rates lower than capital growth, you could borrow to buy property and literally make money out of thin air, without even bothering to rent out the place. What was the catch? Money was not easy to borrow back then, but if you could, the sky was the limit.

The story was very different by the 80s. Capital growth of 11.5% still exceeded inflation at 8%, but interest rates of 13.5% were now higher than both. Why so high? Following deregulation of the financial markets in 1983, money became more freely available — but at a cost of higher real interest rates (relative to inflation).

The 90s saw a return to low inflation at 2.1%, but capital growth at a seemingly low 4.7% continued to exceed it, with interest rates at 8.5%. For the many investors and commentators who witnessed high growth in the 70s and 80s, the idea that property as an investment in the 90s could be just as good may come as somewhat of a shock.

Chapter 22: Understanding the 'What Ifs' 233

Looking back over the past four decades, several obvious similarities appear but also some glaring differences. The common thread was the fact that capital growth consistently exceeded inflation by several per cent in the major capital cities. This difference can be attributed to factors other than inflation that also cause property to increase in value, namely scarcity and improvements (such as rezoning or renovations), as discussed earlier.

So what can we learn from the past? Is there a link between inflation, interest rates and capital growth and, if so, what is it? I'll try to describe this connection so that we can look at what might happen to property investment under changing inflationary conditions.

While interest rates were lower than capital growth during the 60s and 70s, to undertake a conservative analysis in a far less regulated financial environment such as exists today, the combination of inflation, interest rates and capital growth, would show the relationship to be:

Interest rates > capital growth > inflation

Using this worst-case scenario let's select a broad range of inflation rates (2%, 5%, 8% and 11%), and their respective combinations of capital growth and interest rates, so that we can then analyse investment property under different inflationary regimes. These combinations are as follows:

Selected Combinations of Inflation, Capital Growth, and Interest Rates

Inflation	2.0%	5.0%	8.0%	11.0%
Capital growth	4.5%	7.5%	11.5%	14.5%
Interest rate	8.5%	10.0%	12.5%	15.0%

Many readers who have been unduly influenced by the media may have difficulty accepting my contention that investing in property is still great, even with low inflation. Consequently, I have been very conservative in constructing this set of combinations. For lower inflation, I have set the difference between inflation and capital growth at 2.5% compared to 3.5% for the higher rates. Also, I have recognised that with low inflation, banks increase their margin (the difference between inflation and interest rates), because of what they term 'market tolerance' — you are more likely to accept an interest rate of 8.5% when inflation is 2% (a margin of 6.5%) compared to 15% when inflation is 11% (a margin of 4%).

Using the above set of rates, we are now in a position to compare the rates of returns from property investment across the spectrum of low to high inflation. To simplify the process, I have used the PIA computer program described in Appendix B to produce a spreadsheet for each of the four combinations listed, and these are shown on the next two pages. Each spreadsheet is for our example $160,000 property as described on page 127.

234 *More Wealth from Residential Property*

Computer Projections at 2% Inflation

Year	Initial	1yr	2yr	3yr	5yr	10yr
Property value	$160,000	167,200	174,724	182,587	199,389	248,475
Purchase costs	$4,500					
Outlays	$0					
Loan amount	$166,000	166,000	166,000	166,000	166,000	166,000
Equity	($6,000)	1,200	8,724	16,587	33,389	**$82,475**
Capital growth rate	4.50%	4.50%	4.50%	4.50%	4.50%	4.50%
Inflation rate (CPI)	2.00%	2.00%	2.00%	2.00%	2.00%	2.00%
Gross rent /year	$10,400	10,400	10,608	10,820	11,257	12,429
Cash deductions						
Interest (I/O)	8.5%	14,110	14,110	14,110	14,110	14,110
Property expenses	25.00%	2,600	2,652	2,705	2,814	3,107
Pre-tax cash flow	$0	-6,310	-6,154	-5,995	-5,667	-4,778
Non-cash deductions						
Deprec.-building	2.50%	2,000	2,000	2,000	2,000	2,000
Deprec.-fittings	$15,000	2,700	4,039	2,610	1,128	189
Loan costs	$1,500	500	500	500		
Total deductions	$0	21,910	23,301	21,925	20,052	19,407
Tax credit (single)	$47,000	3,626	3,998	3,540	3,242	3,238
After-tax cash flow	$0	-2,684	-2,156	-2,455	-2,425	-1,550
Rate of return (IRR)	23.15%		**Weekly cash flows**			
Real rate of return	**20.73%**	**-$52**	**-$41**	**-$47**	**-$47**	**-$30**

Computer Projections at 5% Inflation

Year	Initial	1yr	2yr	3yr	5yr	10yr
Property value	$160,000	172,000	184,900	198,768	229,701	329,765
Purchase costs	$4,500					
Outlays	$0					
Loan amount	$166,000	166,000	166,000	166,000	166,000	166,000
Equity	($6,000)	6,000	18,900	32,768	63,701	**$163,765**
Capital growth rate	7.50%	7.50%	7.50%	7.50%	7.50%	7.50%
Inflation rate (CPI)	5.00%	5.00%	5.00%	5.00%	5.00%	5.00%
Gross rent /year	$10,400					
Cash deductions						
Interest (I/O)	10.00%	16,600	16,600	16,600	16,600	16,600
Property expenses	25.00%	2,600	2,730	2,867	3,160	4,033
Pre-tax cash flow	$0	-8,800	-8,410	-8,001	-7,119	-4,500
Non-cash deductions						
Deprec.-building	2.50%	2,000	2,000	2,000	2,000	2,000
Deprec.-fittings	$15,000	2,700	4,039	2,610	1,128	189
Loan costs	$1,500	500	500	500		
Total deductions	$0	24,400	25,869	24,577	22,888	22,823
Tax credit (single)	$47,000	4,410	4,716	4,527	4,480	3,244
After-tax cash flow	$0	-4,390	-3,694	-3,474	-2,639	-1,256
Rate of return (IRR)	29.20%		**Weekly cash flows**			
Real rate of return	**23.05%**	**-$84**	**-$71**	**-$67**	**-$51**	**-$24**

Chapter 22: Understanding the 'What Ifs' 235

Computer Projections at 8% Inflation

Year	Initial	1yr	2yr	3yr	5yr	10yr
Property value	$160,000	178,400	198,916	221,791	275,737	475,191
Purchase costs	$4,500					
Outlays	$0					
Loan amount	$166,000	166,000	166,000	166,000	166,000	166,000
Equity	($6,000)	12,400	32,916	55,791	109,737	**$309,191**
Capital growth rate	11.50%	11.50%	11.50%	11.50%	11.50%	11.50%
Inflation rate (CPI)	8.00%	8.00%	8.00%	8.00%	8.00%	8.00%
Gross rent /year	$10,400	10,400	11,232	12,131	14,149	20,790
Cash deductions						
Interest (I/O)	12.50%	20,750	20,750	20,750	20,750	20,750
Property expenses	25.00%	2,600	2,808	3,033	3,537	5,197
Pre-tax cash flow	$0	-12,950	-12,326	-11,652	-10,138	-5,158
Non-cash deductions						
Deprec.-building	2.50%	2,000	2,000	2,000	2,000	2,000
Deprec.-fittings	$15,000	2,700	4,039	2,610	1,128	189
Loan costs	$1,500	500	500	500		
Total deductions	$0	28,550	30,097	28,893	27,415	28,137
Tax credit (single)	$47,000	5,717	6,118	6,043	6,149	3,563
After-tax cash flow	$0	-7,233	-6,208	-5,609	-3,989	-1,595
Rate of return (IRR)	31.86%		**Weekly cash flows**			
Real rate of return	**22.10%**	**-$139**	**-$119**	**-$108**	**-$77**	**-$31**

Computer Projections at 11% Inflation

Year	Initial	1yr	2yr	3yr	5yr	10yr
Property value	$160,000	183,200	209,764	240,180	314,882	619,691
Purchase costs	$4,500					
Outlays	$0					
Loan amount	$166,000	166,000	166,000	166,000	166,000	166,000
Equity	($6,000)	17,200	43,764	74,180	148,882	**$453,691**
Capital growth rate	14.50%	14.50%	14.50%	14.50%	14.50%	14.50%
Inflation rate (CPI)	11.00%	11.00%	11.00%	11.00%	11.00%	11.00%
Gross rent /year	$10,400	10,400	11,544	12,814	15,788	26,604
Cash deductions	3.50%	67,000	69,345	71,772	74,284	76,884
Interest (I/O)	15.00%	24,900	24,900	24,900	24,900	24,900
Property expenses	25.00%	2,600	2,886	3,203	3,947	6,651
Pre-tax cash flow	$0	-17,100	-16,242	-15,290	-13,059	-4,947
Non-cash deductions		3,785	2,901	3,432	3,365	4,466
Deprec.-building	2.50%	2,000	2,000	2,000	2,000	2,000
Deprec.-fittings	$15,000	2,700	4,039	2,610	1,128	189
Loan costs	$1,500	500	500	500		
Total deductions	$0	32,700	34,325	33,214	31,975	33,740
Tax credit (single)	$47,000	7,024	7,521	7,564	7,805	3,461
After-tax cash flow	$0	-10,076	-8,721	-7,726	-5,254	-1,486
Rate of return (IRR)	33.03%		**Weekly cash flows**			
Real rate of return	**19.85%**	**-$194**	**-$168**	**-$149**	**-$101**	**-$29**

236 *More Wealth from Residential Property*

Effect of inflation on returns

How do the different inflation rates, and their associated capital growth rates and interest rates, affect the returns on your investment dollar? To understand how rates of return are calculated, you might need to read pages 251 to 253 in Appendix C. Essentially, though, the return is calculated by relating the bottom line, which is your investment, or after-tax cash flow, to the end result or equity after any given period of time — in this case 10 years. The table below summarises these results taken from the spreadsheets on the previous pages.

Effect of Inflation on Rate of Return (IRR)

Inflation	2.0%	5.0%	8.0%	11.0%
Capital growth	4.5%	7.5%	11.5%	14.5%
Interest rate	8.5%	10.0%	12.5%	15.0%
Cost/wk in 1st yr	$52	$84	$139	$194
Equity after 10yrs	$82,475	$163,765	$309,191	$453,691
Return (IRR)	23.15%	29.20%	31.86%	33.03%

We'll look at these results first on an 'in-out' basis. When inflation is high (11%), interest rates are high (15%) and the after-tax cost is also high ($194 per week in the first year). Correspondingly, the equity built up over 10 years is high at $453,691. When inflation is low (2%), interest rates are low (8.5%), the after-tax cost is low ($52 per week in the first year), and likewise the equity after 10 years is low at $82,475. Can you see that as both inflation and interest rates fall, so does the cost per week?

It is a mistake to appraise the performance of property during high and low inflation by simply looking at the end result. It's easy for anyone to see that during high inflation and high capital growth, the equity achieved is greater than during low inflation and low capital growth. This is just stating the obvious. A true property investment analysis must also take into account the amount invested — and this is not easy to calculate by hand, or with a calculator, as it involves a myriad of factors, such as tax benefits and the investors' personal income. However, the PIA computer program does make it quick and easy.

With low inflation of 2%, the rate of return is 23.15% per annum compound; while at the other end of the scale, with high inflation, the rate of return is 33.03%. Compared to alternative investments, these returns are great! But does this mean that property investment is a very good investment in low inflation and an even better one in high inflation? I'll go one step further. Let's look at the *real after-inflation* rate of return.

Real effect of inflation

Don't forget this: at the same time as you are making a good return on your investment, inflation is affecting what your money can buy. So, to compare different inflationary eras, we should convert the rates of return to *after-inflation* rates of return. The table below gives you the *real* rates of return, taking the inflation rate into account.

Effect of Inflation on Real Rate of Return (IRR after Inflation)

Inflation	2.0%	5.0%	8.0%	11.0%
Capital growth	4.5%	7.5%	11.5%	14.5%
Interest rate	8.5%	10.0%	12.5%	15.0%
Rate of return (IRR)	23.15%	29.20%	31.86%	33.03%
Real rate of return (After inflation)	20.73%	23.05%	22.10%	19.85%

Note: The real return after inflation can not be found by subtracting the inflation rate from the IRR. For those interested in technicalities, the formula is this: [(100% + IRR)/(100%+Inflation)] - 100%. Otherwise, suffice to say there is a small variation because the base money has grown by the inflation rate and the return must be divided by the new dollar value.

There are several points to note here. First, if you look solely at the IRR, it appears as though there is a better return from investment property during times of high inflation. With high inflation, the return is 33.03%; however if we reduce this return by inflation of 11%, we have a real return of 19.85%.

On the other hand, when inflation is low at 2%, the return is 23.15%, and if we reduce this by the inflation rate, we have a real return of 20.73%! Without this mathematical explanation, intuitively you should realise that in times of high inflation, you really *need* to get better returns in order to compensate for the devaluing of the dollar, compared to times of very low inflation, where you can tolerate lower returns because the dollar is not devaluing as quickly.

From these analyses, you should be appreciating why the effect of inflation on property investment must be looked at in conjunction with the related factors of capital growth and interest rates. And while there is a link between these economic factors, I don't believe that low inflation, or high inflation or anything in between, makes much difference to the rates of return on investment property, as judged by the IRR.

238　*More Wealth from Residential Property*

More what ifs ...

There are thousands of 'what ifs' that investors worry about. Here are just a few more that come to mind:

What if I have to lower the rent to get a tenant?
I believe that 80% of something is better than 100% of nothing, and besides, the 'loss' is tax deductible, so a $20 reduction may only be a $12 drop in after-tax income!

What if I buy a unit instead of a house?
In general, capital growth of units is lower, while the yield is higher, primarily because of the smaller land content. However, we have both and consider them to be just different, with one not better than the other. It really depends on what tenants are looking for in that area.

What if there's a rental guarantee for two years?
Some guarantees are fine and it may be the developer's way of showing confidence in their product. Just make sure it's not built into the price!

What if the property drops in value after two years?
Property values do not rise continuously in a straight line, but are more likely to stagnate in some years and boom in others. Compared to shares, it's highly unlikely you'll be left with a worthless investment. Don't be dismayed, though, if a valuer thinks your property is worth less than you paid for it. This is common, as valuers have everything to gain and nothing to lose by undervaluing. (See pp. 156 and 165)

What if capital growth is low relative to inflation?
The overall returns should take into account growth *and* yield. Lower growth is usually accompanied by a higher yield; do your own sums.

What if I lose my job?
Having cash reserves or credit lines set up in advance is usually all that is necessary to carry people over for the few months that they need to find another job. But at least property, unlike superannuation, is a redeemable asset that you can sell should you have to.

What if I miss out on a bargain?
It's my view that the 'once in a lifetime' bargain comes along once a month, but also remember the real cost of chasing a deal. If you invest for the long term, paying 'fair market value' is all that is needed.

What if the mortgage company goes bust?
You have their money so you can not lose it in the same way as if the company has yours. The title of the property is in your name and the mortgagee has no right of claim to your property, unless you default. Usually another company takes over the defunct lender, or you may have the slight inconvenience and expense of refinancing elsewhere.

Chapter 22: Understanding the 'What Ifs' 239

What if I earn less than $20,000 per year?
The ABS statistics show that low-income earners can and do borrow to buy investment properties. People on higher incomes usually don't have any more spare money. Their living expenses simply have another zero or two tacked on the end!

What if a flat rate of tax is introduced?
All things being relative, all tax effective investments will be similarly affected. Remember too, that tax benefits are a bonus, not a necessity.

What if I buy a holiday unit?
Is it for investment or lifestyle? If purely for investment, the returns can be as good as permanent lettings. Rents will be higher but so too will the cleaning and management costs, and the time it is vacant.

What if I mortgage the family home?
Without trying to frighten you, there's a risk that you could lose your family home even if it's *not* mortgaged, by creditors forcing you to sell. However, I believe doing nothing represents the greatest risk to your long-term financial security.

What if we move upmarket and rent out our original home?
Technically, if you borrow against your 'old home' to buy your 'new home', the debt is non-deductible as the purpose of the loan is to buy your principal place of residence, not a rental property.

What if I buy a property in partnership with a friend?
Usually, this is one sure recipe for losing a friend. If the investment is worthwhile, do it yourself, as the after-tax cost should be affordable. Different people will have different ideas on investments. However, if it is the only way that you can afford to buy investment property, have a go, but beware of the pitfalls.

What if interest rates rise?
I recommend fixed-interest loans for at least two thirds of the total debt. If rates rise, you are insulated; on the other hand, if rates fall, you should still be smiling as you won't be out of pocket. I see this extra amount that you may have had to pay as insurance against rising rates.

What if I don't like real estate?
Real estate is only the vehicle for building wealth — a means to an end, not the end itself, so you don't have to love it. The great thing about property investment is that you can do as little or as much as you like. You can do the maintenance and bookwork, or you can get someone to do it for you. The returns from property can be so great that you can afford to pay to have things done that you either don't like doing, or don't have time for — they're tax deductible anyway. As Ian says:
Life's too short to drink cheap beer or paint rental properties!

240   *More Wealth from Residential Property*

One more what if

Most 'what ifs' have logical answers. This chapter has covered a few of the more common ones. An earlier book, *Building Wealth in Changing Times,* contains detailed answers to many more; the Property Investment Analysis (PIA) computer program enables investors to answer their own 'what ifs', simply by inserting figures into an easy-to-use spreadsheet; and at the end of my seminars, people have the opportunity to hear my answers to more 'what ifs'. So there are umpteen ways and opportunities to answer all the 'what ifs' that worry people. However, perhaps the most important 'what if' that only *you* can answer is:

What if you don't?

What lies in store for you when you retire if you don't start a wealth building plan today? Let's revise some of the alternatives so you can see that the answer to 'What if you don't?' is not a pleasant one.

If you do nothing, you run the risk that there'll be no pension when you retire. And with an ageing population, it will *not* be economically possible to extract enough in taxes from a dwindling workforce to pay for even a basic age pension — let alone one that you would like.

Ah! You say. What about the Superannuation Guarantee Charge; isn't the government making sure I'll be OK? The government is just making sure it doesn't need to pay *you* the pension. The reality is that the money generated by the SGC will be totally inadequate, and at best will provide an income equivalent to the age pension, except that you will have paid for it.

What if you just top up your super? With the introduction of the Superannuation Surcharge, the government has made it clear that it will provide tax concessions to allow you to save for your own pension — but no more. And without the ability to borrow and leverage your money, superannuation will never make you wealthy — unless, of course, you're a politician whose super is subsidised almost 70% by the public purse!

What if you pay someone else to do it all for you by investing in a managed fund? I suppose it will be better than doing nothing, but your returns will be significantly reduced by the fees you pay. You could invest in shares, but their volatility increases the risk and decreases your capacity to borrow, curtailing your wealth building strategy.

Ultimately, I believe that the best way for the average person to build wealth is through residential property. Do you fancy being one of the 95.3% of couples who never achieve the income they want in retirement? Or will you be one of the 4.7% who retire with more that $50,000 a year?

Appendix A: Returns from Shares and Property

This appendix provides a detailed comparison of the investment returns from shares and residential property between 1980 and 2000. The study is presented in summary form in Chapter 7 (pp. 64-65) where it compares shares and residential property as potential investment vehicles.

Investment returns can be measured and reported using various indices (eg growth, yield, internal rate of return and net present value) and time frames, so it is important that any objective comparison incorporate and explain as many measures as possible. In this analysis, I will not only present the various measures of return but also follow the results of two separate investment scenarios for a fictitious couple called Tom and Jenny, so that you can relate to the figures more easily. In the first investment scenario the couple embark on a mission to invest as much money as they can afford into shares, while in the second scenario, they do precisely the same but with residential investment properties. I will use the Property Investment Analysis (PIA) software (described in Appendix B) to carry out these two simulations, and the parameters used will be derived from the statistical history of the two asset classes in Australia over the 20 year period between 1980 and 2000.

Shares

The most quoted index for Australian shares is the All Ordinaries (All Ords). Most people would be familiar with the All Ords Index as changes to it are reported daily as part of most evening news bulletins. While I will use the annual changes in the All Ords Index as the measure of capital growth in shares, it is important to remember that capital growth is only one aspect of investment return. We must also consider things such as dividend yields and the costs associated with this form of investment. As you will see, it is also important to understand what the All Ords actually measures and how it is derived.

In compiling this analysis, the Australian Stock Exchange (ASX) was most cooperative in providing a detailed history of the All Ordinaries Index, the Gross Dividend Yields, the All Ordinaries Accumulation Index (a combination of the previous two), and of all of the companies that have been part of theses indices over the years. Information was also obtained from *The 1999 ASX Delisted Companies Book 1929 to 1999*.

Based on the All Ords Index, the average annual capital growth of shares between 1980 to 2000 measured **8.7%**. However, using the All Ordinaries Accumulation Index, which also takes account of the dividend yield (**4.5%**), the gross return measured **13.2%**.

242   *More Wealth from Residential Property*

However, before we can compare these returns to those from property, we must understand what it is that is being measured. In fact, the All Ords is not representative of all shares bought and sold, but rather a select group of larger, supposedly more stable companies — those with at least 0.02% of market capitalisation and 50% turnover. In 1980, only 265 of the 1,029 companies listed on the stock exchange were in the All Ords.

You might think: If I invested only in companies in the All Ords in 1980, for the next 20 years I should get the same returns. Wrong! Of the 265 companies in the All Ords in 1980 only 124 remained in 1990, and by 2000, there were only 109 left, allowing for mergers, acquisitions, name changes and takeovers. The other 156 companies either dropped out of the All Ords or were removed from the ASX altogether through privatisation, off-shore acquisition, or just plain failure. So which companies would you have invested in? The ones in the All Ords today or yesterday?

How can we overcome these inconsistencies? Easy, you say. If the composition of the All Ords is unstable, I could just invest in the top 10 blue chip companies and I couldn't miss. Wrong again! Of the top 10 companies in 1980 only six remained in 1990, and by 2000 only two were left — BHP (Broken Hill) and WMC (Western Mining Corporation).

Surely there must be a way of maintaining a share portfolio that will produce results similar to the All Ords. According to Prof. Terry Walter from the Faculty of Economics at the University of Sydney, to mimic the returns of the All Ords Index you need to invest in 10 to 30 different shares from the All Ords, then buy and sell daily to rebalance your portfolio (pers. com. Mar, 2001). But this can cost up to 3% of the gross returns due to transaction fees, *not* including CGT! For an investor, there is also an opportunity cost in the considerable amount of time needed to do this.

One way of cutting transaction costs is to invest in a managed indexed equity fund where the economies of scale might help — but then there are management fees. According to the Australian Shareholders Association (*www.asa.asn.au*), the average Management Expense Ratio (MER) for managed equities is 1.8% annually. However, this does not include entry fees, which can be as high as 4% of your investment, nor Capital Gains Tax (CGT). Furthermore, with so many transactions, the investor would probably be treated by the ATO as a trader whose profits would be taxed at their full marginal rate with no CGT concessions available.

Whether you try to mimic the All Ords as an individual investor, or through a managed fund, the costs of maintaining your share portfolio are large. Nevertheless, for the purposes of this study, I have conservatively discounted the gross return by *just* 1.7% to allow for these costs, reducing the **net return for shares** from 13.2% to **11.5%**.

Property

There is no equivalent measure to the All Ords for residential property in Australia but the most commonly used and relevant index is that of median price, though these data are available for individual cities only. The Real Estate Institute of Australia (REIA) maintains a comprehensive database of median house prices and median rents for all Australian capital cities, from which I have drawn. My analysis of the REIA data was helped enormously by the efforts of Professor Graeme Newell from the University of Western Sydney, who has compiled a quarterly Residential Investment Property Index (RIPI) for the REIA since 1982 for all capital cities.

The RIPI index incorporates capital growth of median-priced property together with *net* yields. While the RIPI index is an appropriate index in its own right for measuring *net* returns, we must go back to the original data from which it is derived to obtain a true comparison with the *gross* returns from shares. To ensure a complete data set from 1980 to 2000, I have also used supplementary information on rents from the research firm BIS Shrapnel (*Residential Property Prospects*).

Based on the annual changes in median house prices and rents over the period from 1980 to 2000, the average annual gross return from residential property (growth plus yield) for each of the capital cities ranged between 15.0% and 17.1%. The most striking aspect about these gross returns is their remarkable uniformity across the major capital cities. Residex, a company that has received international recognition for its research into residential property markets, calculated average gross returns of about 15% in Sydney going back to 1901 (*Past Returns from the Sydney Housing Market, 1992*). They found that during times when capital growth was high, rental yields were low and vice versa.

While Hobart, with gross returns of 15.8%, falls within the same range as other capital cities, I have excluded it from further analysis because its capital growth (5.7%) and rental yield (10.1%) are outside the range of the other six cities. Hobart-type parameters have been dealt with previously in Chapter 9 in a revealing study of the growth and yield connection. Thus, for comparison with shares and for use in our property investment simulation, I will adopt the six-city average **gross return of 15.6%**, representing an average **capital growth of 7.8%** and a **gross rental yield of 7.8%**.

In contrast to shares, where one must incur ongoing transactional costs to mimic the All Ords Index, the property indices encompass *all* properties bought and sold. For property, however, we must take into account the ongoing rental expenses and we will use the net rental yield in the same way as Professor. Newell.

244   *More Wealth from Residential Property*

Residential rental expenses can vary enormously from 10% to 30% of gross rents, depending on the style and age of the property. However, to be consistent with Professor Newell's RIPI index, I have used a figure of 20% of rental income to represent rental expenses, which means that a gross rental yield of 7.8% is equivalent to a **net rental yield of 6.2%**. Thus our **estimated net return from residential property** drops from 15.6% to **14.0%**. Here is a summary of the gross and net returns from shares and residential property over the 20 year period.

Returns of Residential Property and Shares (1980-2000)

	Syd	Mel	Bri	Ade	Per	Can	*6-City*	*Shares*
Cap growth	7.8	9.2	8.3	6.7	7.0	7.5	7.8%	8.7%
Net growth	7.8	9.2	8.3	6.7	7.0	7.5	**7.8%**	**7.0%**
Gross yield	7.6	7.9	7.4	8.5	8.0	7.7	7.8%	4.5%
Net yield	6.1	6.3	6.0	6.7	6.4	6.2	**6.2%**	**4.5%**
Gross return	15.4	17.1	15.7	15.2	15.0	15.2	15.6%	13.2%
Net return	13.9	15.5	14.3	13.5	13.4	13.7	**14.0%**	**11.5%**

This table clearly demonstrates that the net returns from residential property were consistent across all major capital cities (averaging 14.0%), and all have been higher than those for shares (11.5%). However, the net returns are not the end of the story as the effective use of finance and tax benefits can magnify these returns for the individual investor. Therefore, to progress further, there is another factor that we must address before we can follow the two alternative investment scenarios for our couple, Tom and Jenny. This is the element of risk and its impact on the ability to borrow money using the asset as collateral, or security.

Risk and gearing ability of shares and property

The relative risk of shares and property has already been dealt with in detail in Chapter 7. Suffice to state here that lenders much prefer to use property rather than shares as security for loans. To a certain degree, you can reduce the inherently higher risk of shares by investing in a spread of companies such as we have assumed here, and by continually manipulating your portfolio so that the gross returns mimic the All Ords Index. But this of course incurs substantial transaction costs, as we have already noted. Nevertheless, the All Ords Index itself still reflects a volatile share market compared to median-priced residential property. Consequently, lending institutions will generally lend to a maximum Loan to Value Ratio (LVR) of around 50% where shares are used as collateral, compared to 80% or more for residential property.

Wealth accumulation

In this comparison of shares and property, we will use the parameters previously described and apply them to a specific couple, Tom and Jenny, to see how much wealth they could have accumulated between 1980 and 2000 through investment in either one or the other.

Let us suppose that, in 1980, Tom and Jenny had just paid off their home worth $40,000, the average of median-priced property in all capital cities in 1980. Tom earned the average male wage of $13,500 and Jenny worked part-time earning $6,500, giving them $20,000 per year. In both wealth building scenarios, they start by using their own home as security to borrow and buy the assets. With asset equity and cash flows increasing in line with the relevant inflationary statistics, they continue to borrow to buy more investments as Loan to Value Ratios (LVRs) and Debt Services Ratios (DSRs) permit.

We will use the PIA software to simulate the two investment scenarios, and at the end of the 20 year period, we will compare the investment wealth that the couple would have achieved under each. The overall rate of return for each portfolio will also be calculated.

The two scenarios have many common variables that have been drawn from the averages of the era. For example, the marginal rate of tax was assumed to be 30%. Although higher in the early eighties and lower in the late nineties, this is a reasonable average over the time and since it was applied in the same way to both shares and property, the actual rate used was not significant. The couple's living expenses were initially taken as 30% of their total income, or $6,000 annually, and assumed to increase at the average inflation rate of 5% over the 20 years. In both cases, the rates of increase used for expenses and wages were assumed to be the 20 year averages, as provided by the Australian Bureau of Statistics. So the inflation rate on all expenses, including property expenses, was 5% while wages increased at 6.5%.

The lending criteria were based on the couple's Loan to Value Ratio (LVR) and Debt Service Ratio (DSR), which is explained in detail in Chapter 14. For their property acquisitions their LVR was kept below 80%, eliminating the need for mortgage insurance, and their DSR at 100% or less, qualifying them for a loan with most lenders. For shares, their LVR was kept to a safe level of below 50% and their DSR at 100% or less, again qualifying them for a loan with most lenders. The interest rate was fixed at 10% in both cases, the average over the period, and any cash available after paying for all living and investment expenses was paid into the loan.

246   *More Wealth from Residential Property*

Share investment between 1980 and 2000

While the PIA software is optimized for property investment analysis, it was possible to use it to simulate the share investment scenario by making the reasonable assumption that shares were purchased in lots of $5,000. At the outset, Tom and Jenny were able to borrow against their $40,000 home to buy $35,000 worth of shares, the maximum possible without the LVR exceeding 50%. Their initial LVR was 48% and their initial DSR was 48%, qualifying them for the loan. The purchase costs of stamp duty and brokerage fees amounted to 1.3%, or $455, and borrowing costs were 1.0% of the loan, or $350. The total loan of $35,805 included $35,000 for the shares and $805 in purchase and borrowing costs.

The initial dividend yield was 4.5% and, after franking, came to 5%, or $1,750. By the end year one, their share portfolio had grown in value to $37,450 and they had reduced the debt to $28,756. Thus, at the beginning of the second year, they were able to purchase another four lots of shares (now worth $5,350 per lot) without the LVR exceeding 50%.

Over the 20 years, they directed all spare cash into their loans and at the beginning of each year, borrowed as much as possible to buy more shares. By the end of 20 years, they had acquired 86 share lots which were now worth a total of $1,663,964. With outstanding debts of $603,327, the net wealth that they would have accumulated through shares was **$1,060,637**.

Wealth Accumulated from Shares
(1980 to 2000)

Start of year	1yr	2yr	3yr	4yr	5yr	20yr
Home value	40,000	43,120	46,483	50,109	54,018	166,654
Share lot price	5,000	5,350	5,725	6,125	6,554	18,083
Total share lots	7	11	14	18	22	86
Total loans	35,805	50,649	60,771	77,725	95,936	629,781
Total value	75,000	101,970	126,626	160,363	198,205	1,721,761
LVR	**48%**	**50%**	**48%**	**48%**	**48%**	**37%**
Dividends	1,750	2,888	3,859	5,209	6,685	54,329
Wages	20,000	21,300	22,685	24,159	25,729	66,172
Total income	21,750	24,188	26,543	29,368	32,415	120,501
Living expenses	6,000	6,300	6,615	6,946	7,293	15,162
Tax	5,430	5,703	6,096	6,420	6,772	17,067
Loan payments	3,581	5,065	6,077	7,772	9,594	62,978
Total expenditure	15,010	17,068	18,788	21,138	23,658	95,206
Cash savings	6,740	7,120	7,755	8,230	8,756	25,295
DSR	**48%**	**58%**	**61%**	**68%**	**73%**	**98%**
End of year						
Total share value	37,450	62,970	85,753	117,972	154,281	1,663,964
Total loans	28,756	43,203	52,660	69,117	86,779	603,327
Net share value	8,694	19,767	33,093	48,854	67,502	**1,060,637**

Appendix A: Returns from Shares and Property 247

Property investment between 1980 and 2000

At the start, Tom and Jenny bought three median-priced residential investment properties at $40,000 each by using their $40,000 home as security, keeping their LVR below the acceptable limit of 80%, at 78%. A DSR of 93% then qualified them for the loan. The purchasing costs of stamp duty and solicitor's fees were 3%, or $1,200 for each property, and the borrowing costs of 1% came to $400. The total loan of $124,800 included $120,000 for the three properties and $4,800 for the three lots of purchasing and borrowing costs.

In the first year, rent for each property was $3,120 (7.8% gross yield), with rental expenses of 20% and a vacancy rate of 2.9% (the capital city average during the period). By the end of the year, the total value of their three investment properties had increased by 7.8% to $129,360 and they had managed to reduce the debt to $119,060. Refinancing and borrowing more money allowed them to buy an additional investment property, the LVR coming in at 76% and the DSR at 97%.

Following this investment strategy over the next 20 years enabled them to accumulate 17 investment properties with a total value of $3,054,106. Subtracting the associated debt of $1,159,912 means they would have accumulated a net wealth through investment property of **$1,894,195.**

Wealth Accumulated from Residential Property (1980 to 2000)

Start of year	1yr	2yr	3yr	4yr	5yr	20yr
Home value	40,000	43,120	46,483	50,109	54,018	166,654
I.P. Value	40,000	43,120	46,483	50,109	54,018	166,654
Total I.P.s	3	4	5	5	6	17
Total loans	124,800	163,905	206,313	200,171	248,841	1,188,586
Total value	160,000	215,600	278,900	300,654	378,123	2,999,777
LVR	**78%**	**76%**	**74%**	**67%**	**66%**	**40%**
Rent	9,089	12,724	16,700	17,535	22,094	130,143
Wages	20,000	21,300	22,685	24,159	25,729	66,172
Total income	29,089	34,024	39,385	41,694	47,824	196,314
Rental expenses	1,872	2,621	3,440	3,612	4,551	26,806
Living expenses	6,000	6,300	6,615	6,946	7,293	15,162
Tax	3,248	3,039	2,825	3,941	3,689	8,071
Loan payments	12,480	16,390	20,631	20,017	24,884	118,859
Total expenditure	23,600	28,350	33,511	34,516	40,417	168,897
Cash savings	5,489	5,674	5,874	7,179	7,406	27,418
DSR	**93%**	**97%**	**100%**	**92%**	**96%**	**94%**
End of year	1	2	3	4	5	20
Total value I.P.s	129,360	185,933	250,545	270,088	349,386	3,054,106
Total loans	119,060	157,971	200,171	192,663	241,096	1,159,912
Net I.P. value	10,300	27,963	50,375	77,425	108,290	**1,894,195**

248 *More Wealth from Residential Property*

Shares or property?

After 20 years, if Tom and Jenny had borrowed to buy shares, their net investment wealth would have been $1,060,637. Indeed, this is a great result compared to most of today's retirees and would be enough to offer a degree of financial independence in retirement.

However, if they had borrowed and bought residential properties, they would have accumulated a net investment wealth of $1,894,195 — almost double the wealth created by investing in shares and more than enough to have complete financial independence in retirement. Let me explain the main reasons why it was possible to accumulate so much more through residential property than shares.

First, the net return for residential property (14.0%) exceeded that for shares (11.5%). While this may not seem much, it makes a big difference when it is compounded each year for 20 years. Suppose you believe that you would have been exceptionally lucky and would have picked shares that mimicked the All Ords Index exactly without the need to ever buy or sell. How much wealth would have been accumulated using net returns for shares of 13.2%, instead of 11.5%? In the same 20 year period, the net investment wealth would have been $1,316,123 — with investment in residential property still producing about 43% more!

Another reason why property fared better than shares was the different levels of gearing. While gearing for property saw LVRs of up to 80%, for shares, the LVR was held below 50%. Gearing magnified the 14.0% net return on property to 17.2% as measured by the internal rate of return (IRR) in the property simulation. In the case of shares, the net return of 11.5% was increased to an IRR of just 11.9%. However, had the gearing ratio for shares been lifted to a risky, and probably unacceptable level of 80%, the IRR would have been 12.5% and the wealth accumulated would have been $1,128,246, still well short of that of property. The twist in the tale to the gearing story is that while LVRs make a big impact on how much can be borrowed to buy either shares or property in the first ten years, the limiting factor for both in the latter 10 years is the DSR.

If the share simulation had used unadjusted net returns of 13.2% and LVRs of up to 80%, the wealth accumulated would have been $1,423,246, still a long way short of the $1,894,195 from property!

Clearly, the wealth accumulated by long-term investment in residential property was greater than that for shares during this 20 year period. Unlike investment in shares, it may not have been exciting and there would have been little opportunity for making windfall astronomical gains. However, if 'steady as she goes' suits your personality, investment in residential property has been shown to give you more wealth with less risk.

Appendix B: PIA Computer Program

There are probably many reasons why more people have not discovered the wonderful benefits of investing in residential property. One possible reason is that most people don't know how to calculate investment returns on property (or shares for that matter). Nor do they understand how those returns can be magnified by the creative use of collateral and borrowed money. While the analytical procedures are not rocket science, they can be very intimidating to inexperienced investors and it could conceivably take a few days to fully evaluate just one investment property proposal.

The Property Investment Analysis (PIA) computer program that has been used extensively throughout this book to perform various cash-flow analyses and evaluate 'what ifs' was developed by my best friend, Ian. The fact that his experience in mathematical modelling and computer software design dates back further than he'd care to remember and the fact that he also happens to be my husband, has made it so much easier for me to put this book together. He may be backward when it comes to doing laundry, but he is brilliant at making difficult property investment calculations easy to do *and* understand. His skills and effort resulted in the PIA computer program that is so simple to use but so powerful in what it can do for investors. Even novice property investors can find the answers to virtually all of their questions about investment property with just a few of clicks of a mouse and the entry of a few key variables.

Briefly, PIA can help you evaluate and make objective decisions about any property investment. You can quickly estimate your rate of return, tax savings, true after-tax cost and affordability. Furthermore, you can easily answer all 'what ifs' by making changes to the variables such as capital growth, inflation and interest rates. Finally, you can print a professionally structured report showing all your assumptions and cash-flow projections to present your investment proposal to your bank manager or accountant.

While the program comes in three versions (see page 255), I have used the Personal Professional Version in this book as it enabled me to produce a spreadsheet for each stage of Bill and Mary's wealth building strategy. Firstly, using the Home Loan Analysis spreadsheet, we could examine ways in which they were able to pay off their home loan sooner. Then, using the Investment Analysis spreadsheet, we were able to analyse the cash flows for each rental property they bought. Finally, the spreadsheet in the Wealth Builder, gave us the tool to appreciate how it was possible for them to accumulate a portfolio of properties by buying more and more whenever they could afford them. Using the computer program in this way, we easily mapped a plan by which they could become millionaires in 10 to 15 years.

250 *More Wealth from Residential Property*

The diagram below portrays the screen image for the main Property Investment Analysis spreadsheet which can be used for analysing any property investment.

PIA Screen Image

Investment Analysis	Input	1yr	2yr	3yr	4yr	5yr
Year	2001					
Property value	$160,000	167,200	174,724	182,587	190,803	199,389
Purchase costs	$4,500					
Outlays	$0					
Loan amount	$166,000	166,000	166,000	166,000	166,000	166,000
Equity	$-6,000	1,200	8,724	16,587	24,803	**33,389**
Capital growth rate	4.50%	4.50%	4.50%	4.50%	4.50%	4.50%
Inflation rate (CPI)	2.00%	2.00%	2.00%	2.00%	2.00%	2.00%
Gross rent /wk /yr	$200	10,400	10,608	10,820	11,037	11,257
Cash deductions						
Interest (split)	8.50%	14,110	14,110	14,110	14,110	14,110
Property expenses	25.00%	2,600	2,652	2,705	2,759	2,814
Pre-tax cash flow	$0	-6,310	-6,154	-5,995	-5,833	-5,667
Non-cash deductions						
Deprec.-building	2.50%	2,000	2,000	2,000	2,000	2,000
Deprec.-fittings	$15,000	2,700	4,039	2,610	1,705	1,128
Loan costs	$1,500	500	500	500		
Total deductions	$0	21,910	23,301	21,925	20,574	20,052
Tax credit (single)	$47,000	3,626	3,998	3,540	3,258	3,242
After-tax cash flow	$0	-2.684	-2.156	-2,455	-2,575	-2,425
Rate of return (IRR)	40.99%					
Real rate of return	38.23%	52	41	47	50	47

The items in the Menu bar across the top access further functions that allow you to save files, produce reports and graphs, use the wealth builder, calculate Capital Gains Tax, view different spreadsheets such as the Home Loan Analysis, and change settings to cater for different state stamp duties. Beneath the menu bar is the Tool bar consisting of a series of icons, each of which provides quick access to commonly used functions. The left hand column of the spreadsheet contains the names of the items or rows. The second column is referred to as the input column and it contains a set of initial values associated with the rows. The five remaining columns show projections over future years, capable of being projected up to 40 years. The bottom three rows collectively represent the 'bottom line'. The 'After-tax cash flow' is the cash flow out of your pocket each year. The 'Rate of return (IRR)' is a measure of the return on the investment and is explained in detail in Appendix C over on the next page. The real IRR shows the equivalent after-inflation rate of return. Your cost/income per week shows you the projected weekly net cost or income resulting from the investment — the real bottom line.

Appendix C: Internal Rate of Return (IRR)

Working out the Internal Rate of Return, or IRR, on any investment is basically a matter of analysing what you put in compared to what you get back at the end. In the very simple case of cash invested in a bank, what you put in are the deposits and what you get back at the end will be the sum of these deposits plus the interest accrued each year, less the tax you pay. The rate of return is effectively the interest rate that the bank offers minus the tax you would need to pay at your marginal rate.

With property investment, the rate of return is still calculated on the basis of what you put in compared to what you get back at the end for a predetermined period; but the equations are much more complicated than those for cash in a bank. They must take into account all the annual cash flows in and out of the property and relate this to the money made at the end — which is your equity in the property.

So it is important to consider *all* the variables relating to both the property and the investor. We need to include not only variables such as property value, capital growth, rent and inflation, but also the investor's personal tax. The rate of return can therefore be different from property to property, and the same property can even produce a different rate of return for different investors.

For a property where you have a large initial cash deposit, the property would probably generate a positive cash flow (net rent plus tax refund, less loan payments) from day one. In this case, your only investment would be the initial cash deposit, and what you get back would be the positive annual after-tax cash flows plus the equity build-up in the property. Where you have little or no initial cash deposit, the annual after-tax cash flows would most likely be negative. In this case, what you put in would be your regular contributions to cover this deficit, while what you get back would simply be the equity build up.

The rate of return in either case is effectively the 'interest rate' you would need to get on these after-tax contributions to attain the equity at the end. This percentage is termed the internal rate of return (IRR) which is calculated by trial and error such that the sum of your regular investments or 'deposits' plus the 'interest' each year is equal to the equity at the end.

You don't need to understand how the rate of return is calculated for investment property in order to be a successful investor. Think of it as like driving a car. You certainly don't need to know what goes on under the bonnet to get a licence, but there are some people who might want to know. This section is for those who would like to know how the engine works for property. I will explain it as simply as I can.

252   *More Wealth from Residential Property*

To see these concepts in practice, let's go through an example using the $160,000 investment property described on page 127 and we'll look at the IRR over the next five years. Bill was earning $47,000 per year when he borrowed $166,000 (including costs of $6,000) with an interest-only loan at 8.5% and payments of $14,110 annually.

Suppose that in the first year the annual rent is $10,400 and expenses are $2,600. For the next five years, rents and expenses are projected to increase at 2% per year. At the end of the first year, Bill is eligible for a tax refund of $3,626, however, in calculating the cash flow, it is assumed that he applies under Section 15-15 of the Tax Act to have the refund in the form of a reduction in his PAYG tax. After five years, with annual capital growth at 4.5%, we find that the property increases in value to $199,389. Let's look at the 'ins and outs' of the cash flow situation, with the figures taken from the spreadsheet on page 250.

What You Put 'In' Over 5 Years

The shortfall in the first year would be $2,684 (rent of $10,400 plus a tax refund of $3,626, less interest of $14,110 and expenses of $2,600). Over five years, the interest is constant (interest-only loan), but both rents and expenses increase with inflation (2%), while the tax refunds decline. The negative after-tax cash flows, which are the 'ins', would then be:

The 'Ins' over 5 years

	Yr 1	Yr 2	Yr 3	Yr 4	Yr 5
After-tax cash flows	-$2,684	-$2,156	-$2,455	-$2,575	-$2,425

What You Get 'Out' at the End of 5 years

For an interest-only loan, the debt of $166.000 is constant over the five year period. Consequently the equity, or what you get 'out' after 5 years, would be $33,389, which is the difference between the property value after five years and the loan. You do not need to sell the property to measure how much you have made; you only need to estimate its value. (Note that with time, the rents should gradually overtake the loan payments and the property expenses; your 'outs' then will also include this surplus.) Here is the calculation:

The 'Outs' over 5 years

	At purchase	After 5 Years
Property value	$160,000	$199,389
Loan	$166,000	$166,000
Equity	-$6,000	$33,389

Appendix C: Internal Rate of Return (IRR) 253

Relating the 'Ins' to the 'Outs'

We can now calculate the 'interest rate' needed to turn the 'ins' into the 'outs'. In the first year, $2,684 ($52 per week) is invested, and 'interest' is added. Then $2,156 is contributed in the second year and again 'interest' is added, and so on until you know what 'interest rate' was needed to reach an equity of $33,389. This 'interest rate' is the so-called Internal Rate of Return or IRR. If you have a few days to spare, the IRR can be worked out by hand using trial and error, however the computer can do it in a few milliseconds. In this example, the IRR over five years would be 40.99% compound per year, and over 10 years, it would be 23.15%.

Obviously, the IRR on a negatively geared property gradually declines with time. The reasons for this are twofold. Firstly, with rents rising, the tax benefits diminish to the point where tax is paid. Secondly, the equity in the property increases with time so the leverage effect is reduced. In the first year, Bill has no equity (in fact it is -$6,000). After 5 years the value to equity ratio is $199,389 to $33,389, almost 6:1; and after 10 years it is $248,475 to $82,475, or about 3:1. To maintain higher overall gearing ratios with higher rates of return, further properties should be bought when cash flow permits. This will regain the tax benefits and increase leverage.

Sensitivity Analysis

It is important to understand the effect of changes in the various inputs on the rate of return, and, using the computer program, it is possible to perform a sensitivity analysis to look at all the 'what ifs' of property investment. The examples in this table show how both the weekly cost and the IRR over 5 years change by varying some assumptions.

Sensitivity Analysis

Change to inputs	Cost per wk 1st Yr	IRR per yr
No Change	$52	40.99%
Deposit of $40,000	$7	12.41%
Vacancy rate of 10%	$64	30.69%
Mortgage insurance of $3,000	$49	38.15%

As you can see, the rate of return is very sensitive to the deposit size, with large deposits significantly lowering the IRR. Contrary to what many people believe, the IRR is not greatly affected by such factors as vacancy rates or even mortgage insurance, primarily because the impact of these is lessened as a result of the corresponding tax credits. There are thousands of scenarios that can be evaluated using the PIA software, but these few at least should give you an idea of what can be done.

254 *More Wealth from Residential Property*

About the publisher...

Somerset Financial Services Pty Ltd* is a publishing company that specialises in helping residential property investors. Formed in 1989, its role is one of research, analysis and education. While many organisations use our material to assist their clients with investment in property, our company is completely independent and does not sell property, finance, or personal advice. Instead, through the publication of software and books, it provides investors with all the objective, well-researched information and tools they will need to be self sufficient in their investment decisions.

The PIA (Property Investment Analysis) computer programs developed by Ian in 1988, have been enhanced and updated continuously and have become the industry standard in property investment analysis.

More Wealth from Residential Property is Jan's fifth book in the series on investment in residential property. Her first book, *Manual for Residential Property Investors* was released in 1989 to a limited market in Brisbane. This manual was so well received that it was expanded into a second book, *Building Wealth through Investment Property*, and distributed Australia wide in 1992. It was an instant best seller, becoming one of the top selling self-help books of the 90s. Both these books were adapted and released in New Zealand in 1993. By the mid 1990s, economic conditions had changed in Australia, and with it came a barrage of 'what ifs' by the media and cynics who questioned the validity of Jan's strategy in times of low inflation. In 1994, Jan released her third book, *Building Wealth in Changing Times*, in response to those questions.

With hundreds of thousands of books in circulation, Jan became inundated with stories from people who had successfully invested in property — and some from those who could have or should have. As a result, 101 of these fascinating stories were published in 1998 in her fourth book, *Building Wealth Story by Story*, the final story being Jan and Ian's own, describing the types of property they bought and the kinds of finance they used.

With a large following of devotees, and a whole new wave of investors interested in property, Jan received numerous requests for her earlier books to be updated. While still totally committed to the principle of building wealth through residential property, Jan recognised the need for people to be reassured that the recipe was still relevant in the new millennium. The result is her latest book, *More Wealth from Residential Property*, which not only updates and consolidates the information in her first three books, *Manual for Residential Property Investors*, *Building Wealth through Investment Property* and *Building Wealth in Changing Times*, which are all now out of print, but also contains a wealth of new information.

---

* Somerset Financial Services Pty Ltd (ABN 25 623 732 311)

Current publications available

Our publications include both software and books aimed at helping investors make their own decisions about property investments. More information is available on our website *(www.somersoft.com.au)* where you can download demonstration versions of the software and read the introduction to each book. In keeping with our belief that investors learn from the experience of others, the website includes an interactive forum.

Computer Programs *PIA (Property Investment Analysis)*

PIA helps you analyse and evaluate prospective property investments. You can quickly estimate your rate of return, tax savings, after-tax cost and affordability. Furthermore, you can very easily test the sensitivity of your results (playing 'What if') by making changes to variables such as growth, inflation and interest rates. Finally, you can print out a professionally structured report to help present your investment proposal to your bank manager or accountant. PIA is available in three different versions to run on either the PC (Win 95 or later) or Mac (Mac OS 7.1 or later) platform. The current software is optimized for both Australia and New Zealand.

PIA Personal is the basic version of the software for investors who want to perform cash flow analysis on any investment property.

PIA Personal Professional is a more powerful version for serious investors who want extra functionality. It has all the features of the PIA Personal plus additional spreadsheets for home-loan analysis, linked loan analysis and a wealth builder for interactively building a portfolio over a number of years. It also has extensive graphics, a suite of property and finance calculators, and a much wider array of report options.

PIA Professional is designed for industry professionals who want to use PIA to help investors understand all the benefits and implications of investing in property. It has all of the features of the PIA Personal Professional plus additional client-related features and a site license.

Books

More Wealth from Residential Property (2001)

This book should be the first investment that any potential property investor makes and gives a meticulous step-by-step guide of why and how to invest in residential property

Building Wealth Story by Story (1998)

Some of the best information and tips about property come from the exploits of other property investors. This book contains 101 such stories. Some of them will warm your heart. Other stories may make you squirm. Story by story you will learn a little more about the many strategies and wonderful benefits of investing in residential property.

ORDER FORM

(All prices are in A$ and include GST and P&H within Australia)

PLEASE SEND ME:

Computer Program: *PIA Personal* $140 [   ]

           PIA Personal Professional $245 [   ]

           PIA Professional $495 [   ]

           Mac [   ]   Win [   ]

Book: *Building Wealth Story by Story* $29 [   ]

        Add-on price with software $22 [   ]

Book: *More Wealth from Residential Property* $32 [   ]

        Add-on price with software $25 [   ]

TOTAL AMOUNT (Prices include GST, P&H within Australia) [A$_____]

I am paying by cheque [   ] Bank Card [   ] Master Card [   ] Visa Card [   ]

l__l__l__l__**l**__l__l__l__**l**__l__l__l__**l**__l__l__l__**l** Exp___/___

Card Holder's Signature _____

PLEASE NOTIFY ME:

If you want to be informed of new publications, please tick the box. [   ]

Mr/Mrs/Ms_____ First Name _____

Surname _____

Company Name _____

Address _____

_____

State _____ P'code _____ Phone No. _____

Email Address _____

Please send your order to:

Somerset Financial Services Pty Ltd	**Telephone:**	(07) 3286 4368
P.O. Box 615,	**Fax:**	(07) 3821 2005
Cleveland	**Email:**	sales@somersoft.com.au
Qld 4163.	**Web: www.somersoft.com.au**	